THE FIRST HELLCAT ACE

CDR HAMILTON MCWHORTER III, USN (RET.)

with

LT. COL. JAY A. STOUT, USMC (RET.)

CASEMATE

Pennsylvania & Yorkshire

Published in the United States of America and Great Britain in 2024 by
CASEMATE PUBLISHERS
1950 Lawrence Road, Havertown, PA 19083, USA
and
47 Church Street, Barnsley, S70 2AS, UK

This is a revised edition of *The First Hellcat Ace*, published by Pacifica Press in 2001.

Hardcover Edition: ISBN 978-1-63624-409-9
Digital Edition: ISBN 978-1-63624-410-5

A CIP record for this book is available from the British Library

Printed and bound in the United Kingdom by CPI Group (UK) Ltd, Croydon, CR0 4YY
Typeset in India by DiTech Publishing Services

For a complete list of Casemate titles, please contact:

CASEMATE PUBLISHERS (US)
Telephone (610) 853-9131
Fax (610) 853-9146
Email: casemate@casematepublishers.com
www.casematepublishers.com

CASEMATE PUBLISHERS (UK)
Telephone (0)1226 734350
Email: casemate@casemateuk.com
www.casemateuk.com

Cover image: U.S. Navy

For my beautiful wife, Louise, whose undying love and devotion sustained me through sixteen months of combat in the Pacific and continues to this day. And for my children—Donald, William, Georgia, Hamilton, and Jon—for their love, and with the fervent prayer that they and none of their descendants will ever have to experience combat.

Contents

Introduction

At Pearl Harbor, the lucky failure of the Japanese intelligence apparatus, and the withholding of our own intelligence, set the stage for the Pacific War. The attack, whatever its "infamy," was a masterpiece of planning and execution. That the Japanese tactics were borrowed from our own made them no less effective. The subsequent horrible destruction of our battleship fleet, and the providential escape of our aircraft carriers, forced our effort from the surface to the air. The battleship and the battle line gave way, of necessity, to the aircraft carrier and the air strike. Ironically, given the ascendancy of air power at that point in history, the Japanese, in a sense, did us a favor.

Mac McWhorter's story helps to illuminate one of the least appreciated but most fundamental aspects of World War II—the fight to regain control of the Pacific Ocean. This charge fell in large part onto the shoulders of a very few—the pilots and aircrew of the United States Navy. Theirs was the responsibility. They came from no special stock. Farm boys and college lads alike were converted into naval aviators. Augmented by a few "grizzled" twenty-five-year-old-or-so veterans from the surface fleet, these young men were all rigorously schooled. Some did not make it. Those who did went on to become the nation's finest combat aviators.

And they went on to prevail over their Japanese adversaries, who—despite the fact that they were often derided merely as "Japs"—were pushovers in no sense of the word. Pearl Harbor and many subsequent actions proved that. Prevailing over the Japanese involved air strikes of incredibly long range, with a clever and capable enemy waiting at the far end. But the fight against the enemy made up only part of the danger. Incredibly enough, just finding the aircraft carrier on the return trip, often in pelting rain and darkening sky, was sometimes more stressful than the combat itself.

Combat was too busy for stress! Combat required instant decisions; finding the carrier demanded anxious hours. Each meant life. The latter half of the Pacific War saw the Hellcat—and its stablemate, the Corsair—dominate the skies over the Pacific Ocean. Rugged and dependable, the Hellcat embodied all that we had learned in the early bitter years of combat. It was a winner. But without its pilot, the airplane was just a machine. For it was the pilot who sought and scanned, who tracked and shot, who ultimately was the deciding factor upon which success or failure rested.

Thankfully, success rested with us. And for that success we honor those who delivered it. And among those who delivered it, we honor the first. Here, we honor *The First Hellcat Ace*!

Noel A. M. Gayler

Admiral, U.S. Navy (Retired)

Author's Note: Noel Gayler was McWhorter's first commanding officer in VF-12. Prior to that, during the dark, early days of the war, he proved himself in combat as he earned the Navy Cross three separate times in just a few months during 1942. Flying the F4F Wildcat, he downed five Japanese aircraft to become one of the Navy's first aces. When his aircraft carrier, USS Lexington, was sunk during the battle of the Coral Sea on May 8, 1942, he abandoned ship as ordered by the captain. After some time, he grabbed a rope and hauled himself up out of the water and back to the flight deck of the listing ship. When queried by his puzzled squadron mates he answered: "I didn't know any of the guys down there and got kind of lonely. When are you coming down?"

Gayler had an exceptional career. As he rose in rank, eventually becoming an admiral (four stars), he held numerous commands of increasing size and importance. In due course he served as the head of the National Security Agency under President Nixon, and later commanded all U.S. forces in the Pacific. Following his military career, he became a staunch and respected advocate of nuclear disarmament. He passed away in 2011.

Glossary and Guide to Abbreviations

ACTG	Aircraft Carrier Training Group.
Aileron	Aerodynamic control surfaces mounted on the wings that control roll.
Aileron Roll	A 360-degree roll about the airplane's longitudinal axis. Although the airplane rolls from upright, through inverted, and back to upright flight, its altitude and heading do not change.
API	Armor-piercing incendiary ammunition.
Avenger	Navy/Marine Corps TBF Avenger single-engine torpedo bomber manufactured by Grumman.*
B-24	U.S. Army Air Forces Liberator four-engine heavy bomber manufactured by Consolidated.
Betty	Imperial Japanese Navy G4M twin-engine land-based medium bomber manufactured by Mitsubishi.
Breguet 521	Three-engine French maritime reconnaissance biplane flying boat.
CAP	Combat Air Patrol.
Chandelle	Steep climb at the top of which the airplane's heading is abruptly reversed, and the airplane transitions into a dive in the direction opposite that at which the maneuver was begun.
Corsair	Navy/Marine Corps F4U single-engine carrier fighter manufactured by Vought.
CPT	Civilian Pilot Training (Program).
CV	Fleet carrier.
CVE	Escort carrier.
CVL	Light carrier.
Curtiss Hawk 75	Export version of the U.S. Army Air Forces Curtiss P-36.
Dauntless	Navy/Marine Corps SBD single-engine dive bomber manufactured by Douglas.

DC-3	Douglas twin-engine commercial transport (C-47 or R4D equivalent).
Dewoitine 520	French single-engine fighter.
Division	Naval aviation term for a flight of four aircraft.
Elevator	Control surface at the tail of the airplane that causes an airplane to climb or dive.
F2A	Navy/Marine Corps Brewster Buffalo single-engine carrier fighter.
F4F	Navy/Marine Corps Grumman single-engine carrier fighter.
F4U	Navy/Marine Corps Vought Corsair single-engine carrier fighter.
F6F	Navy Grumman Hellcat single-engine carrier fighter.
FDO	Fighter direction officer.
Finger Four	Four-plane aerial formation arranged similarly to the tips of a hand's fingers
Flak	Antiaircraft fire (from the German; *Flieger Abwehr Kannonen*).
Ford Trimotor	Three-engine commercial monoplane.
Forecastle	Forward part of a ship.
Frances	Imperial Japanese Navy P1Y twin-engine light bomber manufactured by Yokosuka.
FW-190	German single-engine fighter manufactured by Focke-Wulf.
G	Force of gravity—1 G equals the force of gravity on a body at rest.
Half-Cuban Eight	Variation of the loop whereby the airplane is rolled upright at the top of the loop and continues to dive in the direction opposite that in which the maneuver was begun.
Hellcat	Navy F6F single-engine carrier fighter manufactured by Grumman.
Helldiver	Navy SB2C single-engine carrier dive bomber manufactured by Curtiss.
HVAR	High-velocity aerial rocket.
IJN	Imperial Japanese Navy.
Immelmann	A half-loop in which the airplane is rolled upright at the top of the loop—essentially a climbing vertical turn resulting in a 180-degree change in heading. Named after the German World War I aviator credited with inventing it.

Irving	Imperial Japanese Army Nakajima J1N twin-engine reconnaissance airplane.
J3	Light American single-engine monoplane.
Kingfisher	Navy OS2U single-engine observation floatplane manufactured by Vought.
LeO 451	French twin-engine bomber.
Liberator	U.S. Army Air Forces B-24 four-engine heavy bomber manufactured by Consolidated.
Lightning	U.S. Army Air Forces P-38 twin-engine fighter manufactured by Lockheed.
Loop	A 360-degree turn in the vertical plane. The airplane is pulled into a vertical climb, through inverted flight (headed in the opposite direction), down into a dive and back into upright flight in the original direction and at the original altitude.
LSO	Landing signal officer.
Mae West	Rubberized inflatable life jacket.
Mariner	Navy two-engine flying boat patrol plane manufactured by Martin.
Me-109	German single-engine fighter manufactured by Messerschmitt.
Myrt	Imperial Japanese Navy C6N single-engine reconnaissance airplane manufactured by Nakajima.
Napalm	Jellied aviation gasoline weapon.
N3N	Navy single-engine biplane trainer.
NAS	Naval air station.
Ohka	Imperial Japanese Navy MXY7 manned flying bomb manufactured by Yokosuka.
OS2U	Navy single-engine observation floatplane manufactured by Vought.
P-26	U.S. Army's first metal single-engine monoplane fighter manufactured by Boeing.
P-36	U.S. Army Air Forces Hawk single-engine fighter manufactured by Curtiss.
P-38	U.S. Army Air Forces Lightning twin-engine fighter manufactured by Lockheed.
P-39	U.S. Army Air Forces Airacobra single-engine fighter manufactured by Bell.

P-40	U.S. Army Air Forces Warhawk single-engine fighter manufactured by Curtiss.
Paul	Imperial Japanese Navy Aichi E16A long-range reconnaissance floatplane manufactured by Aichi.
PBM	USN Martin-built flying boat patrol plane.
Pete	Imperial Japanese Navy F1M2 single-engine biplane observation floatplane manufactured by Mitsubishi.
Pipper	Center aiming dot of a gunsight.
Port	Left.
Quonset Hut	Prefabricated corrugated metal building in the shape of a half cylinder.
R4D	Navy/Marine Corps version of Douglas DC-3 transport airplane.
R5D	Navy/Marine Corps version of Douglas C-54 twin-engine transport.
Rudder	Vertical control surface mounted on the rear of the tail that controls yaw.
SB2C	Navy Helldiver single-engine carrier dive bomber manufactured by Curtiss.
SBD	Navy/Marine Corps Dauntless single-engine dive bomber manufactured by Douglas.
SBU	Navy/Marine Corps two-seat, single-engine biplane dive bomber manufactured by Vought.
SCAR	Sub-Caliber Aerial Rocket; small, cheap practice rocket.
Section	Naval aviation terminology for a flight of two aircraft.
Snap roll	An abrupt, rolling turn usually executed with a preponderance of rudder control.
SNJ	Navy advanced trainer. (AT-6 in the U.S. Army Air Forces) manufactured by North American.
SON-1	Navy two-seat, single-engine scout observation biplane.
Split-ess	A diving vertical half-loop. At the start of the maneuver the airplane is rolled inverted and pulled down through a vertical dive and back into upright flight. The maneuver finishes with the airplane lower and heading in the direction opposite that in which it started.
Starboard	Right.
Strafe	Air-to-ground gunnery.
TBD	Navy Devastator single-engine carrier torpedo bomber manufactured by Douglas.

TBF	Navy/Marine Corps Avenger single-engine torpedo bomber manufactured by Grumman.
TBM	Navy/Marine Corps General Motors–built Avenger single-engine torpedo bomber (same as TBF).
Thach Weave	Defensive response to an enemy attack by two or more fighters whereby each airplane protects the other.
Tracer	Phosphorescent bullet which enables the pilot to visibly trace the path of his machinegun fire.
USAAF	United States Army Air Forces.
USMC	United States Marine Corps.
USN	United States Navy.
V5	Navy pilot training program.
V-mail	Victory mail.
VB	Navy bombing squadron.
VBF	Navy fighter-bomber squadron.
Vertigo	Spatial disorientation.
Very pistol	Flare-firing signal pistol.
VF	Navy fighter squadron.
VT	Navy torpedo squadron.
UPF 7	American biplane trainer manufactured by Waco.
Wildcat	Navy Grumman F4F single-engine carrier fighter.
Willie Pete	White phosphorous marking round.
YE/ZB	USN aircraft radio navigation system used to home on the aircraft carrier.
Zero	Imperial Japanese Navy A6M single-engine fighter manufactured by Mitsubishi.

Identified manufacturers are the companies which designed the associated aircraft. Wartime exigencies were such that many aircraft types were manufactured by more than one company. Those additional manufacturers are not identified here.

Chapter 1

It had been raining hard for two days and the water rushing out of Lake Okeechobee had risen so much that it covered the railroad tracks. And though the clack of steel wheels on steel rails told me otherwise, it seemed as if we were skimming free of the tracks across the surface of the still-rising water.

Only an hour earlier, my mother, my brother, and I waved goodbye through the rain to my father. Alone and wet among a crowd of strangers, he waved back from where he stood under the eaves of the station platform.

It was September 17, 1926, and I was five years old. Only a year earlier my father brought us—my mother, younger brother, and me—to Moore Haven, Florida, on the southern shore of Lake Okeechobee. A series of boll weevil-ravaged cotton harvests drove us from the family plantation in northeast Georgia, a region that had been home to the McWhorter clan since they arrived from Scotland in the late 1700s. Consequently, the move to Florida was not made lightly.

But my father had to make a living, and South Florida in the mid-1920s seemed to be a place where one might be made. There was a land boom underway and rampant speculation had created a booming economy. My father went to work for a dredging company that clawed canals out of the mucky landscape in order to drain parts of the Everglades for farming. I remember going out to visit him one day and becoming fascinated by the huge suction dredges that floated in the canal. They made a tremendous roaring noise as they sucked up the black muck and pumped it onto the edge of the canal. While I was there, the big intake pipe on one of the dredges became clogged and my father had to dive beneath the horrid glop to clear it.

But now, a great hurricane—in concert with economic realities that would lead ultimately to the Great Depression—was delivering a wake-up call to the

The Miami hurricane of 1926 destroyed much of Southern Florida and compelled McWhorter's parents to move back to Athens, Georgia, and family. (Library of Congress)

developers and businessmen, and those of us who hoped to ride their coattails to riches. Or at least to a decent living.

The hurricane struck South Florida with a force and fury that was nearly beyond belief. In Moore Haven it pushed the lake over the levees and through the town in the form of a 26-foot storm surge. Most of the houses, ours included, were swept off their cinderblock foundations like so many matchboxes. What was left of our house was found more than a mile from where it had stood. Nothing but sludge and water and rotting ruins were left of the devastated town.

Categorized by modern standards as a Category 4 hurricane, the storm was one of the worst to hit the United States during the 20th century. All told, the hurricane destroyed millions of dollars of property, including the city of Miami. Worse, more than 400 people were killed.

***

After salvaging what little he could from the ruins of our house—some silverware and a shotgun—my father joined us in Hillsboro, Georgia, the home of my maternal grandparents. He had weathered the storm in the third story of a brick office building with a group of other men. His stories of the devastation left behind, the wreckage and death, were incredible.

We lived in Hillsboro for a year and I started school there. Although I was only five, I got into the first grade because my grandfather was head of the school board. It was a one-room schoolhouse and each row in the room was a different grade. We left Hillsboro in 1927 and moved in with my grandfather McWhorter in Athens, Georgia, where he owned a huge, four-story Victorian mansion situated on a 160-acre estate. It had been a country club when he bought it in 1901, and he remodeled the house almost immediately. It was a

Cloverhurst, in Athens, was owned by McWhorter's grandfather, Judge Hamilton McWhorter. Young McWhorter enjoyed playing in its many halls and rooms. (University of Georgia Digital Library)

wonderful old building that my brother I regularly explored during the two short years we lived there. The ledges that ran around the roof were perfect for climbing, and we disappeared at play for hours at a time in the seemingly innumerable rooms and hallways.

After my grandfather passed away in 1929 the house was torn down, the acreage was developed for sale, and we moved to a more modest home in Athens. It was the house where I finished growing up.

***

One summer Sunday in 1928 a ragtag flying circus came to town to fly out of the little grass field that served as Athens's airstrip. It was to be the day of my first airplane ride. The circus operated a Ford Trimotor that took people for rides for five dollars apiece. My uncle bought tickets for himself, my cousin, and me. I was so excited that I could barely contain myself. After waiting forever in line, I nearly ran up to the big airplane when it was our turn to board. That old trimotor sat at a very steep angle, and it was about all I could do to climb into the airplane and then up the steep aisle in the center of the passenger cabin to find a seat. With a fuselage full of townspeople, the

McWhorter's first airplane ride was in a Ford Trimotor when he was a young boy. (Wikimedia Commons)

Trimotor, one of the premier commercial airliners of its day, bumped itself into the air and took us for a short flight over the town.

I was fascinated by this new perspective of the world—despite the noise created by the old airplane's three roaring engines. The noise and the bumpy ride through the hot summer air caused more than a couple of my fellow passengers to become rather queasy. After we landed, the pilot explained that the bumps we felt were caused by "air pockets."

***

The idea of flying had always interested me, but that flight really lit the fire. Now I really knew what I wanted to do with my life; I wanted to become a pilot. This aspiration was quite a reach for a Depression-era youngster. It was doubtful that I would ever get the opportunity or the education I needed to take to the skies. Nevertheless, I built model airplanes whenever I had the 25 cents it cost to buy them. When I didn't have the money—which was most of the time since we were soon to be in the middle of the Depression—I carved them out of blocks of soft white pine. I got pretty good with those carvings.

After the summer of the Trimotor ride, I often pedaled my bike the five miles out to the airstrip to watch the planes. It wasn't much of an airport, but back then airstrips weren't much to look at as a rule. The field was situated on a rounded hill, and its newly built runways sloped down at both ends. Although there weren't any military units based there, military flights sometimes passed through. When this happened, everyone in town rushed out to watch.

On one of my excursions to the airport I was impressed by a flight of Army P-26 fighters. The Army's first monoplane fighter, the P-26, was a

A Boeing P-26, the nation's first all-metal, monoplane fighter. A flight of these inspired McWhorter to become a fighter pilot. (Wikimedia Commons)

tiny little kite with beautiful aerodynamic fairings over its fixed landing gear and a big radial engine out in front of the pilot. I thought it was wonderful. These P-26s had just started, and one of them was parked facing in the wrong direction. The pilot simply added power, raised the tail, and in a roar of dust and debris, kicked the rudder and spun the little airplane around until it faced the other way. Seconds later, the whole flight roared down the airfield and we earthbound mortals were left with nothing but the smell of aviation gasoline and the sting of grit in our eyes and dust on our skin. From that moment I not only wanted to fly, I wanted to fly fighters!

***

Another passion I had was hunting, particularly quail hunting. My brother and I roamed the woods around our home with .22-caliber rifles and BB guns. We hunted all sorts of small game, and I'm certain that the shooting eye that I developed during that time helped me years later, during the war.

My father was an avid hunter. One of my clearest memories is of an early hunting trip with him. On that particular day he borrowed a couple of bird dogs and took my brother and me with him. After a short time, the dogs went on point and marked quail hidden in the brush. With my brother to my right, I crunched carefully through the brush and dry grass toward where the dogs were frozen in their stance. As prepared as I was, knowing full well that at any instant the bird, or birds, would explode out of the cover, my heart was still parked halfway up my throat. Then, at the very moment when it seemed I could stand the tension no longer, a pair of quail rocketed up from almost beneath my feet. I am sure they brushed against my legs as they took flight.

Almost instinctively, I raised my shotgun, released the safety, and swung to the left to follow their flight path. I drew the barrel just past the trailing bird and, seemingly without aiming, squeezed the trigger and felt the gun rock back into my shoulder. Without hesitating, I kept the gun barrel moving, put it just in front of the other bird, and squeezed the trigger a second time. The gun recoiled into my shoulder again. I was barely aware of the stink of burned gunpowder when I lowered my gun and realized that I had dropped both birds.

It takes little more than a crisp autumn day and dry grass underfoot to bring that memory back.

Chapter 2

In Georgia during this time, the public schools went only to the 11th grade. To be honest, at least in Athens, they didn't do a very good job of preparing students for higher education in the state's university system, which was quite demanding. However, I was a decent student, driven in part by my desire to become a fighter pilot.

I also did my part to help in the household; I took on a paper route, delivering the Athens *Banner Herald* newspaper. Every day after school I rode my bike down to the printing plant and wrapped and stacked more than 140 papers. Then I jumped back on my bike and delivered them all. I did a lot of bike riding back then. The papers sold for two cents apiece. I didn't get rich, but every little bit helped.

I was always quite a bit bigger than most of the other kids. Partly for that reason I enjoyed playing pickup games of baseball and football, but I never really had a lot of time for, or interest in, organized sports. The only extracurricular activity I participated in was shooting, as part of the high school's ROTC rifle team. Practice took place late in the evenings and did not interfere with my paper route. I did quite well and earned my only high school letter.

After I graduated from high school in 1937 at the age of 16, I enrolled at Georgia Tech in Atlanta. My goal was to become an aeronautical engineer, which I felt would help me in pursuit of my goal to become a fighter pilot. I'm not sure that I got into Georgia Tech totally on my own merit. I had decent grades and recommendations, but I had a relative—also named Hamilton McWhorter—who was the speaker of the Georgia House of Representatives. I'm sure that his influence didn't hurt my chances for admission.

My higher education got off to a fitful start. I did decently well in everything but math. And, of course, math is pretty important to anyone who wants to get a degree in aeronautical engineering. I was very concerned that I wouldn't be able to handle the curriculum.

It didn't help that I was on a co-op program. Because money was tight, I attended school for three months, then worked for three months. I worked for the Georgia Power Company in Athens, putting up power lines and poles, clearing brush, digging holes, or doing whatever they needed me to do.

After about a year and a half of studying in the co-op program, my money ran out completely, and I returned home to Athens. That was an unsettling time for me. The country hadn't yet clawed its way out of the Depression and I wasn't sure what the future held for me. I worked at a local service station for six or eight months, earning fifty dollars a month, before I saved enough money to enroll at the University of Georgia, right there in Athens.

***

One of the biggest reasons I chose to go to the University of Georgia, rather than return to Georgia Tech, was the Civilian Pilot Training program. The University of Georgia had it and Georgia Tech did not.

The Civilian Pilot Training Program, or CPTP, began in 1939, when the nation realized it was going to need a great many pilots in a hurry. The military was unable to provide basic flight training to the huge number of available and qualified candidates, so the resources of the civilian flying establishment were enlisted. The Civil Aeronautics Administration, which managed the program, oversaw the training at hundreds of civilian flight schools. Several hundred colleges and universities included the CPTP as a part of their curricula. Later in the program a military obligation was incurred, but during the time of my training there still was no such requirement. I don't think it mattered; most of the men and women that I trained with went on to military service.

Happily, for the government, the CPTP program proved to be very cost-effective. It cost Uncle Sam only 375 dollars to train a person well enough to qualify for a private pilot's license; for an additional 870 dollars, the program produced a licensed secondary pilot with more extensive training in larger, more powerful, and more complicated aircraft.

The requirements for enrollment in the program were not stringent. You only had to be at least an average student and able to pass a cursory physical. If enthusiasm had been a requirement, I would have been able to give enough to supply another dozen students.

I started flying during the spring and summer of 1939, my sophomore year, at the same airfield where I had my first airplane ride in the Ford Trimotor so many years before. The airplane we flew during our primary training was the J-3 Cub. Originally built by the Taylor Aircraft Company, and later by

Piper Aircraft Corporation, the J-3 was a simple little airplane. A high-winged, single-engine aircraft, the earlier versions had only a 40-horsepower engine. I really liked it; it was forgiving, easy to fly, and simple—a perfect primary trainer.

Bill Quinby, my instructor, was a wonderful guy. Although he was quiet-talking and considerate, he was also very demanding, which made him a great instructor. I always felt completely at ease with him, and after each lesson I was eager to get started with the next.

This was a wonderful time for me, probably my best summer ever. When I wasn't at class I was at the airfield. If I wasn't scheduled to fly, I was at the hangar talking with the other students, or outside watching the flying. To top it off, I was young, healthy, responsible for no one but myself, and I had my whole life in front of me.

During the summer of 1940 it often took three of us to land the little J-3 Cubs. On many afternoons the wind picked up and gusted to 30 or 40 miles per hour as thunderstorms swept through the area. The gusts were about the same speed as that at which the little J-3 landed. So, when some hapless student came in for a landing—almost hovering in the wind—a pair of us raced out onto the field, grabbed a wing strut, and pulled the airplane down to the ground. With one of us on each wing, we walked it back to the ramp and held it in place until it could be tied down.

We did all of our flying right around the field. There wasn't much of anything but farmland nearby so we didn't have to waste time getting away from populated areas. The flights lasted about 30 minutes each, and although that didn't seem like very long, Quinby was able to teach me a great deal about flying in that short time.

We were flying back to the field one day at less than 1,000 feet when Bill said, "Watch this," and pulled the power off, picked the nose up, and kicked the airplane into a one-turn spin. We lost only about 100 feet. A typical pilot would have lost 300 or 400 feet. I'm still impressed. Unlike most instructors, when Quinby gave us a simulated engine failure, he made us take it down and actually land in a pasture or field. That was a real truth-teller—not much arguing about whether you would have made it or not. I'm not certain how the farmers in the area felt about their fields becoming ad hoc landing strips.

There weren't television newscasts or nearly the amount of news coverage that we have today, but we weren't living in a vacuum in 1940 and 1941. We had newspapers, and the radio programming was fairly timely and extensive. Most of us felt that the United States couldn't stay out of the war in Europe, and that the time when we would become combatants wasn't too far off. Events in Europe made the big news, and very few of us gave much thought to war with Japan.

After school started in the fall of 1940, I continued to mix flying with studies. This was at the height of the Battle of Britain. Perhaps it was this, or my enthusiasm for flying, or both, but whatever it was carried over into my schoolwork and my academic performance improved through the year.

I got a big ego boost on one occasion when I was hanging out at the airfield. I wasn't doing much beyond taking up space when Quinby approached me.

"Hamilton, what are you doing?"

"Not too much." In my mind there wasn't much that I could do that would take priority over doing something for Bill. "What do you need?"

"One of the other students got lost on his cross-country flight and landed in a field about thirty miles out. I need you to go out with me to ferry his airplane back."

Well, that put me on top of the world. The idea that Bill trusted me above several others who were also available really felt good. We took off in one of the J-3s and located the other airplane which the student had landed in a wheat field.

We landed next to it, and after checking to make certain that it was undamaged, I climbed in while Quinby hand-cranked the engine. After the engine started, he ran around to the tail section and held the aircraft back while I ran the throttle up to full power. I wanted as much power as I could get; the field wasn't too big, and the ground was soft under the wheat, which was almost two feet high.

I looked back at Bill, whose face was screwed into a grimace against the propwash and debris that the little airplane was kicking up. Behind him, the propwash buffeted the wheat so that it flashed gray and green as it whipped back and forth. It looked like the surface of a pond hit by a big gust of wind. After a few seconds, I signaled and Bill released the straining little airplane. A few yards later I was safely airborne and on my way back to Athens. In my own eyes, my personal stock was a notch or two higher.

When I finally got my private pilot license on September 15, 1940, the first thing I did was take my parents for a ride. I think they were quite proud of me—and impressed. I built up a respectable amount of flight time during this period. It cost only about five dollars an hour to fly the J-3, and while it may have been questionable legally—private pilots were not supposed to charge to fly passengers—I took friends up for rides and they gave me money to pay for the gas. It was a mutually beneficial arrangement.

One day in April 1941, I was sitting around in the hangar at the airfield with my friends Sam Forrer and Bill "Bing" Crosby. We had been pondering what the future held for us. With war raging all around the globe, things seemed particularly uncertain.

"We'll have two years of college finished after this term," I said. "We'll be eligible for the military flight programs. I think I'm going to sign up with the Navy."

The other two knew that I had always liked the Navy. The challenge of landing on aircraft carriers appealed to me. The traditions and customs also seemed special. On top of that, I had two distant relatives who were naval aviators, and that fact also influenced my thinking.

"Are you sure you don't want to give the Army a chance?" Sam tested me.

"No," I answered. "Their uniforms aren't as nice." I did like the Navy uniforms, but of course that wasn't the reason I wanted to join.

"That's as good as any reason I've heard," Bing said. "I'll go with you. Sounds like a lot of fun. Odds are that if we don't do something, we're going to get drafted anyway. I'd rather pick my own poison."

That afternoon, all three of us piled into Sam's dad's car and drove to the Naval Reserve Air Base in Atlanta. There wasn't much of a fuss to get signed up; we filled out some long forms and made arrangements to get a physical examination. We were told to go back to Athens and finish our sophomore year. If we completed that successfully, then we'd hear from them. For the next month or so, time seemed to drag while I waited to hear from the Navy.

I kept myself occupied with my studies and, of course, with my flying. By this time, I was enrolled in the secondary program, training with the CPTP in the Waco UPF-7. The Waco was a very powerful airplane compared to the J-3. It was a biplane with a 220-horsepower engine and was capable of aerobatic flight.

Up to then I had not flown an airplane with an engine more powerful than 60 horsepower, so it was a great thrill to get into a *real* plane! The training syllabus concentrated on precision flying, figure-eight turns around a point, short- and soft-field landings, cross-country flights, and the like. There followed a great deal of aerobatics.

My instructor was Ben Bradley, a tall, lanky man who spoke with a Southern drawl so pronounced that even I, who had spent my entire life in the South, took notice. But this didn't affect his ability to teach; he was an outstanding pilot and flight instructor, and he thoroughly taught me the fundamentals of aerobatics, which proved invaluable in combat.

At about the time I finished my sophomore year, in early June 1941, a letter finally came from the Navy. It directed me to report to the Naval Reserve Air Base in Atlanta. Accordingly, on June 16, 1941, I went to Atlanta, put my name on the dotted line, and officially became a seaman second class.

This was the first step in the Navy's V-5 Aviation Cadet Program. Through this standardized program, the Navy screened and trained tens of thousands of young men for wartime service in aircraft at sea. During this time the base at Atlanta was one of several Elimination Bases, or E-Bases, operated by the Navy. At the E-bases, candidates for aviation duty were brought together and evaluated for their suitability. Each candidate was tested for their physical and mental aptitudes for aviation and went through a short syllabus on flying. For those who passed, the E-Base was the first of many steps in becoming a naval aviator. It was a huge success.

There wasn't yet a high-pressure boot camp mentality. They assigned us to a barracks and gave us the usual duties that a seaman second class would have—peeling potatoes in the mess hall, standing fire watch, and other chores of that nature. We did a lot of marching and were given indoctrination classes to get us accustomed to Navy life. But there wasn't the rushing around and shouting that characterized the training a couple of years later, when they were putting thousands upon thousands of young men through flight school.

Those of us who had participated in CPTP didn't do any flying; we had already demonstrated that we had the aptitude and talent for piloting airplanes. While it was gratifying to know that we had the initial hurdle cleared before we really started, it was difficult to watch the other boys go flying while we stayed on the ground.

During this period the Navy pooled its CPTP graduates until there were enough to start a complete class of about 120 students. On August 6, 1941, I was sent to Pensacola, Florida, to begin flight school. The class I was assigned to was class 8A41P(C). The "8" stood for August, the eighth month of the year; the "A" stood for the first class to be formed in August; the "41" stood for the year, 1941; the "P" stood for Pensacola; and the "C" indicated that all cadets in the class were graduates of the Civil Aeronautics Administration CPTP.

The move to Pensacola was quite an event for me. I hadn't been out of Georgia since I was five, when my family fled the great Florida Hurricane of 1926. A bunch of us who were friends at the E-Base in Atlanta were sent to Pensacola together. We were billeted in a big, redbrick barracks that still stands. There was quite an emphasis on our physical training, and every morning they woke us up at 0530 to go out behind the building in our skivvies for about half an hour of calisthenics. It wasn't so bad initially, but by the time November rolled around, it was rather chilly out there!

At Pensacola we were designated aviation cadets. The rank of aviation cadet was an odd animal. We were not considered enlisted men, nor were we quite yet officers. We were in a sort of netherworld of the military pecking

Aviation Cadet Hamilton McWhorter III at NAS Pensacola in August 1941. McWhorter began flight training a few months before the Japanese sneak attack on Pearl Harbor. Training intensified subsequent to the attack, at the cost of many aviation cadet lives. (McWhorter Family)

order. No one really seemed comfortable with how they should treat us. Technically, I suppose, we outranked all the enlisted personnel, but we had very little experience compared to them. In fact, much of our academic instruction was given by enlisted sailors. And although we were earmarked to become commissioned officers, it would not have occurred to us to pull rank on enlisted men.

At the other end of the spectrum, the best the officers seemed to be able to do was exercise a form of tolerance toward us. We were destined to join them with a commission when we finished flight training, but we had yet to achieve that goal. Until then, we were held at a distance and treated as students who had yet to prove themselves.

Chapter 3

Our training began in earnest at Pensacola; we studied subjects that dealt directly with flying—navigation, aerodynamic theory, engineering, meteorology, and a host of other disciplines. One of the least popular classes was celestial navigation. It was difficult, and it was useless as far as I was concerned, because I was sure I was going to become a fighter pilot. Fortunately, I never had to use it, but I'm sure it was important to patrol airplane pilots.

Again, as CPTP students, we got very little primary training because we were already rated pilots. Once in a while we got to fly a familiarization flight in whatever aircraft was available, just to keep our heads in the game. One of these airplanes was the seemingly ancient SBU-1, built by Vought. Intended as a two-seat scout bomber when it entered service in 1935, it was obsolete by the time we flew it. It was a biplane constructed largely of wood and fabric. That, along with all the wires and struts that held it together, certainly made it *look* obsolete. Still, with its 700-horsepower engine, it was a bigger, more powerful beast than anything I had flown before. And flying it was better than not flying at all.

Such flights were infrequent, though, and because we weren't studying for primary training like the other students were, we had a lot of free time. Pensacola wasn't a bad place to have free time. Founded by the Spanish in the late 1600s and taken in turn by the British, the Spanish again, the French, the United States, the Confederate States, and finally by the United States once more, Pensacola is one of the oldest towns in the country. Blessed with miles and miles of sugar-white beaches, plenty of places to have a drink, and a relaxed Southern attitude, it provided numerous diversions for hundreds and later thousands of young pilots-to-be.

Among those diversions were women who came from all over the surrounding area in hopes of meeting someone they might like. It didn't hurt

Cadet McWhorter, front cockpit, checks out an SOC floatplane with another cadet at NAS Pensacola in October 1941. (McWhorter Family)

our feelings to give them the opportunity. Being a young man, I felt like I was dead center in the perfect time and place. It was just a shame that it took an impending war to make it happen.

***

My class finally began regular flight training at the end of September 1941. In the mornings after formation, we boarded big, open-sided trailer rigs we called "cattle cars." They had long wooden seats down the middle and horizontal grab bars for us to hang onto. Packed inside, we bounced our way out to Saufley Field. We normally spent all day at the field, flying twice, before we were crammed back into the cattle cars for the return trip to Pensacola.

Our training began a little more than one-third of the way through the program at what was called the "33-hour check." We did most of our basic training in the N3N, and our later instrument and cross-country training in the SNJ. Our basic training included aerobatics, formation work, and all sorts of takeoffs and landings.

The N3N was a simple little biplane. Similar in many ways to the Stearman, it was built by the Navy in its own factory in Philadelphia. Powered by a 235-horsepower, Wright-built radial engine, it could do about 110 miles per hour on a good day. Interestingly, there was no wood in its structure;

The N3N had an all-aluminum structure and was manufactured by the Navy in its own factory. McWhorter remembered it as a docile, easy-to-fly trainer. (U.S. Navy)

it was all aluminum, the Navy having quite a bit left over from its defunct dirigible program. The instrumentation in the cockpit was minimal, and communication between the instructor, who sat in the front seat, and the student, who sat in the back, was done mainly through a Gosport tube. This tube had a mouthpiece on the instructor's end and earphones at the student's end. One-way communication was pretty much the standard.

Things went along really well for us. Historically, the CPTP classes experienced a washout rate of only seven percent; much lower than the typical classes, and I don't remember any washouts from my own class. I was doing well also. The only real trouble I had was of my own making.

Our training syllabus included plenty of solo flights. These were intended for us to practice various aspects of our flying and to help us develop our confidence. Because I didn't feel particularly challenged, I often grew bored with the officially sanctioned solo flying. Confidence wasn't much of a problem for me either, and I wasn't alone in this.

It was quite common for cadets in search of excitement to meet over predetermined points at an agreed-upon time—or to take advantage of chance meetings—and engage in mock dogfights. These were wonderful, twisting, turning affairs that actually were good training. But if mistakes were made, they could be dangerous. Because of the danger, these encounters were officially frowned upon, and we were admonished against them.

But the temptation was too great. One sunny October morning I was cruising above the pine trees of the flat Florida panhandle when I spotted another N3N flying in the same direction. Fair game! I banked hard toward the other pilot just as he saw me and turned into my pretend attack. The fight was on. We swirled around each other, rolling and twisting. The wire and fabric of my airplane was singing—straining against gravity and against the engine. Still, we coaxed our aircraft at each other in slashing attacks, picturing ourselves as wing-borne Knights of the Sky. This went on for what I am sure was several minutes, until I saw another aircraft descending toward us.

Both cockpits of this aircraft were manned, so I knew that it had an instructor aboard. The jig was up. I forgot the other student, hauled back on the stick, and kicked the right rudder hard. My airplane responded perfectly and immediately went into a spin. Once, twice, three times the airplane spun around its vertical axis. I held the controls hard against the stops and watched for the instructor's airplane. Four, five, six revolutions now. There he was, still following me down. Seven, eight, nine; the ground was rushing up at me. Caught between the instructor's airplane and the earth, I had only two choices; neither was good. I couldn't win an encounter with the ground, so I neutralized the stick and kicked the rudder against the direction of the spin. Again, the N3N responded perfectly. After the spin tightened for just a fraction of a second, the airplane hesitated, swung once or twice, then steadied into a nose-low dive. I hauled back on the stick and leveled out above the landscape, which was very much closer than it had been.

I gave a sheepish look over my shoulder, and just as I had feared, the instructor was flying off my wing. He was frowning as he signaled me back toward the field, indicating that I should land. I saw his student looking at me with commiseration on his face.

My heart fell into my stomach as I nodded and turned back toward the field. I suddenly felt very foolish. What if I had just ruined my lifelong dream? What if the Navy decided to wash me out of the flight program? After all, what good is a pilot who can't follow instructions? What good is a pilot who willfully disobeys orders?

I was sure that I was finished. Carefully, I landed back at the field, parked my airplane with all the other bright yellow N3Ns, and started back toward the flight line shack to put my gear away.

"Hey, Cadet!"

I turned and recognized the instructor who had sent me back to the field. "Yes, sir," I answered, stiffening to attention.

"That spin was really a pretty good trick," he said. "You almost lost me."

I was flabbergasted. I had expected to be roughly upbraided. His remark was almost a backhanded compliment. "Well, sir, . . ." I started, then stopped. There really was no good thing for me to say.

"Do you know the rules regarding unauthorized dogfighting, Cadet?"

Here it came. "Yes, sir."

"I'm guessing that those rules don't apply to you, Cadet?"

"No, sir, I mean, yes, sir . . . I mean . . ." How was I supposed to answer that?

"I think it would probably be a good idea if you went up to visit with the commanding officer," he said.

I dropped off my gear, then headed to the operations building and made my way upstairs. After smoothing my khaki uniform with my hands and straightening my tie—we flew in uniforms then—I stepped into the CO's office.

I got lucky. Rather than chew me out, the commanding officer calmly spelled out the perils of doing anything unauthorized, *especially* dogfights. He emphasized that nearly every rule or regulation in the books was written in blood. That is, that someone had died doing the things that were forbidden or controlled.

My punishment seemed surprisingly light. In order to emphasize his point, he "secured my liberty." That is, he restricted me to the base for 10 days. He also gave me the opportunity to further consider the importance of the rules and regulations of naval aviation, as well as the roles that trust and responsibility played in the life of a naval officer. That opportunity came in the form of an order to march for two hours on the parade deck after each working day, for two weeks, with a 1903 Springfield rifle on my shoulder. I was to be a one-man parade.

Considering the punishment I could have received, I didn't particularly mind my daily dates with the Springfield. Looking back on the whole incident now, and thinking back to the instructor's first remark about my "neat trick," I wonder if the whole incident might have worked in my favor. Maybe by demonstrating an aptitude for aerobatic flight, illicit as that demonstration was, I had increased my chances of being selected for training in fighters.

As it turned out, I learned that the other student was my classmate, Sam Logan. Sam was a Marine who also was picked to fly fighters and ended up flying combat in the Solomon Islands. In 1943, while chasing a Zero, he was shot down from behind by another Zero. While Sam descended in his parachute, his attacker turned on him and made several passes to try to chop him out of the sky with his propeller. In the end, the enemy pilot slashed off one of Sam's feet and mangled the other.

Remarkably, Sam kept his cool. Upon splashing down into the water, he managed to climb into his life raft and administer first aid to himself until he was picked up by a floatplane. Ultimately, he was able to keep the Marine Corps from discharging him and after his convalescence he returned to flying as a transport pilot.

***

By November 1941, we were flying the North American SNJ trainer. Also built as the AT-6 Texan for the U.S. Army Air Forces, and as the Harvard for the British, the SNJ was a fairly advanced trainer for its time. An all-metal, low-wing monoplane, it had retractable landing gear and was powered by a 600-horsepower Pratt & Whitney R-1340 Wasp radial engine. We did instrument training, formation work, and advanced navigation in the SNJ. It also had a single .30-caliber, cowl-mounted machinegun for gunnery. For us, it was an exciting airplane to fly—almost a real fighter.

But for communication between cockpits, the old Gosport tube was still the standard. On one instrument training flight, when I was flying under the hood in the rear seat of an SNJ, my instructor tested me by putting the airplane into an unusual attitude. Somehow, I missed his signal for me to

North American made outstanding advanced trainers for both the Navy and the Army Air Forces. The Navy's variant, the SNJ, was virtually identical to the Army's AT-6. (U.S. Navy)

take control and recover the airplane. So, there we both sat, wondering what the other was doing while the aircraft rolled inverted and started into a steep dive. Finally, I heard him shout at me through the Gosport to "do something about this!" Startled into understanding what had happened, I grabbed the controls and brought the straining airplane upright before we got into too much trouble. Such were the vagaries of the Gosport tube.

***

On December 7, 1941, I was behind the barracks, throwing a football around with a bunch of the other guys. We heard shouting and looked up and saw a group of cadets waving wildly from the windows. Confused, we stopped playing ball and waited until someone ran out and told us that the Japanese had bombed Pearl Harbor. This was a shock to us, as most of the war news came from Europe. Some of us weren't even sure where Pearl Harbor was. And although we guessed correctly that the attack meant we were in the war, we weren't too sure what that would mean to us.

We found out quickly enough. Almost immediately, the training schedule shifted to an eight-day week—we trained for eight straight days, then had a day off. Also, the workdays stretched to ten or twelve hours, rather than the eight-hour days we had gotten used to.

It all had a dramatic effect. Some of the guys didn't adjust and partied on the very next Saturday night as if they were on the more relaxed schedule. The result was deadly. The next day, Sunday, there were five fatal accidents. Most of them involved cadets who just flew straight into the ground. I can only guess that they were hungover and had blacked out under heavy maneuvering. One evening, the personal effects from one of the boy's bodies were brought back. Someone showed me his room key, which was in his pocket when he crashed. He hit the ground so hard that the key was bent at a 90-degree angle.

***

The stepped-up training tempo produced the results the Navy was looking for. My class finished training on December 18, two weeks ahead of schedule.

I was overjoyed when I learned that I had been selected to fly fighters. I had thought about little else, and my flying marks, combined with some pretty good work in the aerial gunnery pattern, were enough to get me assigned to Naval Air Station Miami at Opa-locka, Florida, for fighter training. I departed Pensacola on December 23, 1941, and rode down with a classmate, Bill Bonneau, in his 1936 Ford convertible. Bill and I had been together since the class began in August and, unbeknown to us, we would be together for a long time thereafter. We checked in at NAS Miami on December 26, 1941.

At that time, every fighter pilot in naval aviation took his training at Opa-locka. Located more or less in Miami, it had more to offer in the way of social life than even Pensacola. And we tried out every bit of it.

But there wasn't one of us there who, if given the choice between flying fighters and partying, would have hesitated at choosing flying. We were all tigers and were excited to be getting on with our training. There was a war on, and each of us knew in our heart-of-hearts that he, personally, was going to win that war.

The transition from the Grumman F3F biplane fighter to the Brewster F2A Buffalo at Opa-Locka had been completed just before we arrived. As the years have passed, the F2A has had heaps of criticism piled onto it as a poorly performing, tough-to-maintain, badly constructed piece of junk. Rightly so. It had been, and would be, terribly mauled by the Japanese. But at the time it was still a front-line fighter with some flying organizations, including the U.S. Marine Corps, and we were excited to get our hands on it.

Built by the Brewster Aeronautical Corporation, the first F2A Buffalo had been delivered less than three years earlier as the Navy's first monoplane fighter. Armed with four .50 caliber machineguns and powered by a 1,200-horsepower Wright Cyclone radial engine, it could do about 320 miles per hour.

McWhorter recalled the Brewster F2A fighter as a difficult-to-fly and unreliable aircraft. This example flies over NAS Miami where he trained. (U.S. Navy)

The Buffalo's performance numbers weren't that bad on paper, but in practice it just couldn't compete. I wasn't particularly fond of it either; it just didn't handle very well. It was also rather unforgiving if it was only slightly mishandled when you were pulling high Gs. More than once I came in on a gunnery run and perhaps skidded a bit too much, or didn't have the yaw trimmed just right—or something—and that airplane snap-rolled so quick that it made my head spin.

We did not have G-suits at that time, and it was very easy to pull too many Gs and black out during gunnery runs. I lost consciousness more than once and came to in some rather unusual attitudes. The time I spent training to recover from unusual attitudes proved to be well spent. More often than not I regained consciousness from these gut-wrenching episodes as a mere passenger in an inverted airplane.

***

I returned from a gunnery flight one morning and set myself up for landing. I put the landing gear down and checked that it was down and locked. The only indication that it was down was a pointer on a braided wire that ran across the bottom of the instrument panel as the gear went down. When it wouldn't move anymore, and the pointer on the wire lined up with a mark on the instrument panel, the pilot was supposedly assured that the gear was down and locked in place.

With the flaps lowered and the aircraft trimmed—no small feat in itself—I checked the windsock one more time and aligned the nose of the stubby little fighter with the landing area. I brought the nose up slightly an instant before touching down and waited for the airplane to settle to earth.

It did settle—all the way down. In a screeching, frightening roar, the landing gear folded, the propeller blades flailed at the ground, and the airplane hit the grass field and skidded several hundred feet in a huge cloud of dust. Of course, the engine stopped and the silence that replaced the screeching of the tortured metal was nearly as unsettling. Instinctively, on pure muscle memory, my hands went through the shutdown procedures and I scrambled out of the damaged bird. The short trip down to the ground felt distinctly peculiar.

Fortunately, I was exonerated of any wrongdoing. What happened—and it had happened quite a number of times before—was that the over center locks on the landing gear did not push the gear into place. When the weight of the aircraft transferred to the landing gear, it simply folded.

Eventually, manufacturing problems and poor management got so bad at the Brewster plant that the Navy physically walked in and shut it down in

1944. That this happened at the height of the war, when aircraft were badly needed, is telling evidence of how bad the problems were at Brewster.

***

We trained right through New Year's Day at Opa-locka. For me, other than my sledding episode in the Brewster Buffalo, things went well. I finished training on January 22 and received my wings and designation as a naval aviator. Finally, on February 9, 1942, I was commissioned as an ensign in the United States Naval Reserve and received orders to Fighting Squadron 9 (VF-9) at Norfolk, Virginia. We really didn't do much celebrating after we were commissioned, but it was a kick to be saluted by every enlisted man around. The tradition was that you had to give a dollar to the first person who saluted you after being commissioned, and every sailor went out of his way to salute us.

My classmates and I would have been commissioned a bit earlier, but we were held back until they could expedite the students out of the Trade School at Annapolis—our nickname for the Naval Academy. The Navy wanted to get them commissioned the day before us hurriedly indoctrinated pagans from the V-5 program. That sort of subtle favoritism toward Naval Academy graduates rubbed a lot of us the wrong way, but it was something that was with us throughout the war and beyond.

Most of us were just too anxious to get home on leave to worry about partying. I went straight back to Athens and stayed with my parents. They were very proud—but anxious at the same time. The nation had been at war for only a couple months and things were not going well. Wake Island had fallen a couple of weeks after the attack on Pearl Harbor, and our forces in the Philippines were taking a drubbing.

Nevertheless, I was young and felt nearly invincible. About the only real danger I faced in Athens was getting my back patted off. I stopped at the airfield, of course, and visited with all my former instructors and flying buddies. I spent quite a bit of time answering questions and, without meaning to, recruiting a few more pilots for the Navy. It felt pretty good to strut around in my new uniform with its shiny gold ensign bars and aviator wings. And I think that helped my stock quite a bit when I visited my old girlfriends!

Chapter 4

By March 3, 1942, I had put aside the role of Hometown Hero and reported to the Aircraft Carrier Training Group—the ACTG—at Naval Air Station Norfolk, Virginia. While there, I would receive my last bit of training before being sent to join VF-9. The ACTG was where I was introduced to the Grumman F4F Wildcat.

The F4F was originally designed for the Navy as a biplane fighter, the follow-on to the F3F. The configuration changed in 1936, when the Navy decided that the biplane design had reached its limits and that the monoplane was the answer to increased performance. After being redesigned as a monoplane, the Wildcat competed in a fly-off against the Brewster XF2A and the Seversky XNF-1. The Wildcat came out as the loser to the F2A because it was equipped with a weak engine.

Nevertheless, the Navy saw promise in the Grumman design and ordered a modified version featuring a more powerful engine. This new version, with square-tipped wings, a more powerful Pratt & Whitney radial engine, and a two-stage supercharger (necessary for high-altitude performance), was more to the Navy's liking. In August 1939, it ordered 54 production models. The Wildcat went on to become the Navy's front-line fighter through the first part of the war, and variations served in a secondary role all the way to the end.

Like the Brewster Buffalo, the Grumman Wildcat wasn't a pretty airplane. It was shaped like a beer keg with wings, and takeoffs and landings could be a bit touchy, but it was an honest plane otherwise. It was reasonably fast and maneuverable for its time, and had good high-altitude performance, a respectable combat radius, and was reasonably well armed with four .50 caliber machineguns—later increased to six. And Grumman built a toughness into it that enabled it to withstand tremendous battle damage and still bring its pilot home. That toughness saved a lot of lives.

The Grumman F4F Wildcat fighter was inelegant in appearance, but made up for it with reasonable performance, good armament, and legendary ruggedness. (U.S. Navy)

***

My first flight in the Grumman was uneventful and the rest of the transition from the Buffalo was no big deal, though I did have one "near thing" while at the ACTG. I was out on a familiarization flight one afternoon and was putting the airplane through its paces—loops and rolls and half-Cuban eights, that sort of thing. I stomped on the right rudder for a real hard snap roll, and it did. Snap, that is. Not the airplane, but the rudder pedal. The rudder pedals in the Wildcat hung down from a bar that ran horizontally beneath the instrument panel. I guess my big, size-13 foot came down a bit too hard, because the right rudder pedal broke off and was rolling around somewhere in the bottom of the airplane.

In the air you could fly the Wildcat around without the rudder pedal as long as you weren't doing anything fancy. It wasn't a big deal to trim the aircraft to balanced flight. But taking off without the rudder was impossible, and landing without it was very difficult because the right rudder was required to counter the torque from the engine. The Wildcat was a stubby little airplane, with a fairly narrow landing gear. That configuration, combined with a relatively powerful engine that generated a lot of torque, made directional control on the runway rather difficult at times—and impossible without rudder control.

Fortunately, the airfield at NAS Norfolk was a huge circular mat rather than a set of runways. I gingerly nursed the aircraft back to the field, descended, and set it down on the mat without too much trouble. As soon as the wheels were on the ground, I pulled the fuel-mixture control back and stopped the engine in order to prevent damage to it if the plane nosed over. From that point on, though, I was just a passenger.

Sure enough, the airplane started to drift left because of the torque of the still-spinning propeller. With no right brake—the brakes were actuated with the rudder pedals—I could not stop the turn. The airplane turned slowly at first, then more sharply until it spun around in a complete 360-degree turn and came to a stop. I saw a tow tractor already leaving the flight line to come retrieve me, so I let out my breath and congratulated myself. Home safe.

***

Though we flew a lot of familiarization flights and practiced a bit of air-to-air gunnery, the primary reason for us to be at the ACTG was to train to be carrier aviators. To do so, we spent quite a bit of time with Lieutenant Commander William A. Stewart. He was already something of a legend within the fleet as one of the best landing signal officers (LSOs) around, and he would go on to make even more of a name for himself later in the war. He was quite a character—stern, professional, and totally in control. He was the type of man who made you feel safer just by being around.

As an air group LSO, Stewart was in charge of your life when you arrived, gear and flaps down, hanging on the prop at 75 miles per hour, at the back end of the ship. His word was law. But his word wasn't passed via the radio. Rather, he had a pair of paddles, similar to shortened tennis rackets, with strips of fabric stretched across the face instead. This enabled him to wave them about without having to wrestle against the 20-plus knots of wind that blew constantly across the deck of the carrier.

The LSO could pass a number of signals with the paddles: both paddles held out horizontally at arm's length meant to continue—everything was looking good; crossing them over his head meant a mandatory wave-off, or go around; dropping the left paddle to his side and bringing the right paddle sharply across his chest meant to cut power and land the aircraft on the deck into the arresting wires; both paddles raised above the horizontal meant that you were too high; and both paddles held below the horizontal meant that you were too low. There were many other signals; it was almost a distinct language.

After we were lectured more than we thought was necessary, we were finally turned loose to practice on dry land. A flight of four or five of us took off to find some obscure grass field in the surrounding countryside, where Lieutenant Commander Stewart waited for us. Through good fortune we managed to find it, even though we had no navigational aids or two-way radio contact with him. I took my turn and banked into a left downwind—the carrier pattern is always to the left—for my first pass. I busily set my Wildcat up for landing: gear and flaps down, mixture set, trim set, propeller pitch set. Carefully, I double-checked my distance and altitude. Looking good. This wasn't going to be too difficult. Everything was setting up nicely and I was flying what I thought was the proper pattern.

Until I turned onto final approach. Stewart was there at the edge of the field. For all practical purposes he was jumping up and down. So were his paddles—chopping up and down on the ground. It was the signal to land. I remembered that much from his lecture. Suddenly, I wasn't so sure that everything was going as smoothly as I had thought.

A few seconds later I put the airplane on the ground and taxied to where he stood waiting for me with his hands on his hips. The canopy of my aircraft was open, and I leaned over and watched him scramble up onto the wing and pull himself up to the cockpit until his face was only a few inches from mine.

"Ensign, how's the weather in Tennessee today?" he shouted over the idling engine.

"Sir?"

"Listen, Ensign, this is a carrier landing pattern you're supposed to be working on—not a low-level, cross-country navigation flight! You were so low and so far out that I could barely see you."

This bothered me. I thought I had done a pretty fair job of flying what I believed I had been taught. Nevertheless, he was a lieutenant commander with more experience than nearly the entire Navy, and I was just a wet-behind-the-ears ensign.

"Okay, sir. I'll tighten it up," I answered, pretending that I suddenly remembered every procedure and nuance associated with landing on an aircraft carrier.

Fortunately, he didn't buy it. He spent a few more minutes with me and in no uncertain words made it plain how I was supposed to fly *his* carrier pattern.

And that did the trick. From that time on, I really never had any more problems with carrier landing procedures. After a week or so, we were all qualified at the field, and a few days later, on April 20, 1942, we got to try it for real.

We were sent to qualify aboard the escort carrier *Long Island* in Chesapeake Bay. In the spring of 1942, the German U-boat campaign was really taking a toll on American shipping up and down the Atlantic coast. Chesapeake Bay was considered safer than the open ocean. Later in the war, carrier training was moved into even safer waters—Lake Michigan.

***

As I flew in formation with my instructor as flight lead, I sneaked peeks downward as we made our way over Chesapeake Bay. When I finally caught sight of the carrier my reaction was typical: I blinked my eyes and tried to lean closer. A nervous flutter went through my stomach—the ship looked so tiny! From where we orbited thousands of feet above, the little wooden-decked escort carrier didn't look like much more than a toy.

But landing aboard the carrier wasn't child's play. Partway through the day one of the ensigns made a rough approach, bounced hard, and rode his airplane over the side. There was a frantic scramble aboard the ship as sailors rushed to the edge of the deck to throw rescue equipment overboard, watching for the hapless pilot to scramble clear of the airplane. Unfortunately, the pilot perished. He was either knocked out by the crash or he got hung up in the airplane, because he never came up.

After crisscrossing the water for a while, the carrier and its escorts were brought back on course. The ensign was given up as lost, and flight operations resumed. My own landings—eight of them—went well, but the loss of one of our ensigns was sobering, a reminder to the rest of us of just how dangerous our profession was. A few days later, on April 24, 1942, my stint at the ACTG was complete and I reported to VF-9, ready for combat. It had been only 10 months since I had enlisted in the Navy.

Chapter 5

VF-9 was among the first of the many new squadrons formed during the expansion of the wartime Navy. It came into being with the commissioning of Carrier Reserve Air Group 9 on March 1, 1942, along with Bombing Squadron 9 (VB-9) and Torpedo Squadron 9 (VT-9).

Initially, VF-9 shared Hangar 4 with the ACTG at East Field, so it was just a simple matter of walking across the building to check in. The first person I met was Jake Onstott. He was very cordial and took me around to introduce me to the commanding officer and the other pilots. Naval aviation at this point in the war was so shorthanded that Jake, only a lieutenant, junior grade, and a transfer pilot from a dive bomber squadron, was assigned to duty as the executive officer. As such, he was second in rank behind the commanding officer.

The commanding officer, or skipper, was Lieutenant Commander Jack Raby, affectionately known as "Captain Jack." Raby was a fantastic man, a full-blown extrovert. He was genuinely friendly and full of energy, and he made it his business to learn the strengths and weaknesses of his officers and sailors. His affability extended into off-duty hours as well; he loved a party as much as anyone I knew. If he had any fault at all, it was that he liked to bend his elbow a bit too much.

Nevertheless, Raby was an excellent leader. He had been around for quite a while and was a very experienced flier. He earned our loyalty and respect with his experience and commonsense attitude toward getting things done right. There was no intimidation in his leadership style, and our small nucleus of officers and enlisted men quickly took to his lead as we worked to fill the squadron to full combat strength.

***

On April 30, less than a week after I arrived, the squadron received urgent orders to ferry some new F4F-4s to the West Coast. An R4D transport, the

Jack Raby was the commander of VF-9, McWhorter's first squadron. An excellent leader and pilot, Raby was noted for playing hard and working harder. (U.S. Navy)

Navy equivalent of the civilian DC-3 airliner, flew 12 of us up to the Grumman plant at Bethpage, New York.

After we signed for the factory-fresh fighters, we left Bethpage the next day and stopped at Naval Reserve Aviation Base Atlanta, the same place where I had signed up for the Navy. I had a great time showing off "my" new F4F-4 fighter to my parents, who had driven over from Athens. To make things better, they brought my girlfriend along, although, lamentably, she and I didn't get any time alone together. I also met one of my high school and college classmates, who had joined the Navy and was going through training at the base. It was nice to see the envy in his eyes when I led him up to the cockpit and let him sit at the controls.

We arrived in San Diego on May 4, after 16.8 hours of flight time. I was directed to report to the base operations officer the next morning. He took me outside and pointed to an airplane sitting on the ramp in front of the building.

"Ensign, you're going to take that airplane back to Norfolk."

Shading my eyes against the bright Southern California sun, I peered out at an awkward-looking, too-big-and-ugly-to-be-a-fighter biplane. "What is it?" I asked.

"Don't worry about what it's called. We'll get someone to show you how to start it, and you can leave this morning."

"Hey," I shouted at him as he turned to walk away, "how did I get this job? Why me?"

"Your skipper volunteered you."

Being the junior ensign in the squadron sure had its drawbacks.

A short time later another pilot came out and ran me through the start-up checks, pointing out the more important instruments. The airplane turned out to be an SON-1, a Navy-built version of the Curtiss SOC-1A. It was a scout-observation biplane and was fairly dated. Nevertheless, I did some flight planning and got airborne that morning, cutting a blistering pace across the sky at about 90 miles an hour. With fewer than 300 flight hours under my belt I was now all alone with 2,700 miles, several weather systems, and no end of opportunities to fail in front of me. Fortunately, by using my Navy navigation training and, admittedly, a good dose of Army Air Corps IFR (I Follow Railroads) navigational technique, I found my way back across the continent to Norfolk, 24.8 flight hours later, on May 9.

***

There is an old saw that the demeanor of any military unit is a direct reflection of its leadership. That was certainly the case with VF-9. As the squadron grew, it became more and more like Jack Raby. At least once a week the officers held a party. If it wasn't at the Raby household, it was at the home of one of the other married officers, the beach, or some other convenient place. Any event of significance—a birthday, someone's child's birthday, you name it—automatically became a good reason for a squadron get-together. These parties brought us closer together and engendered a great comradeship and loyalty that lasts to this day.

I believe that one of our greatest strengths lay in our diversity. Like the formulaic Hollywood movies, we came from a hodgepodge of geographic, ethnic, and economic backgrounds. We had our Texan, Marv Franger, who we all agreed was probably the world's foremost authority on the art of barbecuing. "Honest Hal" Vita came from Long Island, New York. He was a smart, gregarious type and an aggressive fighter pilot. Hal and his inseparable pal, Joe Sheehan, had actually reported to the squadron a few days late after being waylaid by a big party in Atlantic City. They were promptly dubbed "The Gold Dust Twins," after a cartoon strip, popular at that time, which featured a pair of flighty, mischievous characters. Lou Menard was from Palmetto, Florida, a fellow Southerner and one of my closer friends. Chick Smith hailed from North Carolina and was one of the sharpest pilots in the squadron; he was a very friendly and dependable fellow, a good leader. Mike Hadden, one of our senior pilots, was more reserved—very droll, but still very nice. Stu Ball and George Blair, both Northerners, were much the same, a bit more reserved than the rest of the squadron, with dry wits, but still very sympathetic. John "Tubby" Franks, our classic Midwesterner, was a graduate of Purdue University and one of the happiest, most gregarious people I've ever known. He could pull off a practical joke at a funeral without rubbing anyone the wrong way.

Early on, probably because I was the biggest officer in the squadron—and the most junior—but also I think because he liked me, I was semiofficially assigned as Raby's "handler." That meant that I was responsible for keeping Jack out of trouble. At the end of the evening I was charged with making sure that he got to his car in an upright position and was driven home by someone more sober than him. Back then, there wasn't much thought given to drinking and driving, but we still kept an eye on one another.

***

If we played hard, we worked even harder. I quickly realized that although we had been trained with a vengeance before we were sent to the fleet squadrons, what we learned really only gave us the tools we would need to absorb the real training we would receive as young wingmen. Raby worked us hard, three flights on most days and sometimes as many as six. We practiced everything from formation tactics to aerial gunnery and strafing. At the end of most flights, on the way back to the field, the flight leader wagged the tail of his airplane back and forth. That was the signal to fall back into a trail formation for a tail chase. We then followed him through every aerobatic maneuver he could think of—loops, Cuban eights, loops with a snap-roll on top—whatever he thought might shake us off his tail. It was great fun as well as superb training, and it was something we always looked forward to.

It wasn't all training for us, though. This was early in the war, and we weren't winning. German submarines were still a huge threat and we often sat submarine alert, a couple airplanes at a time. We were scrambled a few times after ships were torpedoed off the Virginia coast. Other than investigate the area, I'm not sure what we were expected to do if we actually ever found a submarine as we weren't armed with bombs or depth charges, just our .50 caliber machineguns. As it turned out, we never found any enemy subs.

We also flew as training aids for the local antiaircraft batteries. At night we flew at a given altitude on a certain course until the searchlights picked us up. First one beam would reach out and find us, then another, and then more—until there were so many that you thought you would go blind. It often got so bright that you couldn't see outside the airplane or in. It was very disorienting and quite dangerous.

One of our pilots came back from one of these flights and forgot to lower his landing gear. When he touched down, he skidded along the runway in a stream of sparks that turned into a sheet of flame when the fuel trapped behind the drain petcock on the belly ignited. Fortunately, the fire burned itself out and he climbed clear without any injury. That Grumman was built so tough that it was back airborne only a few days later.

***

This early in the war, the military was building or planning to build thousands of installations, airfields among them, to meet its enormous and growing needs. One of these new bases was the little airfield the Navy built about 10 miles east of Norfolk, at Oceana. On May 11, 1942, it became VF-9's new home.

Today Naval Air Station Oceana is the Navy's premier jet base, home to more than 200 fighter aircraft. When we arrived, it was little more than a cleared swamp with three short macadam runways, each only some 2,000 feet long, forming a triangle. Surrounding the entire airfield was a deep perimeter ditch, a perfect breeding area for mosquitoes. We were billeted in small Quonset huts, eight men per, and we worked out of similar structures. The ground around the airfield was so wet most of the time that the Navy built wooden boardwalks between all the buildings to keep us from soaking our feet in the mud whenever we went outside.

Amenities aside, Oceana was a great place to train a fighter squadron. We were the only squadron there and were isolated enough that we weren't bothered much by higher headquarters. Still, we were close enough to Norfolk and Virginia Beach that there was entertainment aplenty. And if, for whatever reason, we couldn't get into town, we could entertain ourselves in our squadron bar.

The bar was actually a little officers' club we had carved out of part of the administration shack. We added some furniture, a stone fireplace, and a couple of not-too-well-rendered landscape murals. We were lucky enough to get an electric icebox, donated by a neighbor-lady, and thereafter we always had plenty of cold beer on tap, distributed and paid for as the rolls of the dice dictated. With the addition of a Victrola and a wine mess, we had a comfortable little club. Over the next year or so it was the site of quite a bit of revelry.

I was in the club one night with some of the other pilots when we heard a rumbling sort of roar approaching from a distance.

I turned to Lou Menard. "What's that noise?"

"I don't know. If it's an airplane, it's in trouble."

I shook my head. "No, it's not an airplane."

"Train?"

"No."

"Tornado?"

By then, most of us had run outside to try to identify the source of the noise.

"Look!" someone shouted and pointed.

Quite a distance down the road that led to our squadron area we saw a huge spray of sparks racing in our direction. As the glowing spray and its accompanying roar approached, we stepped back and peered into the dark, still trying to make out what was causing the clamor.

It was Bill Bonneau's 1936 Ford convertible sedan. He had loaned it to Charlie Moutenot and a couple of the other boys for a night on the town. Now here they all were, hooting and hollering and drunker than any 20 people should have been. The right rear tire went flat on their way from town, but that hadn't even slowed them down. It wasn't long before the wheel shed what was left of the tire and began to roll on the metal rim. Of course, this made an incredible noise and threw up enough sparks to set a wet dog on fire, all of which delighted the drunk young fighter pilots.

By the time the abused car careened to a stop in front of our makeshift bar, the wheel itself was ground down almost to nothing, and what was left was glowing red-hot. It was a wonder the car hadn't caught fire. Poor Bonneau didn't know whether to get mad, laugh, or start crying.

***

Being a car owner in a flying squadron had its perks. Although gasoline was rationed and not too easy to come by, there was always a good bit of aviation fuel that was found to be "contaminated" and not "suitable" for use in our fighters. Well, rather than just disposing of this contaminated gasoline, we put it to good use in the automobiles of various squadron members. Naturally, the aviation gasoline caused the cars to run a bit hot, but it was free and plentiful.

***

In the early summer of 1942, our new executive officer, Lieutenant Hugh Winters, reported for duty and took over from Jake Onstott. Winters was a 1935 Annapolis graduate. After serving what was then an obligatory two-year period on battleships and destroyers, he went through flight training at Pensacola. He then served two years in VB-5 on the fleet carrier *Yorktown*

(CV-5), then returned to Pensacola and served as a flight instructor for one year prior to reporting to VF-9.

Hugh Winters was really a great guy, easy to talk to and nearly always smiling. He was also an avid hunter, and it just so happened that the Back Bay area of Virginia, a few miles southeast of Oceana, was one of the finest waterfowl hunting regions in the country. A resourceful type, Hugh often scouted the area in the squadron's little NE-1 Cub, with his trusty Irish Setter, Copper, who assumed copilot duties.

Despite Hugh's scouting efforts, when he actually went hunting the ducks and geese usually just sat on the water and fed rather than flying around in front of his gun. He quickly solved that problem by pinpointing the location of his duck blinds to the squadron pilots. On the days that Hugh went hunting, most of us found time at the end of a mission to drop down to just a few feet above the water and roar up and down in front of his blind at a couple of hundred miles an hour. Of course, this terrorized the ducks and geese. They got up in the air thicker than flies at a picnic. This was perfect for Hugh. There weren't many days that he didn't come back with a full limit.

***

As the summer wore on, we continued to train hard. One of our favorite diversions was tangling with the Army P-40s based out of nearby Langley Field. Sometimes we called ahead and met them in prearranged mock air battles. More often we jumped them, or were jumped by them, whenever we happened to be in the same piece of sky. These battles were wonderful whirling affairs that were as close to the real thing as possible. And although on paper the P-40 equaled or bettered the Wildcat in almost every respect, we nearly always bested the Army pilots. This seemed to validate our tactics as well as further boost our already heady egos.

By July 1942, other ensigns had reported to the squadron and I was no longer the junior officer. I was made a section, or two-plane, leader, which meant that I flew as the third airplane in a four-plane division. It also meant that I got my own wingman. My assigned wingman was Ensign Jim Feasley. Jim looked a lot like the movie star Fred Astaire and was a very outgoing sort, always pulling wild gags or practical jokes—a truly fun guy to be around.

Feasley and I were assigned to fly in Lieutenant Danny O'Neil's division. O'Neil transferred to VF-9 from VF-5 on the old *Yorktown*, which was sunk that same June at Midway. He was older and a combat veteran. Of course, anyone above our rank seemed old to us new ensigns. And the fact that he had seen combat made him even more estimable in our eyes. O'Neil was a good leader in that he would not put up with any foolishness; he demanded that we do things right. Still, he was friendly in a gruff sort of way and we were happy to be assigned to his division.

An interesting sidenote was that Feasley and I were assigned to photo-reconnaissance duties. We flew the photo version of the Wildcat, the F4F-3P, in a short course back at NAS Norfolk. It was very basic, with just a brief introduction to photo-reconnaissance theory and some fundamentals on how to operate the cameras. I remember that we used a piece of tape attached to the airplane's canopy to aim the cameras—very crude. Nevertheless, this training would eventually set me up for one of the most exciting missions of my career.

***

Sometime during the summer someone decided that the usual round of parties was starting to lose its edge. To liven up things it was decided to try something different—a turnabout party. This meant that the men were to come to the party dressed as women, and the wives and girlfriends were to come to the party in uniform.

McWhorter, far right, was not a petite figure, yet his fashion-forward ensemble of a bandeau and print skirt—with dress uniform white shoes—was one he wore with elan. VF-9 partied regularly. In this instance they enjoyed a "turnabout" party. The dog seems confused. (McWhorter Family)

It turned out to be a great success. There were beautiful, shapely women in uniform giving orders to great, hulking, hairy men in skirts. The change in roles, helped along with a little booze, really eased the tension and made for great laughs. Some of the guys really pulled off the transformation, too. After that party I never quite looked at Bill Bonneau the same way. And in all my life I don't recall seeing so many different kinds of artificial breasts: apples, oranges, grapefruits—we could have stocked a grocer's cart.

***

An episode that occurred during these early days at Oceana pretty much showed the state of our maturity. One day early in the summer we were issued brand-new Colt .45-caliber pistols. We were supposed to carry them for self-protection when we flew. Well, being young men, we instantly became enamored with our new toys, and we cleaned and oiled and caressed them almost as if they were babies. Lou Menard and I convinced ourselves that the new pistols enhanced our good looks and already inestimable machismo by a magnitude. So, we decided to carry them into Virginia Beach that same evening to protect it from whatever it needed to be protected from.

We strapped the pistols into shoulder holsters under our green uniform coats and went to one of the hangouts we favored, a little bar called O'Club Inc. We sat around there for a while feeling pretty smug, then walked around town for a bit, just itching for a reason to save the town with our pistols. Fortunately, the opportunity didn't present itself. Just as fortunate, we weren't stopped by the local police. There is no doubt that we would have had the book thrown at us for packing our military-issue weapons around town.

***

By midsummer 1942, the United States was starting to slow the Japanese advance in the Pacific. The Japanese fleet was fought to a stalemate in the Coral Sea during May, and a month later we won a huge victory at Midway, where four Japanese fleet carriers were sent to the bottom.

The Wildcat was the fighter that the U.S. Navy was using to hold the line and, for at least another year, it would continue to be the front-line fighter. It was doing quite well for such a slow, ugly little airplane. While it wasn't the Imperial Japanese Navy Zero's equal in speed, range, or maneuverability, it certainly was much more rugged. When flown well, using the right tactics, it could hold its own against the Japanese fighter. This was in marked contrast to the Army P-39s and P-40s, which were struggling at that same time in Australia, New Guinea, and elsewhere in the South Pacific. Moreover, the Wildcat, with its heavy armament, was more than a match for the other Japanese types—the torpedo bombers, dive bombers, and medium bombers—that, like the Zero, tended to burn when hit by machinegun fire.

German fighters, on the other hand, were somewhat of an unknown to us. From the data that came down to us through intelligence channels and from anecdotal evidence from the fighting in Europe, it seemed to us that the Wildcat was a very inferior machine when compared to the sleek and aggressive-looking Me-109 and FW-190. These two machines were dominating the skies over Europe.

So, while we were satisfied that the Wildcat was an adequate fighter, we knew that there were far better fighters out there, and we were anxious to receive delivery of something more advanced as soon as possible. It was during this time that Marv Franger and I were sent to the Vought aircraft factory in Stratford, Connecticut, to take a look at the new F4U Corsair. The Corsair first flew in May 1940 and quickly set a speed record for military aircraft by reaching a level speed of 404 miles per hour. Powered by a Pratt & Whitney R2800, 2,000-horsepower engine, the Corsair was an unorthodox-looking aircraft, with an abnormally long nose and inverted gull wings that kept its huge propeller clear of the ground.

Although Marv and I didn't get to fly the powerful new airplane, we crawled all over it and got a chance to talk to the engineers, test pilots, and factory personnel. The Corsair was going to be a stellar performer, equal to any fighter flying anywhere in the world. And best of all, once the aircraft completed development trials, VF-9 was slated to be the first squadron to receive it.

Chapter 6

By September 1942 we were starting to become a little restless. We had worked hard together since spring, and fall was fast approaching. By then the Navy and Jack Raby had put together a top-notch fighter squadron in the form of VF-9. The enlisted men, headed by Chief Petty Officer Matty Walsh, had coalesced into a first-rate maintenance crew—one that ultimately paced the rest of the Navy. And the pilots and ground officers . . . well, we were certain that there was no group better prepared to take the war to Japan than us.

McWhorter on the wing of an F4F Wildcat while the *Ranger* steamed for North Africa. (U.S. Navy)

Like every military organization, particularly during wartime, we were besieged by a great many rumors. One week we were bound for garrison duty at Pearl Harbor; the next had us preparing for a raid on Tokyo. On June 23, we received official orders to proceed to Quonset Point, Rhode Island. From there we were to proceed to Malta aboard the British carrier HMS *Victorious*, for operations against the Germans. These orders were quickly cancelled. After a while it became difficult to take gossip of impending orders seriously.

We heard rumors again late in September. This new batch seemed as outlandish as any. We were to prepare for embarkation aboard the aircraft carrier *Ranger* (CV-4). We weren't told what we were going to be doing, or where we were going to be doing it, but we did learn that we were leaving in October. So, on short notice the squadron scrambled to get everything ready to go. Each of the pilots renewed his carrier landing qualifications, first at the airfield and then aboard the *Ranger*. The sailors worked extraordinarily long hours to ensure that the aircraft were in tip-top shape, ready to carry the war to the enemy.

Finally, on October 2, 1942, we flew our aircraft over to NAS Norfolk where they were craned aboard the *Ranger*. The next day we lined the rails of the ship as it slipped its moorings and made its way into the Atlantic.

The *Ranger* was an oddball aircraft carrier. Commissioned in 1934, during an era when international naval treaties restricted the sizes of warships, she was designed as an experimental ship—the first purpose-built aircraft carrier in the U.S. Navy. With an eye on maximum aircraft-carrying capacity, the design sacrificed armor, speed, and guns to stay under a treaty-imposed displacement limit of 22,000 tons. The end result was a ship that displaced only 14,500 tons, was 769 feet long and 80 feet wide, had 8 5-inch antiaircraft guns, and could carry a respectable 86 aircraft.

She was a quirky, one-of-a-kind ship, the only one of her class. Her funnels, or smokestacks, were placed three on either side of the ship—and aft of the carrier's island—rather than the conventional arrangement of funnels on the starboard side, incorporated into the superstructure. Whenever flight operations commenced, the funnels on each side were rotated out horizontally so that they pointed outward, parallel to the water. She was also constructed with only one aircraft elevator. This one elevator operated very slowly, limiting the ship's ability to sortie large numbers of airplanes quickly.

The living quarters were somewhat primitive as well. I was bunked with about a dozen other ensigns in a room only big enough for four. There wasn't much in the way of furniture; we stored a lot of our gear under our bunks. For the head—or restroom facilities—there was one long trough into which

The USS *Ranger* (CV-4) was the Navy's first purpose-made aircraft carrier. It had odd features such as smokestacks along the flight deck which swiveled outward to accommodate flight operations. (U.S. Navy)

you relieved yourself. And there was no air conditioning. All in all, it was very primitive compared to what we enjoyed later in the war.

***

A few days after leaving Norfolk the *Ranger* made a scheduled stop in Bermuda. Our time there was fairly low-key—pretty restful actually. Operating out of McKinley Field we flew only occasionally—some carrier landings and light training. The rest of the time we terrorized the island on little motor scooters. It was a wonder we didn't kill ourselves. Booze, motor scooters, and bored fighter pilots make a pretty volatile combination, particularly when stirred together with the prospect of first combat.

It was in Bermuda that I failed in my duty as Lieutenant Commander Raby's handler. He and the ship's Catholic chaplain were out in town having a great time late one evening, when they decided that the island-wide curfew probably didn't apply to them. Well, the local constable didn't quite see it from their perspective. As it turned out he "took pity" on both of them and provided them lodging "free of charge." We had no idea what happened to them until we got the call the next morning to come get them out of jail. Obviously, my assumption that the skipper couldn't get into trouble while in the company of a man of the cloth was a mistaken one.

The chaplain, Father Joseph T. O'Callahan, later earned the Medal of Honor on board the aircraft carrier *Franklin*, for his heroic actions after that ship was bombed off the coast of Kyushu on March 19, 1945.

***

It wasn't until after we left Bermuda on October 25, 1942, that we were told where we were going. There was to be an Allied invasion of French Northwest Africa—Morocco, Tunisia, and Algeria. The French forces there were under control of the Vichy government, which emerged following France's defeat in 1940, and it operated with some small degree of autonomy only at Hitler's pleasure.

The invasion, codenamed Operation *Torch*, was to take place in early November. It was unknown whether or not the French, traditionally friendly to the Americans and previously allied with Great Britain against

En route to North Africa for Operation *Torch*, VF-9 test-fired the guns of their Wildcats from the deck of the *Ranger*. (U.S. Navy)

the Germans, would oppose the invasion. Unbeknown to us, there were numerous secret negotiations and other clandestine activities taking place in conjunction with the operation. One of the Allies' objectives was to convince the Vichy commanders to support the Allied landings, or, at least, not oppose them.

We joined with the invasion fleet, which was composed of more than 500 ships. It was mostly American—with significant British participation—and included four CVE "jeep" carriers, the *Santee, Suwannee, Sangamon,* and *Chenango.* The invasion force was scheduled to go ashore at three different locations—Casablanca, Oran, and Algiers. American soldiers from British ships were to make the Oran landing, while the Algiers landing was an all-British show. Our convoy of 102 ships, the Western Task Force, was split. The main force was slated to come ashore at Fedala and Mehedia north of Casablanca, while the remainder was to land at Safi to the south.

The *Ranger,* with 54 F4Fs and 18 SBD dive bombers aboard, was assigned to Task Group 34.2 and was charged with launching air strikes against French warships, airfields, and other military targets in the Casablanca area. It was also responsible for providing air cover for the invasion force at nearby Fedala. The *Sangamon,* with 12 F4Fs, 9 SBDs, and 9 TBF torpedo bombers, was also to provide cover for the northern group. The *Suwannee,* with 29 F4Fs, and 9 TBFs, was to stay with the *Ranger* in the Casablanca area. The *Santee,* with 14 F4Fs, 9 SBDs, and 8 TBFs, was assigned coverage of the southern landing force at Safi. The *Chenango* was not capable of launching traditional missions. Rather, she carried 76 Army P-40s that were to be flown ashore as soon as airfields were secured.

During the initial planning stages, in anticipation of the types of missions that were to be conducted, the decision was made to remove the *Ranger's* torpedo bomber squadron, VT-41. The squadron flew obsolete TBD Devastators, which suffered a terrible drubbing at Midway. A fighter squadron took the place of VT-41 to augment the *Ranger's* own fighter squadron, VF-41. Our VF-9 was that additional fighter squadron.

In order to facilitate the scheduling of the air strikes, VF-41 splintered off 9 of its 27 planes, as did VF-9. The 2 sets of 9 planes were combined to form a separate 18-plane unit that we dubbed VF-49. This move was only a temporary expedient, but it gave the planners 3 18-plane squadrons and thereby provided more flexibility in the development of strike schedules and launch and recovery intervals. I was one of the youngsters assigned to "VF-49."

By that time, we had replaced our F4F-3s with F4F-4s. The F4F-4 had folding wings, six .50 caliber machineguns rather than four, armor plates

Grumman TBF Avenger torpedo bombers made up part of the aircraft complement aboard the *Ranger*. Rugged, versatile, and ugly, the type served with distinction through the war and beyond. (U.S. Navy)

Wildcats are parked and ready for action aboard the *Ranger*. (U.S. Navy)

A Douglas SBD dive bomber is loaded with a 1,000-pound bomb aboard the *Ranger*. (U.S. Navy)

behind the pilot, and a couple of other modifications. There wasn't much difference, except that the newer airplanes were 900 pounds heavier, and so overall performance suffered a bit.

The trip from Bermuda to Africa was tedious. There was no flying as the convoy zigzagged to foil enemy submarines for the entire route. These preemptive maneuvers combined with the snail's-pace speed of the transport ships made for extremely slow going. We didn't have much to do other than play cards in the officers' wardroom, tell the same stories over and over again, and eat a lot. The closest thing we did to flying was to line our aircraft along the edge of the deck and test-fire our guns out over the ocean.

As we neared the coast of Africa, our anxiety levels increased. There were only a few veterans of the very early fighting in the Pacific in our ranks; this was to be the first combat experience for nearly everyone aboard the ship. Nerves were also a bit on edge because we had done no flying since we left Bermuda two weeks earlier. Our very next flight, after the extended layoff, would be into combat.

On the evening of November 7, 1942, the night the invasion was to begin, we received the latest intelligence on our part of the operation. Unfortunately, there wasn't much information. Even this late in the game, no one knew what the French were going to do. They had about 170 combat aircraft, including 45 American-built Curtiss Hawk 75 fighters (an export version of the Army's P-36) and 40 French Dewoitine D.520 fighters, along with several warships in and around the Casablanca area. There was no doubt they could do us real harm. On the other hand, the French were traditional allies. The operation had the potential to develop into either a very bloody clash or a reunion of old friends. We just didn't know which.

I'm not sure that any of us slept well that night. The thought that the next day might bring us to the fire and hell of battle, with all of the accompanying terror and fear and hurt—even death—was one that I'm certain plagued all of our minds. I tossed and turned for quite a while. And there was still another fear that was with us: the thought that we might, in the face of enemy fire, fail our squadron mates. The fear that, despite all our training, despite the faith of our nation, despite our own desire to do right, we might freeze or—worse—retreat in cowardice. I think that for most of us, this was a more dreadful prospect than being hurt or killed.

Chapter 7

Thankfully, it was a short night. Flight quarters was scheduled for 0500, so I got up at 0330 to shower, shave, and get breakfast. The ship's doctor had suggested that all hands take a good shower that morning to cut down the chances of infection if we were wounded. I really scrubbed down—as much as I could in a shipboard shower. We weren't allowed the luxury of lengthy hot showers because fresh water was always in short supply. The drill was to wet down, turn the water off, lather up, then turn it back on only long enough to rinse off.

After putting on a clean khaki uniform and black necktie (we had to wear neckties at this point in the war—even in combat!), I went down to the wardroom and found that the galley staff had prepared a superb breakfast of ham, eggs, sausage, waffles, pancakes, and more. This was much more extravagant than our usual fare. Just about the time I sat down to eat, some smart-ass came in and remarked that the scene reminded him of the last meal for the condemned.

After breakfast I went to our ready room, just about amidships on the gallery deck, right beneath the flight deck. I wanted to get there before general quarters was sounded; otherwise all the hatches were battened down, making movement around the ship rather difficult. Although we had done most of our briefings the day before, Mac Wordell, one of VF-41's senior pilots, went over all the details once again. Our mission was not complicated—a combat air patrol (CAP) over the invasion forces at Fedala. We were to keep Vichy airplanes away. During the briefing I reviewed my chart board to make sure that I had all the information I needed—ship's position, patrol position, radio frequencies, and so on.

Information on the current situation ashore was very sketchy. There was much confusion about the progress of the landings, which started a few hours

Jake Onstott (standing left) and Mac Wordell brief Wildcat pilots aboard the *Ranger* at the commencement of Operation *Torch*. Wordell, leading a flight that included McWhorter, was shot down while strafing a French destroyer. He survived, was captured, and repatriated. (U.S. Navy)

before, and, unbelievably, it was still not known whether or not the French would oppose the invasion. After the briefing we all sat in the ready room putting on a brave front and making inane small talk. Nevertheless, nearly every one of us sneaked away to the head more than once to take a nervous pee.

As scheduled, VF-9 launched at 0610, and VF-41 shortly thereafter. I listened as they rumbled down the flight deck just above our heads, envious that they were getting airborne first. It was much better to be flying than sitting around and sweating it out. It wasn't until they were en route to their targets, at about 0640, that VF-9 and VF-41 were given the signal "Play Ball." This meant that the French had not laid down their arms and that the invasion force was being opposed. Hearing this, the knots in our stomachs cinched a little tighter.

After the first two launches were complete, the deck was re-spotted with new airplanes, and we were given our airplane assignments. They were assigned to the pilots in each division in the same order in which they were spotted, or parked, on the flight deck. This kept the divisions together and helped make the rendezvous after takeoff much easier.

At about 0700 we were ordered to man our planes. I strapped on my heavy .45-caliber pistol, put on my cloth helmet (with earphones incorporated into the sides), and donned my Mae West life jacket. Last, I grabbed my chart board and filed out of the ready room with the rest of the pilots.

Up on the flight deck I scanned the pack of parked airplanes as I tried to find the one assigned to me. They were painted a specular gray color. The red dots in the center of the star in the national insignia were removed months earlier; it was feared that they might be confused with the red "meatball" of the Japanese national insignia.

I spotted my airplane near the rear of the pack and walked across the wooden flight deck, around and under other airplanes. After greeting my plane captain and making a walk-around inspection of the plane with him, I climbed onto the left wing and stepped down into the cockpit. I settled into the seat, and

McWhorter sits in the cockpit of his Wildcat aboard the *Ranger*. (U.S. Navy)

the plane captain helped me with my parachute harness and seat belt before he climbed back down to check the aircraft one more time.

Almost without conscious effort—even after two weeks without flying—my practiced hands moved around the cockpit preparing the Wildcat for engine start. Prestart checks complete, I signaled the plane captain that I was ready. Other fighters in front of me had started their engines already, and I had lowered my goggles against their propwash. The heavy thrum on the flight deck grew louder and louder as more airplanes came to life. Checking as best I could that my propeller arc was clear, I reached down, primed the engine, turned the ignition switch on, and hit the starter switch.

Once the engine started, I gave the cockpit instrumentation a quick look to ensure that everything was hot, cool, lubricated, and pressurized in all the right places. Looking forward, I could see the first airplanes of the launch taxiing forward for takeoff. It was to be an all-fighter launch; the SBD Dauntless dive bombers had launched with the first strike. Our mission was combat air patrol. We were to ensure that no enemy aircraft harassed any portion of the invasion fleet or the landing itself.

Finally, at about 30-second intervals, each of the airplanes in front of me taxied into position, ran up their engines, released their brakes, and rolled down the flight deck into the wind. Even without a catapult-assisted launch—the *Ranger* had only one catapult anyway—the fighters were airborne well before running out of deck space.

And then, it was my turn. I moved the throttle forward and let my aircraft slowly roll ahead while I followed the plane captain's hand signals. Finally, I reached the takeoff point. Here I shifted my attention to the flight deck officer. On his signal—the rapid rotation of a small flag in his upraised right hand—I stood on the brakes and pushed the throttle all the way forward with my left hand. At full power, the airplane vibrated madly and strained to break free and race down the deck. I checked the cockpit instrumentation again, double-checked my flap and propeller pitch settings, and saluted the waiting flight deck officer. With a flourish he lowered his right arm and pointed down the deck. Immediately I released the brakes and worked the rudder to keep the fighter pointed down the deck. A few seconds later I felt the airplane grow lighter as it reached flying speed. I eased the stick back with my right hand and was airborne before the last of the flight deck disappeared beneath me.

Once aloft, I scanned the sky around me while I cranked the landing gear up by hand. This was a tiresome effort that required 27 revolutions. It could be dangerous too. If a pilot lost his grip, the handle spun wildly in the opposite

A VF-9 Wildcat launches from the deck of the *Ranger* during Operation *Torch*. (U.S. Navy)

direction with bone-breaking force as gravity pulled the landing gear back to the down position. There were plenty of Wildcat pilots with broken wrists.

Of course, there was much to do besides retract the landing gear. I readjusted the prop pitch and fine-tuned the fuel mixture; at the same time, I monitored my engine and flight instruments and closed formation with the rest of the flight. Sixteen aircraft were airborne and joining as two flights of eight, one a couple hundred feet behind and slightly offset from the other.

***

The division, four airplanes, was the standard Navy unit for aerial combat; it was composed of two sections of two aircraft each. The two sections flew together in a formation called the "Finger Four." It was a formation that was adopted by the British earlier in the war and closely resembled the extended fingertips of a hand. The middle fingertip was the division leader, or the number-one airplane, whereas the division leader's wingman, the number-two airplane, was represented by the forefinger. The ring fingertip was the second section leader, or number-three airplane, and the little fingertip was his wingman, the number-four airplane. This formation was flexible and allowed the division leader to maneuver fairly aggressively without worrying about the other pilots in the formation flying into him or each other.

***

With everyone in sight, I joined Danny O'Neil's division as section leader of the last section of a flight of eight led by Jake Onstott. A short time later, Jim Feasley slid into position on my right wing. Our division flew just a bit behind and offset from Jake's, in order to give him room to maneuver his own division. In turn, Onstott kept our two combined divisions behind and offset from Mac Wordell's eight-ship flight.

On my wing, Feasley was flying the last airplane in the formation. We were still junior ensigns and had been for a while. As such, we had gotten used to being "tail-end Charlies."

Once joined, our two flights of eight proceeded southeast to take position over the invasion beachhead just northeast of Casablanca, near the town of Fedala. Along the way we charged and test-fired our guns. Charging the guns in the Wildcat was tedious and time-consuming. Each of the six guns had to be charged by pulling a handle that was attached to a cable that ran out to the gun. Six separate, hard yanks in all.

When we arrived on station, we set up a loose, left-hand orbit at about 10,000 feet, maintaining the same formation that we used en route. Each pilot divided his attention between flying in position and scanning the sky for enemy aircraft.

Nothing happened. By this time, most of the first strike had made its way back to the fleet. Occasionally we spotted them straggling back in small groups or pairs or sometimes singly. It was obvious from their broken formations and the occasional excited radio call that they had encountered stiff resistance.

Below us, we watched small ships and landing craft shuttling back and forth between the beach and larger ships offshore. They reminded me of water bugs; they busily scuttled here and there with no purpose that was obvious from my high perch. Further away, on the beach, I could see none of the fighting that I presumed was taking place. Still, our CAP encountered none of the enemy.

Finally, after about 45 minutes on station above the beachhead, at 0825, the radio crackled with new information. There were warships underway out of the harbor at Casablanca. Without hesitating, Wordell made a call over the radio and spun us around toward the harbor. Casablanca was only about twelve miles to the southeast, and so, just a short time later, we were able to pick out the wakes of three French destroyers racing out of the harbor and running north along the coastline toward the invasion force at Fedala. They were steaming in a single-file formation.

As we approached the three enemy ships head-on, Wordell took a cut to starboard and set us up for an attack against the lead destroyer's port side. Just before he started his dive, he rocked his wings—the signal for an attack—and pushed over for a strafing run on the lead destroyer. At the same time he called out over the radio, "Okay, gang, this is it!"

The destroyer crews had seen us by this time and started to put up a heavy hail of antiaircraft fire. Accurate antiaircraft fire. About halfway down in its dive, Wordell's aircraft was hit and began to smoke.

"I'm hit, I'm hit—I'm going down," he called out excitedly.

I remember thinking that this wasn't a very good start. Our lead airplane on our first combat attack had just been badly hit and was trailing a stream of smoke and fire. To say that I was frightened might not be entirely accurate, but the pucker factor was certainly up there. I watched Mac guide his aircraft toward the beach as the rest of our flight continued the attack. His aircraft was smoking badly but the fire seemed to have gone out, and he was still making excited calls over the radio. Out of reflex or fear or whatever, he squeezed his trigger, and the smoke from his six machineguns added to the smoke coming out of his plane. The last I saw of him before I started my own dive, he was just beginning to belly into a field behind the beach.

After 14 planes dove to attack, it was finally my turn. I put my wits in place, took a quick look over my shoulder at Jim Feasley, pushed the throttle up, and rolled left, over into a dive. I was diving on the port beam of the lead ship at about a 45-degree angle. The noise of the airstream rushing over my airplane increased dramatically as my airspeed accelerated. Hunched behind my gun sight—a glass reflector with an illuminated center pipper surrounded by concentric rings—and flying through the torrent of antiaircraft fire, I watched the enemy ship grow larger as I waited to come into range. At the same time, I saw other Wildcats in various phases of attack—diving, firing, pulling out. Hurtling ever closer, I spotted the upturned faces of the French sailors from where they crouched in the ship's gun tubs, blasting salvos of antiaircraft fire up at me.

I waited forever for the range to close. Finally, at about 3,000 feet, I took a tiny bit of lead and opened fire on the ship's bridge. The roar of the six guns, added to the already deafening racket from the engine and the airstream, was almost mind-numbing. Fascinated, I watched the tracers from my guns arc toward the ship, seemingly in slow motion. Then, in an explosion of sparkling flashes, my bullets found their mark on the bridge of the destroyer. At the same time, I could see glass from the windows in the bridge rain on the deck and the sparkling, explosive flashes of my incendiary rounds.

In total, each Wildcat carried 1,440 rounds in the ratio of 5 armor-piercing to 3 incendiary to 2 tracer rounds. That meant that for every flash I saw—too many to count—four other rounds of ammunition smashed into the target. The effect of our gunfire was dramatic. Already the lead ship was smoking. As I pulled out of the dive, my face sagged under the increased gravity forces of the pullout. Leveling out at high speed just over the top of the bridge, I could see sailors dashing around, doing whatever sailors do when their ship is under attack.

Under fire from the opposite side of the ship, I double-checked the throttle against the stop. I looked back over my shoulder, where I could see the muzzle flashes from the antiaircraft guns, and I consciously willed my aircraft to climb faster. Unscathed and back at altitude again, I wheeled around to my left and set up for another attack. By now our flight was more or less separated into a bunch of single airplanes pressing attacks against the French ships and being careful to avoid colliding with each other.

Altogether, we made several more runs apiece against all three of the destroyers. On each run, I was amazed at the effects of my guns against the thin-skinned ships. And the other pilots experienced the same success. The decks and superstructures of the French ships were riddled with holes, and soon no one was moving about topside. The antiaircraft fire dropped off dramatically as well. By the time we ran low on fuel and ammunition and began to re-form our flight for the trip back to the *Ranger*, the enemy ships were smoking—flames visible in places—and were turning toward the beach. It was with a good deal of satisfaction later in the day that we learned that they did not reach the invasion beach.

After regrouping and heading back toward the *Ranger*, we found that Mac Wordell was our flight's only loss. With a little reshuffling, Jake Onstott took the lead and brought the group overhead the fleet. A few minutes later we began our approaches and landed aboard ship without incident.

Once I was clear of the arresting wires the deck crew folded my Wildcat's wings and I was directed to a parking spot, where a plane captain put chocks beneath the wheels while I shut the engine down. The propeller barely stopped turning before I scrambled out of the cockpit with my flight gear and went below decks with the rest of the flight. There was nonstop chatter as everyone tried to tell his story to everyone else, who, of course, was only interested in his own story. Hands became airplanes that swept arcs through the ready room—right hands chasing left, or making strafing runs against the duty desk

A VF-9 Wildcat recovers back aboard the deck of the *Ranger* during Operation *Torch*. (U.S. Navy)

or whatever other object was nearby. We were excited and a bit proud that we had turned the French ships away from the beachhead.

***

We didn't have much time to relive the events as we were soon corralled and briefed for another mission. As soon as our fighters were refueled and rearmed, we were back upstairs manning them.

At 1145, we repeated the launch sequence from the early morning. With Jack Raby in the lead of a flight of 12 Wildcats, we were airborne again heading toward the invasion area. Somehow, in the confusion of the day, I ended up back with VF-9.

It wasn't long before the skipper spotted a target. Raising a plume of dust as it raced along one of the coastal roads was a small fuel truck. Raby was on it in an instant. From a fast, shallow dive he opened up with all six guns and sprayed the speeding truck. Almost instantaneously it caught fire and ground to a halt.

What I saw next was one of those images—so vivid and horrible—that etched a permanent place in my memory: the driver was transformed into a human torch. I cringed when I saw him fall out of the truck cab and roll on the ground, waving and slapping at himself as he tried to put out the flames. Even had he extinguished the flames, there was no way he could have survived the burns.

We flew on. A short time later we were given coordinates for a target described as a Vichy command post. It was housed in a big, white, cement-block building set up on a hill. As we dived to attack, guns that were dug in around the building put up torrents of antiaircraft fire. It was intense, but not nearly so thick as what the destroyers put up earlier that day.

From our end, the attack was somewhat frustrating. We could see flashes from our .50 caliber rounds hitting the building, but they had little effect on the masonry structure. We certainly couldn't make it burn.

It wasn't long before I came to the conclusion that our return on this investment wasn't worth it. I saw rounds coming up at me during one of my strafing runs, then heard a loud crack, and felt a gush of air pour into the cockpit.

A small-caliber antiaircraft round had hit the left front quarter-panel of my windscreen, come through the cockpit, missed my face by only inches, and gone right through the rear of the canopy. I could see bits of Plexiglas on the outside of my goggles, trapped there by the hurricane-force wind that was rushing through the cockpit. I really wasn't much interested in strafing that building anymore.

Finally, like a pack of blooded and panting dogs that have lost interest in a treed animal, we rejoined and circled the command post from a distance. It didn't look much different than it had before we made our attack. We were low on ammunition; it was time to head home. We climbed to altitude and started back, a bit disappointed that our efforts hadn't yielded more spectacular results.

There was trouble waiting for us when we reached the *Ranger* at 1425, more than two and a half hours after we launched. Our lack of carrier landing practice during the last few weeks finally caught up with us. The nature of combat being what it is, the launch and recovery cycles had gone askew. Our landing skills had atrophied, and recovering pilots were being given more wave-offs than normal. Consequently, the recovery cycle was running behind and I was sent, along with three others, to the nearby escort carrier *Suwannee*. Though the *Ranger* was small relative to the other fleet carriers, the *Suwannee* seemed absolutely tiny. Fortunately, with the pressure on and despite the lack of practice, our flight recovered aboard the small ship without incident.

Of course, one of the many disadvantages associated with operating aboard a carrier is that there is only one place to take off and land. Unlike

Flight operations demanded the utmost of pilots and support crews alike. Here, a sailor rests in readiness on the wing of a VF-9 Wildcat. (U.S. Navy)

A VF-9 Wildcat is refueled aboard the deck of the *Ranger* during Operation *Torch*. (U.S. Navy)

a land base, a carrier gives you no option to take off on a different runway or in a different direction. Until the *Ranger*'s deck was cleared and ready to recover us, we weren't going to be able to get back aboard to refit and rearm. The *Suwannee*, meanwhile, was busy with her own airplanes. Finally, by the time our Wildcats were refueled, the *Ranger*'s deck was clear and able to recover us.

Back aboard the *Ranger* and still charged with excitement, I was ready to go out again, but the last missions had already been sent; I was done flying for the day. I made my way down to the squadron spaces, hung my flying gear on a peg, and stepped into the ready room, where most of the pilots who weren't flying were already gathered. The mood was mixed. There was a great deal of excitement, as we had scored some good successes, most notably against targets on the ground.

Jack Raby scored the squadron's first aerial victory that morning over an aircraft he identified as a twin-engine French LeO 451. Later, after the French said that none of their planes had been in that area, it was believed that this airplane was most likely one of a few British Hudson aircraft lost on antisubmarine patrol. The two airplanes looked similar, and the roundel markings of the French and British were quite alike. The confusion of first combat and the split-second nature of air combat contributed to this tragic mistake. Raby wasn't the first to make this kind of error, nor he was he the last.

***

If there was a sense of excitement over our successes, there was also the realization that we had lost some dear friends. For good. Tom "Willy" Wilhoite was one of them. Willy was from Kentucky and was one of my good friends. He looked like he had just come off the farm, and he always had a smile for everyone. Just a happy, friendly young man. I had known him since the early days of my enlistment in Atlanta. Born only four days apart, we went almost lockstep through training together, reported to VF-9 at the same time, and become roommates. On his second mission that day he was flying on Hugh Winters's wing on a strike against the airdrome at Port Lyautey. After strafing and destroying a Dewoitine fighter, Willy got caught by French antiaircraft gunners. He called out over the radio, "They got me, Pedro" (Winters's nickname), and a moment later he crashed about a mile from the airdrome.

Willy was posthumously awarded the Silver Star. The citation noted his "conspicuous gallantry and intrepidity" during the strikes that day, as well as his "superb airmanship and tenacious devotion to duty" for the manner in which he pressed his attacks.

"They got me, Pedro," was Thomas Wilhoite's last radio transmission before he was shot down during a strafing run against a Vichy French airfield. Like Eddie Micka, a destroyer escort was named in his honor. (U.S. Navy)

Mac Wordell was still missing as well, from our earlier attack on the Vichy destroyers. Someone saw his airplane belly-land, so there was hope that he survived.

Everyone dealt with these losses in their own way. For many of us, myself included, I don't think it quite hit home that our friends were really gone forever. Consciously, we knew that they were dead, but it would be a while before we would get used to not seeing them up on the flight deck, or lounging in the wardroom or the ready room. Outwardly, few of us showed any emotion, but inwardly all of us grieved in our own fashion. I'm certain that there were quite a few melancholy pilots that night—thinking and staring wide-eyed into the dark.

Like most of the other pilots, I put the deaths of my squadron mates aside during the day. They were something to be dealt with later, when there was time. This wasn't a cold or heartless reaction. It was necessary. Letting grief take the focus of our attention would have been dangerous. I mourned our lost friends. All of us did, and we still do.

Chapter 8

Operation *Torch*, the big scheme, was moving ahead but not spectacularly so. Unexpectedly to some, the French warships in Casablanca sortied in strength. Eight of eleven submarines cleared the harbor and sprayed the American fleet with torpedoes, but without success. A number of destroyers and larger combatants had also cleared the harbor and sunk a couple of our smaller ships.

The French warship *Jean Bart*, a large, unfinished battleship with 15-inch guns, dueled with the task force's capital ships from where she was moored in the harbor. She was quickly silenced on the first morning by a combination of naval shells and bombs from the *Ranger*'s SBDs. Our surface combatants had their hands full all through the morning and afternoon of November 8. Ultimately, though, they prevailed and the invasion beaches remained secure.

The mood the next day, November 9, was very different than it was the morning before. In our minds there was certainly no question about Vichy intentions to resist, nor was there any lingering sympathy for them as our traditional allies. They had killed our friends, they refused to stop fighting, and so there was a bloody task still at hand.

Some of the strikes mounted on November 8 encountered stiff aerial resistance in the form of Vichy fighters: American-built Curtiss Hawk 75s and French Dewoitine D.520s. The score stood in our favor as VF-41 aircraft from the *Ranger* downed eight enemy fighters in the air and destroyed many more on the ground. On the other hand, VF-41 suffered four losses in the fierce aerial combat. Although they were losing, the French were skilled and brave airmen with decent equipment. In fact, Vichy strafers caused quite a bit of damage and confusion on the invasion beach. On this new day, November 9, they were at it again.

Our next mission, then, was to be a fighter sweep over the Vichy airdrome at Port Lyautey, just north of Casablanca. We were to clear the sky of enemy fighters, then drop down and strafe the airfield. This time our flight of 16 planes was led

Ironically, the chief opponent of the Navy's Wildcat fighter during Operation *Torch* was the French Hawk 75, an export version of the U.S. Army's Curtiss P-36. It proved quite capable in competent hands. (Wikimedia Commons)

by the VF-49 executive officer, Jake Onstott. Danny O'Neil's division was now the second division in the four-division flight, and I was his section leader—and no longer a tail-end Charlie. Losing a squadron mate wasn't the best way to advance in the squadron hierarchy, but it was to be a common one.

Once airborne, we headed outbound from the *Ranger* toward Port Lyautey, flying in loose division formation so that we could scan the skies around us without having to worry too much about flying into each other. We were keyed up, anxious to tangle with enemy fighters, but at the same time a little afraid. After all, they took their toll on VF-41 only the previous day.

But the Vichy fighters never materialized. Either we surprised them or they had switched loyalties. Or they could have been refueling and rearming after action earlier that morning. For whatever reason, they weren't there.

The French Vichy forces also flew the Dewoitine D.520, a pretty little fighter that was less successful against the Wildcats than was the Hawk 75. (USAAF)

Jake Onstott approached the airfield from an angle and sized up the best avenue for our attack. We could see antiaircraft fire reaching up at us again, but we were still out of range. Finally, Jake wagged his wings and rolled over into a strafing attack on a group of enemy fighters parked on the eastern side of the field.

The rest of us weren't far behind him. I pushed the throttle full forward, rolled over almost inverted, and pulled down toward the enemy aircraft. They were parked almost at random, rather than in any sort of formation. Whether the French did this intentionally or not, it made it harder to strafe them.

Just before I closed into firing range I checked once more to ensure my fighter was properly trimmed. An aircraft in uncoordinated flight will spray bullets everywhere but into the target. Finally in range, I let loose with all six of my guns and watched as my rounds kicked up debris and found their way into one of the little fighters. After giving it a healthy dose, I lifted my

The tail section of a Dewoitine D.520 which was destroyed by strafing Navy fighters. In fact, it could have been destroyed by McWhorter who shot up several of these aircraft on the ground. (USAAF)

nose up a few degrees and fired again into another fighter farther down the parking ramp. Then, just above the deck, I leveled off and flew to one side of my second target. Like the first, it was badly damaged from the fire of my machineguns.

In the instant or two that I had to look, I saw that it was one of the Dewoitine D.520 fighters. A delicate-looking little airplane, it reputedly possessed pretty good performance and was armed decently with a single 20-millimeter cannon and 4 machineguns. This particular one was bare metallic silver with orange and yellow horizontal stripes on its rudder.

At only 50 feet above the ground, I directed my attention back to flying my own airplane and turned around to look forward. Across the field and directly in front of me I made out a huge Quonset hut-shaped hangar that sheltered a large, three-engine seaplane. I didn't know it at the moment, but the aircraft was probably a Breguet 521, an old biplane design dating from the early 1930s.

I settled my gun sight on the center of the big aircraft—I could hardly miss—and let go a long burst straight into the hangar. The aircraft must have been fully fueled because it caught fire with a flash before I released the trigger and streaked over the hangar, barely missing it.

The radio was clobbered with the whoops and hollers of other pilots as their bullets found their marks or, worse, as the enemy's bullets found *their* marks. The antiaircraft fire was thick and a lot of our airplanes were being holed. Still, we had plenty of gas and ammunition, and there was no lack of targets. Wildcats fired their guns and crisscrossed the field from all directions. The possibility of a midair collision was almost as real, and deadly, as being hit by the antiaircraft barrage.

Finally, with the flight nearly out of ammunition, and smoke from burning aircraft and hangars and such rising up in great billows, Onstott called for us all to rendezvous. After gathering his flight-turned-wild-gaggle, he put us back into a respectable formation and led us back to the *Ranger*.

***

Our losses worsened during the second day of combat. Charlie Gearhardt's airplane was last seen streaming smoke and oil on his way back to the fleet. He slid out of formation and out of sight. He never recovered aboard ship and his fate was unknown.

Eddie Micka's end was not in doubt. His plane disintegrated around him over the airfield at Mediouna when a Douglas DB7 bomber he was strafing exploded just as he passed over it. Like Willy Wilhoite the previous day, Eddie crashed and was killed in his airplane.

McWhorter shot up a Breguet 521 like this which was parked in a hangar. It went up like a torch. (Wikimedia Commons)

Stan Amesbury, flying the tail-end Charlie position on a strafing run against trucks and armored vehicles, was caught by ground fire. And like Willy and Eddie, he crashed and was killed.

George Trumpeter's fate, like Gearhardt's, and Wordell's the previous day, was unknown. He was seen being hit by antiaircraft fire, and he never showed at the rendezvous point when it was time to head back to the fleet. No one saw him crash.

Lou Menard also lost an airplane that day. Actually, he didn't lose it so much as he destroyed it in full view of pretty much everybody. He mishandled his aircraft—again, it was our lack of carrier landing practice working against us—and bounced it into the crash barrier. The Wildcat boomeranged clear of the barrier, into the ship's superstructure, and then broke in half. Amazingly, Lou crawled out of the wreckage with nothing worse than a bruised ego.

For VF-9, in contrast to the first day, there was quite a bit of aerial combat. During the squadron's first mission of the day the French were airborne in numbers—mostly in Curtiss Hawk 75s—and opposed the strike with some ferocity. A number of the boys—Marv Franger, Lou Menard, Hal Vita, and K. C. Childers—each scored a confirmed victory apiece, as well as a handful of probables. Jack Raby scored again as well. It seemed that all the training and hard work we did back at NAS Norfolk and Oceana was validated, as the squadron suffered no losses to the enemy aircraft. I was a little jealous that I hadn't gotten an opportunity to put my skills to the test.

Eddie Micka was killed during Operation *Torch* while strafing a Vichy French airfield. His wife and daughter commission a destroyer escort named in his honor. (U.S. Navy)

Flight operations were hectic aboard the *Ranger* during Operation *Torch*, and were not without incident. (U.S. Navy)

***

By the next day, November 10, resistance from the Vichy aerial units dropped off quite a bit and there wasn't as much concern about coming under enemy fighter attacks. Although we had suffered losses, we had given the Vichy air force a real drubbing, both in the air and on the ground. Partly because of this and partly, I suspect, because most of our losses occurred during airfield attacks, we paid less attention to the French airdromes on this third day of action. Instead, we were turned loose to attack anything of military significance that could threaten the beachhead.

I flew on two different sweeps in the Casablanca and Rabat-Salé area. Again, much to my disappointment—I was still eager to tangle with enemy fighters—we encountered no Vichy aircraft. Our task was to keep the French from moving reinforcements to the beachhead. Surprisingly, the French were still putting up stiff resistance in places and our army units were having some trouble. Even the venerable *Jean Bart* got back into action again with her 15-inch guns before finally being silenced by 1,000-pound bombs.

Operation *Torch* was the first amphibious landing of its size during the war, and it didn't go without problems. Warships and transports alike were shot up by shore batteries and by French warships. And a startling number of landing craft—40 percent—were lost to poor seamanship.

The capability of the French to reinforce their units was not robust, but they nevertheless attempted to move men and equipment to where the fight was. We made strafing runs against men and vehicles and other equipment, but depending on where we were operating, there often weren't a lot of targets. By the end of the day on November 10, most of the operation's objectives were achieved. The only prize that remained was Casablanca. A massive naval, ground, and air bombardment was planned and scheduled for 0715 on November 11, Armistice Day. I was airborne as part of that massive effort. Looking down as our flight approached the coast, I could see our warships in position for the imminent bombardment, the knockout blow.

Realizing that further resistance was futile in the long run, the French raised a flag of truce at 0655. It was only as we were approaching our targets berthed in the harbor at Casablanca that we received word the attack had been called off. We made a wide sweeping turn overhead, not sure what to make of it all, then set a course back to the *Ranger*. It was almost 0715; the cancellation of the attack was a close thing.

Almost immediately after the cease-fire was announced, the *Ranger*, the smaller carriers, and their escorts made preparations to leave. Up to this point the task force had enjoyed incredible luck where Nazi submarines were concerned. Unbelievably, nearly all the shipping associated with Operation *Torch* sailed across much of the Atlantic and parts of the Mediterranean, and arrived unmolested by Hitler's vaunted U-boat wolf packs. But the U-boats finally made their way into the area. We knew our luck couldn't last, and we weren't going to hang around and tempt fate much longer.

Indeed, the *Ranger* escaped disaster only by luck when four torpedoes passed under her stern on the morning of November 10. We jokingly attributed our good fortune to the LSO, saying that he had waved off the torpedoes approaching the stern. There was no joking on November 11, though, when several ships were attacked late in the day and one was sunk.

On November 12, we were steaming well out to sea when our force came under attack again—this time from more than one submarine. I was making a visit to the head that was below the island structure on the starboard side. Right then a ship's gunner spotted a periscope and opened up with the 5-inch guns. I looked out the porthole and saw a torpedo wake coming in from abeam toward the stern of the ship. I braced myself for the explosion, but the torpedo missed. We spotted more tracks and other shadows and shapes over the next couple of hours, but none of our ships was hit.

***

The campaign in North Africa was over for us. We started for home and took stock of what had happened. On the plus side, we achieved our objectives. Vichy air power was held in check and our invasion forces were well protected and supported. Whenever we met the French fighters in the air, we bested them. And despite furious antiaircraft fire, we destroyed the bulk of the remaining French airplanes on the ground. We had won.

On the down side, we lost friends: Stan Amesbury, Eddie Micka, George Trumpeter, and Willy Wilhoite were dead. Thankfully, two days after he disappeared, we learned that Charlie Gearhardt was alive and well; he was rescued by a destroyer after he ditched his airplane on November 9. No one had bothered to let us know.

VF-9 lost seven Wildcats. Four were shot down by ground fire, two were so badly shot up they had to ditch, and one was wrecked while landing back aboard the *Ranger*. All told, the Western Task Force lost about 30 percent of its aircraft. This was a shocking figure for a three-day operation, and it caused a lot of consternation among the planners back in Washington.

Chapter 9

After a brief stopover in Bermuda, we arrived back at Oceana just in time for Thanksgiving. We flew our airplanes off the *Ranger* straight back to the airfield.

Charlie Gearhardt beat us back on one of the fast destroyers and was waiting for us with his girlfriend, Nicki—and a grin that almost split his face. Straightaway Charlie invited us all over to his girlfriend's house for a big party that evening. We were going to celebrate his "resurrection."

When it came to partying, VF-9 never missed a step. Within a couple of hours things got going pretty good; as midnight approached, the party was really traveling along. At about that time there came a knock at the door and Charlie's girlfriend, Nicki, shouted at me, "Hey, Mac, that's my roommate, Louise. She's beautiful. Open the door and give her a great big kiss!"

This idea seemed perfectly agreeable to me. I pushed aside the crowd and flung open the door to a tall, remarkable, obviously-made-just-for-Hamilton-McWhorter blonde. Nicki was right; she was beautiful. I reached right out, grabbed her, and planted a big kiss directly on her lips.

I am a modest man, but I think that she didn't mind that kiss at all. Her name was Louise Edel and she was the daughter of a Navy chaplain. He had been transferred out of the area, but she had stayed behind to go to college and work. She told me right away that she was practically engaged to some Army lieutenant, an aviator. I told her back that the poor slob didn't stand a chance.

I was quite taken with her. She was very attractive and well educated, carried herself like a princess, and wasn't bashful about speaking her mind. For the first time my love of flying had a challenger. My next campaign was to be the pursuit of Louise Edel.

The next morning, Petty Officer Price, an enlisted man in the squadron I had gotten to know, invited me to go duck hunting with him in the Back Bay area. I jumped at the chance. I hadn't been hunting since I left Athens and was eager for a chance to sharpen my shooting eye. We "borrowed" shotguns and shells from the squadron armory, set up in the marshes, and shot our limit of ducks. I took mine over to Nicki's house and we ate them for Thanksgiving dinner.

***

Because of North Africa we were given a few days of leave after Thanksgiving. I used the priority status my military service gave me, put on my uniform, and boarded an overnight train back to Athens. From the outside looking in, things hadn't changed too much. But after a day or two of trying to pick up where I left off, it was obvious that things *had* changed. The biggest surprise, which I should have expected, was that very few of my friends were around. Nearly all the young men my age had been drafted or had joined the service.

Of course, I stopped by the airfield to visit with my old instructors and the new batch of students. Again, I enjoyed the envious looks, but this time my pride was tempered by the loss of my friends in North Africa. Being a Navy fighter pilot was a lot more than snappy uniforms and polished gold wings and fast-flying airplanes; being a Navy fighter pilot was about killing people—and maybe being killed. Nevertheless, I think my being there tipped some more aviators down the Navy's recruitment chute.

I also stopped by to visit my old girlfriend, but it wasn't the same since I met Louise. I was genuinely interested in seeing her but the visit was a little awkward. I had been gone quite a while and I found out that she had a new boyfriend in the Army somewhere. For about five seconds I thought about the poor Army lieutenant that Louise was seeing.

***

Dating during the war was more difficult than it was in peacetime, but not so difficult that anyone gave it up. There were still dinners and movies, but rationing was a factor to consider, as well as blackouts and the scarcity of cars. I didn't own one. Occasionally Bill Bonneau or Charlie Gearhardt generously loaned a car. And there was a trolley line not too far away, so it wasn't that hard getting to Louise when I could get away. But being assigned squadron duty every third day put a crimp in my ability to go out with her every time I wanted to. So did the fact that, despite my winning ways, she was still dating the Army lieutenant and one or two other guys. Nevertheless, we managed to date enough to begin developing a relationship.

This was a good time for me. Not only was I dating a beautiful woman, but I was flying fighters. Not only had I been in combat, but I had survived—prevailed even. There was no doubt a bit more strut in my step than there had been just a few months before.

The first Christmas season since the attack on Pearl Harbor was fast approaching. Because of the war, however—the demands it made on the rail system and the effect it had on gasoline and tire supplies—most people weren't able to travel. As a result, everyone was around for the holidays and we enjoyed quite a bit of squadron togetherness. There were parties and dinners, and the bachelors always received plenty of invitations for dinner from the married officers. Despite the war, and our continued duties, Christmas 1942 was a pleasant one, although a little less joyous for me because of Louise's absence. Despite the difficulty in traveling, she managed to find a way to get up to the Naval Training Station at Sampson, New York, where her father was the chief chaplain.

She was a day late departing because of some, shall I say, "missteps" in the execution of her travel itinerary. A couple of days before Christmas, I borrowed Charlie Gearhardt's car and took Louise to catch the ferry up the Chesapeake Bay to Baltimore. From Baltimore she was scheduled to take the train to New York. We got to the ferry landing about 30 minutes before the scheduled 10 P.M. departure time, and there was a long line of cars waiting for the ferry to arrive. Much to my delight, Louise decided to wait in the car with me rather than stand out in the cold.

Well, it wasn't too long before the car windows fogged up. When we finally looked out to check on the ferry, all the other cars were gone. And so was the ferry! There was nothing to do but wait for the next ferry, which was scheduled to depart an hour later.

I'm embarrassed to admit that when we looked out to check on that ferry, the last one of the day, it had also come and gone. Unfortunately for Louise—but fortunately for me—I drove her back home. The next day, without my help, she was finally able to catch the ferry.

***

The VF-9 squadron history recalls Christmas Day itself through a letter that Stu Ball, a fellow ensign, wrote to his girlfriend:

> Casey Childers was the pilot of an SNJ which brought Chief Walsh, in the role of Santa Claus, and a big bag of toys right up to the front of the squadron ready room. Here the kiddies of the officers and enlisted men stood open-mouthed in wonderment. The children had watched the SNJ circle low above them with Santa waving from the back seat. After landing, Santa distributed the toys from the pack. Then, everyone retired to the ready room to carry on.
>
> "Captain Jack's" memorable affair that night was one for the books. The biggest laugh of the evening was when Ensign Vance Horne, who had just reported, showed up with his pretty wife, Dottie. No one present will ever forget Vance's look when the door was flung open in his face and Dottie was whisked in to be kissed by all hands.

Without Louise I felt all alone. Petty Officer Price took pity on lonesome me and brought me to his home for a wonderful dinner with his family. It was a nice Christmas.

***

On the evening of December 27, after a night out in Virginia Beach, I stepped into my Quonset hut and spotted my friend Jim Feasley in the middle of the floor, clenched into a ball with one of the other ensigns. Another wrestling match. Young men being what they are, full of energy and eager to prove themselves, it wasn't unusual for our hut to be transformed into an ad hoc wrestling ring at the drop of a hat.

Feasley had a cold and had heard that the best way to cure it was to drink and sweat it away. So, he started the night innocently enough, perched up on his bunk with a bottle of bourbon. Well, after several pulls on the cure, he started to realize that he was probably the strongest man in the world, and he challenged his hut mates to wrestling matches. He was taking all comers. By the end of the night, I think all of us had danced him around the hut a time or two. Finally, he crawled up into his bed and went to sleep or passed out—I'm not sure which.

When we got airborne the next day Jim was there with us, his cold not much improved despite his efforts. The flight was an aerial gunnery practice sortie, and my plane was the "target." I flew a straight-and-level profile while the others flew gunnery runs against me—without ammunition, of course—from a starting position high above and to the side. If they flew the pattern correctly, they arrived in a firing position a few hundred feet above me, about a thousand feet behind, and about ten to thirty degrees off of my tail.

The flight went along fairly predictably. We all had done this sort of thing countless times. Still, I kept a sharp watch on each of the airplanes as the other pilots made their runs. Sometimes pilots got fixated on what they were doing, so the possibility of a midair collision was very real.

After quite a few runs I watched Jim bank his fighter around in a left-hand turn and approach a firing position. Rather than bringing the nose of his airplane up to point it toward my airplane, he descended too low and disappeared behind me.

I couldn't see him and instantly became nervous. A couple of seconds later, out of the corner of my eye, I picked up the blue flash that was his airplane as it passed very close beneath me on my left side. I barely had time to register what was about to happen, but not enough time to do anything about it. I felt a terrific impact and instinctively wrestled with the control stick as my airplane was thrown up and to the right. At the same time I heard shouting over the radio.

"Do you have it?"

"Get out!"

"Bail out!"

Within a few seconds I regained control of my airplane and knew that it was flyable. Looking down and left I could see Jim's airplane spinning crazily toward the water.

"Bail out! Bail out!" I added my shouts to the rest.

We all had a sick, helpless feeling as we watched the tiny blue fighter smash into the ocean.

"Did anyone see a chute?" someone called out. No one answered the question. We all knew that Jim didn't get out. But still we descended low over the water and looked for signs of a parachute or life raft—anything that would tell us that our friend was still alive. But he wasn't.

After we landed I learned from the other pilots that, because he went low, Jim had made a flat gunnery run on my airplane. Without any kind of angle off—approaching my aircraft basically in two dimensions—he would have found it difficult to judge distance. He probably realized too late that he was about to hit me and pushed the nose of his Wildcat down to try to pass beneath me. He almost made it. The top of his rudder cut into my left wing just outside of the aileron. But the impact tore off his rudder. Without any rudder and with whatever other structural damage the collision caused, he could not recover from the spin. Whether or not he was conscious to try, we never knew. No one heard any radio calls, and it was a good guess that he was knocked unconscious or had blacked out.

I couldn't help feeling that the previous night's bouts—with the bottle and with the wrestling—were what really killed Jim Feasley. And almost killed me.

Chapter 10

Louise returned just before New Year's Eve, and when she heard about my near miss—and Feasley's death—she was devastated because she hadn't been there for me. I think this was a big turning point in our relationship. I had become completely enamored with her, because she was so lively and fun to be with, but she was still playing the field and dating other guys. She told me later, however, that my almost being killed made her realize just how much she cared for me.

One evening after the New Year we were driving back to her house after a date. Because she was still going out with other guys and I couldn't always get a date when I wanted to, I suddenly said to her, "I guess that if I want to have you all to myself, I'll have to marry you." It wasn't exactly a very romantic, on-bended-knee proposal. I was just trying to find out where I stood with her. To my utter astonishment, she immediately said, "Yes." I had won the battle of Virginia Beach.

Although she answered right away, I knew she didn't make the decision lightly. In the six short weeks we had known each other, one of our close friends had already been killed. She realized that marrying a military man, particularly during wartime, could be tragic. Reinforcing that fact was her younger sister Mary's experience. Mary, who was visiting with Louise during the week I proposed, had a husband on the submarine *Greenling*. Because of the nature of submarine warfare, Mary went months at a time without hearing from her husband. This was all the more heartrending because of the dramatic losses that our submarine forces were suffering this early in the war.

A long engagement was not too practical back then, particularly when combat was just around the corner. We bought a marriage license the next day and, since there was no waiting period required, arranged to be married the following Saturday, January 16. We didn't tell anyone except Louise's and

McWhorter met Louise Edel soon after returning from North Africa. They were married a few weeks later. (McWhorter Family)

my parents, Mary, and Bill Bonneau, who was to be my best man. We wanted Louise's father to marry us, but he could not arrange to get to Virginia in time. On Saturday afternoon, following Louise's shift at work, we went to the church for the ceremony. Just as we were getting started, Bill was suddenly called back to the squadron for some minor emergency. In his absence, Mary was the matron of honor, bridesmaid, best man, and guest.

That evening we went out to Oceana for a squadron party. We still hadn't told anyone in VF-9 other than Bill that we were married. I will never forget the look on Jack Raby's face when we told him. His first response was "What? You can't do that!" He was old-school Navy, from a time when a junior officer normally sought permission from his commanding officer before taking such a step. But after Raby realized that the marriage was a done deed he congratulated us.

Later during the party Louise came up to me with a big smile on her face. She whispered in my ear that one of the other pilots, Bill Blackwell, who had not heard the news, asked her to go out with him. She stopped him cold in his tracks by replying, "You will have to ask my husband first."

In the end, Captain Jack apparently didn't mind too much that I bypassed him on the marriage issue. He gave me a week's leave to take my new bride down to Athens to meet my parents.

My folks immediately took to Louise, and Louise to them. Even Athens received a passing grade from her discerning eye. Unfortunately, we didn't have the time or means to travel to New York to meet her parents. I found out much later that her mother, a Southerner from Virginia, was quite concerned that I might turn out to be some sort of a redneck "Georgia cracker," or "hillbilly." We all got a big laugh out of that.

After marriage there was no more wrestling in the Quonset hut for me as I had a different partner. Housing was tight, but Louise's parents owned a house in Norfolk. When they left for New York, they rented out the bottom half to two Navy couples and saved the upper room in case Louise decided she wanted to move in. We soon moved into that small, one-room apartment.

This practice of renting rooms was very common before and during the war. There were not nearly as many motels and hotels and apartments as there are now, and the shuffling about of people that the war caused exacerbated the problem. Making rooms available for rent was considered patriotic, and it provided a little extra income.

Chapter 11

Things were happening fast. The aircraft carrier *Essex* (CV-9) was commissioned on December 31, 1942. She was to be VF-9's ship. Along with VB-9 in SBDs and VT-9 in TBFs, the *Essex* was to deliver VF-9 to the Pacific Theater for combat. Once there, we would strike out against the Japanese and would continue to strike out until the war was won. Between now and then, however, there was a lot of work to be done.

Probably the biggest item on our agenda—and the most anticipated—was the small matter of trading in our trusty but outclassed Wildcats for new fighters. To say we were excited would be a dramatic understatement. In the ready room there was almost nonstop discussion about what fighters we would get and when. The mood was perfect for the Christmas season; we were like kids who couldn't wait for the big day.

For a number of reasons the Vought F4U Corsair was not yet considered suitable for carrier service. This disappointed some of us who had seen the big fighter earlier in the year. That disappointment was relieved somewhat by the announcement that we were to be the first squadron in the Navy to receive the new Grumman F6F Hellcat.

***

It's been often told that the design work on the Hellcat began after the attack on Pearl Harbor, in a hurried effort to build an airplane that could handle the Zero. In fact, work on the new fighter had started earlier in 1941, several months before America's entry into the war. The Hellcat bore a marked resemblance to the Wildcat but was larger in every respect. At 11,400 pounds, loaded, it weighed almost two tons more than its older sibling. Its wingspan and length—42 feet, 10 inches and 33 feet, 7 inches, respectively—also made it noticeably bigger than the Wildcat.

Bigger doesn't necessarily mean better. But the Hellcat, with its Pratt & Whitney 2,000-horsepower R-2800-8, 18-cylinder radial engine, was more than 80 miles per hour faster than the Wildcat. The Hellcat also had a range of nearly 1,200 miles compared to the Wildcat's 800 miles. The added size allowed for a roomier cockpit, more armor plating, hydraulically operated landing gear and gun chargers, and 2,400 rounds of ammunition—nearly a thousand more than the F4F.

The Hellcat had a very large wing area—nearly 350 square feet—which contributed a great deal to its stability. The Hellcat's wings—which rotated backward to save deck space on the carrier—were mounted on the fuselage at a minimum angle of incidence so as to create as little drag as possible. This ensured good range and excess power. To get an acceptable angle of attack and approach speed for carrier operations, though, the engine was mounted with a negative thrust line. That is, the engine was tipped forward a bit relative to the longitudinal axis of the airplane. As a result of these design characteristics, the F6F flew in a peculiar tail-down attitude while in level flight.

VF-9 was the first squadron to be equipped with the Navy's newest fighter, the F6F Hellcat. Better in every respect than the Wildcat, it dominated the Japanese through the rest of the war. (U.S. Navy)

We got our first Hellcats on January 16, the same day that Louise and I were married. Jack Raby, Herb Houck, and Chick Smith flew the first three down from the Grumman factory at Bethpage, New York. These were F6F-3s, the first production model, of which more than 4,000 were built. Everyone in the squadron checked out on those first three aircraft while we waited for Grumman to build more for us.

My first flight in the Hellcat, on January 23, 1943, was an incredible experience. Being so much bigger than the Wildcat, it of course felt more substantial, more solid. The more powerful engine had a smoother purr to it as well. And everything was powered hydraulically. There was no more wrestling with the landing gear—cranking it up or down by hand and hoping not to bust a set of knuckles or break a wrist or crack a shin. As with the F4F, though, we still had to manually crank the canopy open and closed.

When I poured the coal to the big new fighter, I was amazed at how much power the engine produced. It seemed like the airplane just leapt off the ground; the takeoff roll was so short compared to the Wildcat's. And once airborne, the Hellcat seemed to want to climb and climb and climb. Best of all, it was a dream to fly—so stable and much easier to handle than the Wildcat. Landings were a snap as well. The landing gear struts were widely spaced, so there was little tendency to ground loop on landing. This was a *very* welcome change from the little Wildcat.

As new airplanes became available, squadron pilots continued to travel to New York to bring them back. On February 2, 1943, eight or ten of us piled into an R4D Navy transport to fly up to the Grumman plant at Bethpage to pick up new airplanes. When we got there we found that only one airplane was ready to go. Jack Raby, with his exquisitely tuned ability to recognize an opportunity for a party, volunteered the junior ensign—me—to ferry the airplane back while the rest of them enjoyed a night on the town, courtesy of Mr. Grumman. I didn't mind that much at all. After a briefing with the crew at Grumman, I climbed into the factory-fresh airplane and was on my way.

Along the way I stopped for fuel at Naval Air Station Anacostia, near Washington, D.C. The pilots there hadn't seen an F6F before. The questions and envious looks I got further helped to take the sting out of missing a night in New York with the rest of the boys.

The folks at Anacostia weren't the only envious ones. Some of our fellow fighter pilots in Norfolk wondered how we managed to be the first to get our hands on the F6F, since Raby was far from being the most senior squadron commander. The truth was, since we were assigned to the *Essex*, the first of the newer, larger class of carriers, the powers that be wanted us equipped with the newest fighters.

The VF-9 squadron patch. Light blue sky, orange-gold cat, white clouds and cat muzzle, red nose. (U.S. Navy)

The next month or so was a hectic time for everyone at VF-9. While I was busy learning how to "play house" with Louise, I was also training hard. We flew the new fighters several times a day, and our passion for them never wavered. Like all new designs, the F6F had a few teething problems, but for the most part it was simple to fly, easy to maintain, and very reliable.

Casey Childers very nearly fell victim to one notable exception to that reliability. He was ferrying a Hellcat back from Bethpage on February 5, when his engine quit somewhere over New Jersey. Try as he could, he couldn't get it started again and ended up landing dead-stick, with his wheels up, in a grove of pine trees. Grumman's penchant for overdesigning its aircraft saved his life. The rugged Hellcat plowed right through the trees. Casey crawled out unhurt and waved for the rest of the flight to press on.

All through February and into March we continued to get more airplanes. As we received enough to make it worthwhile, we began our tactical training in earnest—lots of formation flying, strafing, and gunnery flights. The F6F was extremely stable, and because of that it was a superb gunnery platform. I had done quite well in air-to-air gunnery with the F4F, but my scores improved considerably with the F6F.

***

In late February we started getting ready for our carrier qualifications on the *Essex*. We did a lot of field-carrier landing practice and were again overjoyed with our new airplane. It was so stable that it almost flew itself in the carrier landing pattern. The proof was in the pudding on March 7, 1943, when we flew out to the *Essex* and made history. Each of us made our eight qualification landings with no difficulty whatsoever, and VF-9 became the first operational Hellcat squadron to qualify aboard an aircraft carrier.

VF-9 was building a solid relationship all during this period with the rest of the air group and the ship's company of the *Essex*. This particular group of organizations and people clicked in a way that seldom occurs. The chemistry couldn't have been better. Professionally and socially, the air group and the ship's company enjoyed a very satisfying bond that would prove critical to our wartime successes.

Chapter 12

It was March 11, 1943, when we got word that it was time to go. The VF-9 squadron diary does a good job of describing the last day or two. It quotes a letter from Ensign Jack Kitchen to a friend:

> The word finally came through. The afternoon of March 11, our "XO," Pedro Winters, told the squadron that tomorrow morning we would fly our planes to East Field and have them hoisted aboard the *Essex*. What a grand excuse for another farewell party. It happened, and when we woke up the next morning we didn't know whether it was from the night before, or if the weather was really [that fuzzy]. We found out too soon the weather was [actually very poor]. All set to go and someone looked over in one of the planes and there sat "Gerony" [Dick DeMott] in his shorts. He had been awakened too late to pack his clothes or dress, but he was ready.
>
> Several of the planes got airborne and had to return, but most of the flight was held on the ground. Fortunately, Gerony did not take off and found time, with Dr. Keating's help, to pack his clothes and get dressed. All the planes that took off were finally accounted for, so we started working on ideas for a more successful launch for the remainder of the aircraft. This time all planes were launched at certain intervals by a man with a stopwatch standing at the end of the runway and giving each pilot a thumbs up for a "go" signal. Water towers along the route were designated as pylons for the pilots to fly by, so that each one went the same way. By the time we got to Chambers Field [visibility and ceiling were practically nil]. The pilot would fly toward the known vicinity of the field at 25' and when a flare from a Very pistol passed by him he would ease his throttle off, pull his stick back and land. All planes and pilots were accounted for and a very successful transfer of aircraft accomplished. This was so trying on the pilots' nerves that we had another party immediately.

We embarked with the *Essex* and her crew to the Caribbean for her—and our—shakedown cruise. For almost a month in the Gulf of Paria near Trinidad, the ship went through her paces. This was the period when troublesome equipment problems were identified and repaired. It was also the time for the crew to become familiar with the ship and each other—a time to develop procedures and teamwork, to find out what way of doing business worked and what did not. This was the precious bit of time allotted to the ship's crew to iron out her kinks before she was sent to war.

For much of this time, Air Group 9 was put ashore at a small British airfield at Port of Spain, Trinidad. The *Essex* was learning to walk before she tried to run. Having nearly 100 airplanes cluttering the ship sometimes made the task difficult.

The air group started with baby steps as well. We practiced flying small, simulated strikes together, then increased the size and complexity. Along the way, we came to know and respect each other, to work as a team. There was very little of the "us against them" mentality between the pilots of the fighters and the pilots of the dive bombers and torpedo bombers. In fact, one of my closest friends during this time was an SBD pilot named Norm Sandler. We had known each other since early during flight school at Pensacola. Norm was from Des Moines, and although his manner was somewhat reserved, he was a very good friend and we had a lot of fun together.

One notable change to normal operations went into effect during this time. The airplane maintenance sailors from all the different squadrons were detached from control of their parent units and attached to the ship's company, where they fell under the ultimate command of the ship's captain. This helped streamline and balance the maintenance efforts throughout the air group and relieved the squadrons of a significant administrative burden. It was a big success.

For all the success that the *Essex* and Air Group 9 had achieved in coming together, though, the trip ended on a tragic note for VF-9. On April 5, Charlie Gearhardt—who had survived a ditching in North Africa—badly mishandled his landing approach coming back aboard the carrier. This was my friend Charlie Gearhardt. Charlie, whose girlfriend had introduced me to my wife.

He bounced once, then again, going progressively more and more out of control. Finally, he went over the port side and into the water. As is always the case, the deck crew rushed to the edge to watch or do whatever they could to help. Charlie had survived the crash but couldn't get out of his sinking airplane. The impact of the crash had slammed the canopy shut and jammed it. Charlie was last seen struggling with the canopy as his airplane slipped beneath the water. He was gone.

Later, we installed a small metal bar in our Hellcats that could be flipped out over the canopy rail. If the pilot wanted to keep the canopy open, this bar prevented it from slamming closed and possibly jamming.

***

After the *Essex* arrived back at Norfolk on April 9, I took a few days of leave and traveled with Louise to Baltimore, so that I could meet her grandmother.

Afterward we went down to Washington, D.C., to relax for a couple of days. Finally, it was back to Oceana. We flew infrequently the rest of the month; instead, we used the time to take care of details in preparation for our deployment to the Pacific. For this I was very grateful, since it gave me a lot more time to be with Louise.

The time for our departure for the war in the Pacific was fast approaching. Louise and I did our best to feel our way around this fact. While we tried to ignore the impending separation and the unknowns that came with going into combat again, it was difficult. VF-9 had lost five squadron mates in the last six months; now the squadron was leaving for at least six months of what we assumed would be intense combat. I am not sure that all my promises to return were very reassuring to Louise. We just made the best of it and enjoyed our remaining time together as much as possible. That seemed to work, and things didn't get too teary until the night before I left.

On May 9, our airplanes were finally hoisted back aboard the *Essex* and the squadron moved aboard. The following day, May 10, 1943, we set sail for the Pacific.

Louise and two or three of the other wives came out to the beach to watch the *Essex* disappear over the horizon. Shortly after that, she went back down to Athens and spent a month with my parents, then went up to New York and moved in with her parents while she waited for me to return.

Chapter 13

It was now just over a year since I had joined the squadron and once again we were headed out to combat. I felt more prepared than before.

The *Essex* was the first—and thus the namesake—of a class of aircraft carriers that is rightfully considered the finest of its type ever built. She was 877 feet long and 148 feet wide, with a displacement of 33,000 tons. She carried more than 3,200 men and officers to service the ship and her nominal complement of 90 aircraft: 36 F6Fs, 36 SBDs, and 18 TBFs.

The accommodations aboard the *Essex* were considerably nicer than those aboard the *Ranger*. For one thing, I was billeted in a small stateroom with only two roommates—Gene Valencia and Bill Bonneau. The ship was much larger than the *Ranger* and, of course, it was brand new. The wardroom, where the officers ate, was larger and more modern. The heads, or restrooms, were also much more spacious, with hot and cold fresh water. Also, many of the spaces were air-conditioned.

As officers aboard the *Essex*, we enjoyed several amenities, including laundry service. When it was time for a change of uniform, or for a load of laundry to be done, we simply put our laundry basket out for the stewards. As was common in the military at the time, these stewards were mostly Black or Filipino sailors. They picked up our laundry, made out our list, then returned it—washed and pressed—the following day. There was never an excuse for an officer to look rumpled or unkempt aboard the ship.

En route to Hawaii we crossed through the Caribbean to the Panama Canal. Navigating the canal proved trickier than was thought. The ship was too broad to pass through with the gun tubs attached, so the crew had to cut them off with torches. Once the ship made it through—with a clearance of mere inches—the gun tubs were reattached. Following a brief liberty period in Panama City and a few days of exercises in the Gulf of Panama, we were on our way again.

We arrived at Pearl Harbor, Territory of Hawaii, on May 31, 1943. Although it had been more than a year and a half since the Japanese attack, the damage was still very evident. And sobering. Parts of the battleship *Arizona* still stuck out of the water, oil still seeped from the bottom, and the base was crawling with workers rebuilding damaged facilities and building totally new ones.

One sight still remains vividly in my mind. As we approached our mooring at Ford Island, one of the big Pan American Clipper seaplanes roared past us, not too far off our beam. It was a big, romantic-looking aircraft—and it looked more so as it charged through the water sending up great plumes of spray. I could just imagine some important admiral or attaché sitting inside, traveling back to Washington with important plans for the war.

***

Hawaii was closer to Japan than Virginia, but the war was still a long way off. And for Air Group 9 and the *Essex*, it would stay a long way off for a few more months. During the previous year, despite its crushing victory at Midway, the Navy had lost most of its big carriers. The *Lexington*, *Yorktown*, *Hornet*, and *Wasp* had all been sunk, as had the old *Langley*. The *Enterprise* was not yet back after undergoing extensive repairs and refit, so we were left with only the *Saratoga*, the smaller light carrier *Princeton*, and a handful of escort carriers in the Pacific. The Navy was not about to send its remaining carriers piecemeal into battle.

We continued to train, with more work on our tactics and flying proficiency and more simulated strikes. All this was done out of the naval air station at Barbers Point on the southwest corner of Oahu, west of Pearl Harbor and Honolulu. In our isolation, we were being honed to a fine edge.

It was at about this time that one of the smart guys back in the Bureau of Aeronautics figured that an easy way to extend the range of the F6F was to have us really lean out the fuel mixture. That is, reduce the fuel being introduced into the engine's cylinders while keeping the manifold pressure up. We didn't warm to the idea. The Hellcat already had pretty good range—more than a thousand miles—and the engine got extremely hot when the mixture was leaned out too much. We had tried it with a couple of airplanes when we were a day or two from reaching Pearl Harbor. One of the airplanes lost its engine and had to ditch alongside the ship.

The problem was predetonation, or compression ignition. Without enough fuel, the fuel-air mixture in the cylinders became too volatile and exploded before the piston was in the appropriate position, rather than burning in a controlled manner. This could cause tremendous damage.

Well, the engineering types apparently thought that the laws of thermo-dynamics didn't apply to our F6Fs. After our mechanics spent a few days preparing an airplane, I was scheduled to play test pilot. I climbed into my Hellcat on June 9, got airborne, and a few minutes later was at 25,000 feet over Barbers Point. After a brief time, I eased the throttle up to full power with no problem. Then I brought the throttle around the detent into the war emergency power setting. This activated the water injection system, which enabled the engine mixture to burn hotter and produce extra horsepower. This was for emergency use only because the higher temperatures damaged the engine after just a few minutes.

Well, only about three or four seconds passed before I heard a tremendous popping and saw black smoke begin to pour out of the engine. I cut everything back; the poor prop went around a few more times and then just stopped dead.

My fire-breathing fighter had suddenly turned into a 12,000-pound glider. To say that I was distressed would be an understatement. After about three 360-degree descending turns over the field, I lowered the landing gear and wrestled my big blue brick onto the runway. After I rolled to a stop, I was towed ignominiously back to the maintenance shop. When the ground crew pulled the engine cowling, they found that four of the eighteen cylinders were blown completely off of the crankcase. We didn't experiment with exceptionally lean power settings after that.

All through the middle of the summer, we continued to train. We sailed on the *Essex* into nearby waters for a few days at a time for training exercises. We launched mock strikes against various bases or targets in the islands, and land-based aircraft opposed us or launched counterstrikes against our force. It was during one of these exercises, on June 30, 1943, that Herb Houck and Jim Wilkerson collided over the water near Oahu. Houck parachuted immediately from low altitude. His chute opened just before he hit the water and he was rescued. Except for being badly bruised, he was okay. Unfortunately, Wilkerson's plane crashed and Jim was killed.

Just getting ready to go to war was killing my friends, one by one.

***

It was while we were in Hawaii that we first started to practice the Thach Weave. It was a defensive tactic, developed and popularized in the Navy by Jimmy Thach, a hero from the early air battles of 1942. It effectively used teamwork to negate the superior maneuverability of the Japanese Zero.

In practice a pair of airplanes flew a parallel course, about a thousand feet apart. When one airplane came under attack, the targeted pilot turned toward his wingman—away from the enemy—before the enemy fighter came within firing range. At the same time, the untargeted pilot turned toward the enemy fighter in order to protect his besieged wingman. The enemy pilot then had to make a choice; he could continue his attack at the risk of being shot by the untargeted wingman, or he could turn away. In combat, most Japanese pilots elected to turn away.

When the two wingmen passed each other, they resumed their original heading and reestablished their formation, a thousand feet apart, each now on the side opposite from where he started. The Thach Weave was most commonly practiced with a division, or four airplanes, split up so that there was a two-plane section on each side of the formation. The two airplanes within each section flew the weave together as if they were a single airplane.

Hawaii wasn't all hard work, though. On one occasion Casey Childers, who had been to Hawaii aboard a cruiser before the war, arranged a huge luau at Lau Yee Chai's. It was a sumptuous affair with roasted pigs and traditional food and dancing. And drinking.

Marv Franger and I flew a pair of Hellcats down to Hilo on another occasion and picked up about 50 pounds of the most beautiful steaks I had ever seen. Marv was from Texas and had proven to be our chief barbecue expert. Considering that the cost of the fuel for the airplanes made the steaks price out at about 100 dollars per pound, Marv cooked up a feast worth every penny.

While on liberty we did the standard tourist things—Waikiki Beach, the Dole pineapple packing plant, swimming on the black sand beaches, and such. We often took the squadron jeep on tours around Oahu and "borrowed" fresh pineapples from the huge fields that covered so much of the island.

While all of this was going on, the Brass was busy setting up leadership changes. We learned that our indomitably high-spirited skipper, Jack Raby, was being moved up to command all of Air Group 9. His replacement was to be Lieutenant Commander Philip H. Torrey, the son of a Marine general.

The change of command took place on August 14, 1943. After all this time we viewed the loss of the head of our family with some trepidation. But as it turned out that Torrey, who had been our executive officer for a while anyway, proved to be a fantastic squadron commander. He was more subdued than Raby—but who wasn't? He had a quiet, firm air of confidence and aggressiveness about him. A "fighter pilot's fighter pilot," he looked and acted like a leader, and he immediately had our full trust and loyalty.

It was also in August that the new *Yorktown* (CV-10) arrived at Pearl Harbor. The *Yorktown*, with Air Group 5 aboard, was to be our teammate, the other half of our task force for our first strike against the Japanese.

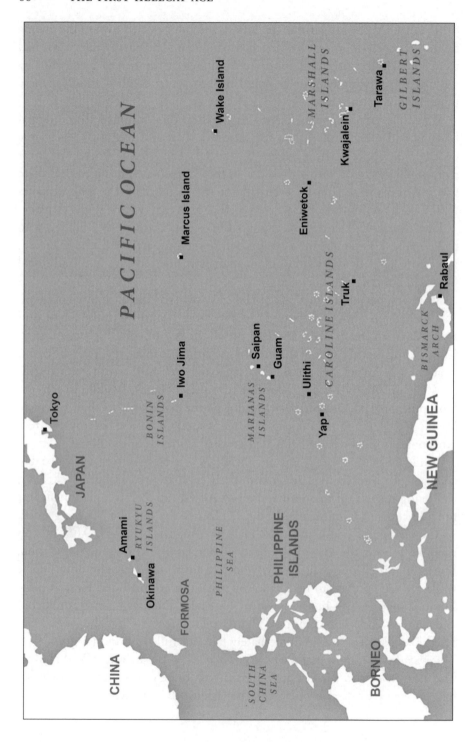

Chapter 14

On August 23, 1943, we sailed from Pearl Harbor in the company of the *Yorktown* and escorting surface warships. Our destination was Marcus Island, only about 700 miles southeast of Japan and home to a Japanese naval base and airfield. While not terribly significant in a strategic sense, it was an important base and would provide us a good opportunity to test our tactics, while at the same time giving the Japanese a wake-up call: the U.S. carrier fleet was back in action!

There were no flight operations along the way. Again, as we had on the way to North Africa and back, we played cards, watched movies, and had training sessions in our ready room. Airplane recognition drills were a regular item on our training menu. I think we spent so much time on airplane recognition because it was an easy lesson for the instructor to prepare, as well as being so crucial to survival, and ultimately to our success as fighter pilots. Life-and-death decisions had to be made in an instant, and time wasted trying to identify aircraft as friend or foe could mean the difference between victory and defeat.

Nevertheless, there was no doubt that the drills got boring. The instructor flashed pictures or silhouettes of airplanes over and over in the front of our ready room. Whether I wanted to or not, I got to the point where I could identify any airplane, American or Japanese, in mere thousandths of a second.

I also got to the point where I could identify every movie star from just about any B movie made up to that time. Hollywood made a big deal about how it was entertaining the troops overseas with free movies. What wasn't well advertised was that the bulk of these movies were not the crown jewels of motion picture entertainment. I watched bad movies night after night—in the vain hope, I suppose, that they might get better. Most of the time they did not.

To make things worse, some of the films were made to be shown on a wide screen. When projected on the small screen that we had, all of the people were about three inches wide! We called these movies "skinnies" and watched them anyway. To this day, Louise has a difficult time getting me into a movie theater.

Another skill we honed during the time we spent splashing from one part of the Pacific to another was skeet shooting. Shooting, especially deflection shooting, was encouraged to sharpen our gunnery skills. One pellet loaded into each one of our shells had a special coating that made it glow like a tracer so that we could see where we were hitting or missing. We set up a skeet thrower on the end of the deck and popped away for hours at a time. This is something I enjoyed quite a bit, and I'm sure that it helped to sharpen my shooting eye.

We received plenty of target briefings during our week-long trip to Marcus Island. The air intelligence officer had solid information about what we could expect to encounter. He also had fairly recent photos of the island and we knew pretty much where the antiaircraft batteries were located. The one thing he could not tell us was how many and what types of airplanes were flying out of the airfield there. It was a small airfield, though, and we didn't believe there would be much aerial opposition.

Since I had been in combat before, the tenseness and uncertainties that I had experienced aboard the *Ranger* were less pronounced now. Flying the F6F helped somewhat as well; it was superior to the F4F in every way. On the eve of combat operations, it was particularly reassuring to know that the

McWhorter and the other squadron pilots kept their shooting skills sharp by shooting skeet from the deck of the *Essex*. (McWhorter Family)

F6F had more armor plate behind, beneath, and in front of the cockpit than the F4F had.

***

By the very early morning of September 1, 1943, our small task force had made its way to a position 150 miles north of Marcus Island. The plan was a predawn launch—one strike group from each carrier. Air Group 5, aboard the *Yorktown*, was to lead the way since its commander, Commander Jimmy Flatley, was senior to our air group commander, Jack Raby.

Flight quarters was scheduled for 0330, so Bill Bonneau, Gene Valencia, and I didn't have to sweat out a long night of precombat jitters. We got up at 0200 and showered, then took turns shaving in the sink in our room. After climbing into my flight suit, I went down to the wardroom for breakfast. Unlike on our first day of combat off the coast of North Africa aboard the *Ranger*, there was no effort by the galley crew of the *Essex* to prepare a special meal.

After eating I made my way up to the squadron ready room, just below the flight deck on the port side of the ship. The room had a dark, morbid glow to it, as only the red overhead lights were on. These lights helped our eyes become night-adapted. I don't know if it was because of the lights or the impending combat, but everyone seemed to be speaking in hushed voices.

Phil Torrey gave us our preflight briefing and passed out our airplane assignments. I checked my chart board to make sure that I had all the required information—headings, times, frequencies, target information, expected task force positions, and the location of the lifeguard submarine. At about 0330 the call came for the pilots to man their planes.

I strapped on my shoulder holster; we now carried Smith & Wesson .38 Specials, Victory models, rather than the big Colt .45 pistols. The .38 was smaller, easier to carry, and easier to shoot. Next, I put on my Mae West life preserver and my helmet, then grabbed my chart board and filed out the small corridor at the rear of the ready room with the rest of the pilots.

I stepped out onto the dark catwalk and into the humid wind as the ship sliced through the dark, gentle Pacific. The night was pitch-black; I almost had to feel my way up onto the flight deck and through the rest of the airplanes until I found mine.

At this point in the war, the Navy was beyond paranoid about losing one of its valuable aircraft carriers to Japanese submarines. Consequently, the light discipline at night was several orders of magnitude beyond unwaveringly rigid. There were no flashlights, floodlights, or running lights for either the ships or airplanes. There was absolutely nothing to give away our position.

In the dark, the plane captain and I half-felt our way around the airplane. We checked to see that the flight surfaces were undamaged and working properly, and that there were no oil, hydraulic, or gasoline leaks that would make the airplane unsafe for flight.

The cockpit was a black hole as well. This was when those blindfold cockpit checks we suffered through during training finally paid off. After the plane captain helped me strap in, I arranged myself and waited. Had I not been waiting to go into combat, I would have enjoyed my seat under the dark tropical sky. The temperate breeze that tumbled into the cockpit and brushed across my face was almost soothing.

Shortly after 0400 we got the signal to start our engines. Flashes of light pierced the pitch black of the flight deck as flames belched from wakening engines. Propellers swung slowly at first, then in a sudden roar of smoke and fire transformed themselves into translucent, whirling, deadly disks.

In minutes the deck was aglow from the exhaust flames of dozens of big radial engines. The ban on lights seemed silly now. Once my engine was started, I checked the dimly lit instrument gauges to ensure that everything was functioning properly. I followed the signals of the taxi directors, who were positioning aircraft with barely visible light wands.

Phil Torrey was taxied up to the takeoff spot and we were led into a line behind him. He launched at 0430 and the rest of us moved into position to follow in 30-second intervals. Once I was taxied up to the takeoff spot the flight deck officer whirled a flashlight in his right hand, signaling me to run my engine up to full power. I stood on the brakes, double-checked that the fuel mixture control was on auto rich and that the propeller pitch lever was full forward, then moved the throttle forward slowly. As I did so, I checked the engine instruments to ensure that the oil temperature and pressure were steady and that I was getting 2,700 rpm and 54 inches of manifold pressure.

I no longer had any trouble seeing the flight deck officer or anything else on the flight deck. The exhaust of my big R2800 produced a flame about two feet long from the aft starboard side of the engine cowling; it really lit the place up.

Everything looked good. On a normal night launch I would have signaled that I was ready for takeoff by flashing my running lights, but that was forbidden for this launch. So, I gave the flight deck officer a hand salute and he dropped his arm, pointing down the deck. I released the brakes and went speeding into the night.

Once airborne, I raised the landing gear handle, cranked the canopy closed, brought the flaps up, and busied myself looking for the rest of my flight.

I strained my eyes against the dark and looked above me to the left, or port, side of the ship. At the same time, I continued to scan the needle and ball mounted on my instrument panel. These two instruments told me whether I was turning or skidding, and in so doing helped me to avoid vertigo and to stay right side up. If I were not careful, with the night so dark, I wouldn't be the first naval aviator to fly blithely into the water.

It was so pitch black that I could only just make out small, blue-tinged exhaust flames from other aircraft. Finally, I spotted a darker shape with an exhaust flame that appeared to be that of a Hellcat in a left turn. I couldn't be sure, though, as there were dive bombers and torpedo bombers airborne, and one exhaust flame looked much like another.

I added power to join. As I adjusted my angle of bank, I scanned my instruments and double-checked my airspeed, altitude, and attitude. Again, if I wasn't careful, I could get disoriented and spin into the ocean. It had happened to others. I closed the distance, and a dark shape soon loomed in contrast to the exhaust flame. I reduced power, readjusted my angle of bank, and slid underneath it and into position on its right wing. Luck was with me; I had joined on another Hellcat. But it was so dark that I couldn't see the identification numbers on its side. I had no idea who I had joined with, but it didn't matter. For the time being I was staying put. I knew that all around me others were joining, breaking formation, and rejoining until they found a like-type wingman. It was truly a miracle that we didn't lose any aircraft to midair collisions.

When the strike group was finally more or less assembled, someone turned us toward Marcus Island, and we were on our way. Moments later the formation nearly came apart when some idiot in the rear accidentally came down on his trigger and sent a huge arc of .50 caliber bullets over the top of the entire formation. At night the tracers looked enormous—like great fiery pumpkins streaming overhead. Disaster was only narrowly averted as airplanes scattered to get out of the way. Again, luck was with us, as no airplanes were hit, and there were no collisions. That episode upset a lot of people.

As it got light enough for us to make out the numbers painted on our airplanes, we shuffled formations again until everyone was settled into the correct position. I finally found my division lead, Mike Hadden, and eased into position as number-three, the section leader. A few minutes later Jack Kitchen joined us in the number-two position. Finally, our formation was rounded out when Bud Gehoe pulled into position on my wing as number four. Our four-ship division was attached to Phil Torrey's division.

For the rest of the flight we were above the bombers in their box formation—SBDs in the lead, TBFs in trail, and F6Fs about 1,000 feet overhead and offset some 500 feet on either side. We kept our heads on a swivel through it all, watching for enemy fighters.

As we approached the tiny island, which was basically taken up by the naval base and airfield, we could see antiaircraft fire reaching up at the airplanes from the *Yorktown* strike group. Many of the targets were already smoking or on fire and there was still no evidence of Japanese fighters. From about 12,000 feet we watched our dive bombers start their dives.

Once the bombers were on their way it was our turn to push over. I followed Hadden's lead as he pushed the nose of his fighter down toward the island. I looked over my shoulder to check that Gehoe was still with me.

We built up airspeed quickly to more than 400 miles an hour. As planned, we passed the bombers in their dives and picked out targets to strafe ahead of them. The idea was that the strafing fighters would keep the heads of the antiaircraft gunners down while the vulnerable bombers were in the delivery phase of their dives.

I leveled off at about fifty feet and aligned my gunsight on a hangar. Fifty feet was probably too low. They could have thrown rocks up and hit me. But being so low and fast, I flashed by the antiaircraft gunners so quickly that they had little time to react. As the hangar came in range, I let loose with all six .50 caliber machineguns and watched my tracers fly right through the open doors.

As I climbed back up to altitude for another strafing run, I could see three or four Japanese airplanes burning on the airfield, but no enemy fighters in the air. Most of the airfield and naval base was on fire. Just as in North Africa, our fighters were flashing back and forth across the airfield, shooting at anything that looked worthwhile, trying to dodge antiaircraft bursts and the streams of tracers that crisscrossed low overhead. After two or three more strafing runs, we rendezvoused and set a course back for the *Essex*.

In a way the strike seemed almost anticlimactic. After all our training and preparations—from Oceana to Hawaii and all points between—and the week it took to transit to Marcus Island, the most frightening part of the flight was the predawn rendezvous. We hadn't even seen any enemy fighters!

Perhaps the mission was less eventful for me than it had been for others. Mike Hadden's airplane was hit in the engine by antiaircraft fire. The Pratt & Whitney and Grumman combination saved another life when Mike was able to make it back to the task force and ditch alongside a destroyer. Mike thought his adventure for the day was over when he climbed clear of his sinking airplane; but while bobbing on the surface in his Mae West he was spooked when he spotted several brown objects in the water near him, and he swam away as fast as he could. We were briefed that the waters around Marcus Island were infested with man-eating sharks, and Mike had no desire to be eaten. He was finally picked up by the destroyer and was told by the skipper that he was the first person that he had ever seen swim away from life jackets! Mike had thought that there were three or four big sharks splashing next to him, ready to finish what the Japanese had started. Mike's airplane was the *Essex*'s only loss.

Chapter 15

By the end of the day, we were on our way back to Hawaii. It seemed to me that we weren't getting much of a return on our investment. We had traveled for more than a week to get into position for the attack, had run one morning's worth of strikes, and now were on our way back. In other words, we traded two weeks of transit time for one morning over the target.

I didn't appreciate the Navy's line of thinking. By this time the United States was holding the line in the Pacific and was carefully building combat power for coming offensives. The Marcus Island strike was considered almost a training mission, an opportunity to evaluate our tactics and readiness without greatly risking our limited carrier assets. Although there were new combatant vessels in the Pacific, and many more on the way, the majority of the men manning them had never been to sea before, much less combat. They needed to be tested.

***

When we got back to Hawaii we moved the squadron from Barbers Point to the little airstrip at Ford Island, right in the middle of Pearl Harbor. This was nice because we were much closer to Honolulu and just about everything else. Including the Big Brass.

One night, after a few drinks at a party, Charlie Moutenot, Gene Valencia, Bill Bonneau, and a couple others thought it might be fun to tour the island. One of the drunks-cum-tourists had seen a jeep conveniently parked down the street from the officers' club, so they all hopped in, fired it up, and went joyriding.

The next morning, Jack Raby informed Phil Torrey that he was somewhat unhappy about a visit he had received from a very irate admiral's aide. It turned out that the borrowed jeep belonged to Admiral Nimitz, who wanted to know immediately the names of the culprits who had stolen it. Fortunately, Raby, in a command performance before none other than Nimitz himself, was able to diplomatically deflect most of that salvo—"Boys will be boys. . . . war heroes blowing off steam. . . . just a harmless little prank. . . ." No one was punished and the jeep was not taken again.

We didn't have that much time to play at being boys anyway. On September 30, 1944, we were at sea again, this time as part of Task Force 14. It was the first time the Navy had assembled six carriers for one operation. Along with the *Yorktown*, the *Essex* was joined by the new fleet carrier *Lexington* (CV-16) and the light carriers *Independence* (CVL-22), *Belleau Wood* (CVL-24), and *Cowpens* (CVL-25). The target was Wake Island.

After repelling a determined attack on December 11, 1941, the American garrison on Wake Island was captured by the Japanese on December 23, two weeks after the attack on Pearl Harbor. The valiant defense put up by the Marines, sailors, and civilians on the island was a rallying point for America early in the war. The opportunity to take revenge was something we looked forward to.

We launched our first strike early on the morning of October 5, 1943. One of the lessons we had learned from the Marcus Island raid was that predawn launches were too dangerous. The first aircraft on the Wake Island strike was sent airborne just at first light.

On this mission, the strike groups from both the *Essex* and the *Yorktown*—more than 100 aircraft—rendezvoused about 150 miles from the island before proceeding on course. Once again, the TBFs and SBDs gathered in their protective boxes while the F6Fs rode herd in a weaving formation a thousand feet overhead.

We were just approaching the island when I looked down through the bomber formation and saw an Imperial Japanese Navy Zero fighter motoring along in the opposite direction about 500 feet below the bombers. It was the first Japanese airplane I had ever seen in the air. The Zero was painted the classic olive-green, with a black engine cowling and big red "meatballs" on the wings and fuselage.

It didn't take me long to figure out what the enemy pilot was up to. Since he had not already pulled up and blasted the bombers from below, I was sure that—left unmolested—he was going to pull up into an Immelmann to get directly behind the bombers or me.

I immediately rolled into a hard right-hand turn. My plan was to meet him in a head-on firing pass. A head-on pass wasn't the best move I could make, because I would be facing his two, 20-millimeter cannons which were bigger and had a greater range than my .50 caliber machineguns. But it was better than having him on my tail.

I had gotten only about two-thirds of the way through my turn when I caught sight of him again. He had completed his Immelmann and was already level at my altitude—headed straight for me! And coming right at me from out of his engine cowling was a long stream of red tracers.

I was flabbergasted that the Zero had gotten through the Immelmann turn so quickly. In an instant I rolled further right, kicked right rudder and split-essed straight down and away at full throttle. This was my only way to escape; we knew there wasn't a Zero made that could stay with the Hellcat in a dive. Luckily, I wasn't hit.

I looked back over my shoulder and saw that the Zero hadn't tried to follow me down. With my Hellcat screaming down toward the ocean at more than 400 miles an hour, the airstream rushing over my airplane was quite loud and the controls were noticeably stiff. I leveled out several thousand feet below the strike force. Using the energy of my airspeed, I kept the throttle full forward, checked again for the enemy fighter, and zoomed back up to rejoin the strike group.

My very first encounter with an enemy aircraft was over. I had almost found out the hard way just how maneuverable the Zero could be, and I was lucky to have ended the engagement in a draw. We learned later that luring us away from our formations was a favorite trick of Japanese pilots. Using a single fighter, they could usually sucker one or two of our planes away before pouncing on them with a large pack of fighters. I never purposely left formation again.

A captured example of the Japanese Mitsubishi A6M Zero. Nimble, and with very long range, it was nevertheless somewhat fragile. It was the fighter most frequently encountered by U.S. Navy flyers. (U.S. Navy)

***

Wake Island, really three little islands, is shaped like a big V. I'm not sure why, but the decision was made to attack down the middle—from the open end toward the point. The problem with this was that every Japanese soldier and sailor on that island had a shot at us. Their radar had warned them we were coming, and now a huge arc of white and yellow and red tracers reached up at us from each arm of the island. It was so thick that in the still-dim early morning light it looked solid!

Our dive bombers tipped over into their dives, and we pushed over after them. A few seconds later we flashed past them and picked out targets as we plunged toward the airfield. The amount of antiaircraft fire was terrifying. It didn't seem possible that anyone could fly through it unscathed.

Mike Hadden led Jack Kitchen, Bud Gehoe, and me on a strafing run against one of the hangars on the airfield. It was satisfying to hear the booming chatter from my guns and see the tracers slam into the structure. As I lifted my airplane up to clear the hangar, I released the trigger and looked to my right before I turned. I was not only looking for antiaircraft fire and enemy fighters, but also checking to make sure I didn't run into another Hellcat. This was a very real danger. Through the war, many of our airplanes were lost because they collided over the target.

Amazed and thankful that I had not been hit, I pulled into a hard, climbing right turn and headed back toward our rendezvous point southeast of the island. As I passed through about 8,000 feet, I spotted a Zero almost at my 11 o'clock position. It was about 2,000 feet above me, crossing from left to right, almost tail-on.

With a quick dip of my right wing, I turned slightly to the right and closed from directly below and behind. It took only a moment or so to close the range to about 300 feet. It felt like a week. Finally, I lifted the nose of my F6F slightly and settled the pipper of my gunsight on the belly of the enemy fighter. I fired a short burst—about one second—and the Zero exploded.

Next, I banked hard left to clear the explosion and checked behind me for another enemy fighter. It would be a tragedy to shoot down a Zero and get bagged by his wingman.

The sky seemed clear of enemy fighters, so I turned back toward our rendezvous point. A short time later I spotted another Zero a half-mile or so ahead of me, going in the same direction in a shallow dive. I started down after him and was gaining slowly when a bright stream of red tracers flashed over my canopy from behind. Without thinking, I kicked my F6F into a hard snap roll to the right and dove away, straight down.

As I rolled and looked back over my shoulder, I was stunned to see another F6F, still well behind me and obviously far out of range of the Zero. Undeterred by the impossible distance, he continued to fire at the enemy fighter, his rounds falling harmlessly in a long arc into the ocean.

I'm sure the idiot never even saw me. Thanks to his bungling, neither one of us got that Zero.

Still seething, I flew to the rendezvous point, joined with the other Hellcats, and escorted the bombers back to the *Essex*. I was very excited about my first aerial victory and made my way around the ship to compare notes with other pilots. The new skipper, Phil Torrey, had gotten into a dogfight with three Zeroes, shot down one, and escaped the other two by dodging into a bank of clouds. After our first strafing run Hadden and Kitchen had tangled with four Zeroes and shared credit for shooting down one. Hadden's plane was badly shot up, though, and he almost didn't make it back.

I found out later that I had missed being the first Hellcat pilot to shoot down an enemy fighter by only a few minutes. That distinction probably belonged to Ensign Robert Duncan of VF-5 from the *Yorktown*. He had bagged two of the enemy fighters on the way into the target. Overall, our Hellcats had performed masterfully against the Zero. VF-9's sole loss was Ensign John McGann, who succumbed to an unknown cause. In air-to-air combat, it seemed obvious to us that the Zero, which remained our primary adversary throughout the war, was starting to show its age against our newer fighter.

***

First flown in 1940, the Mitsubishi-manufactured A6M Type 0 was arguably the world's best fighter when it first flew combat later that same year in China. Powered by a Nakajima Sakae 21, 14-cylinder radial engine, which produced about 1,100 horsepower, the Zero was only respectably fast at 340 miles per hour. But it had other qualities that made it a superlative fighter.

Most notably, the Zero was exceedingly light. This lightness, combined with superb design and engineering, made for an exceptionally maneuverable airplane. All through the war there was not a single Allied airplane that could compete with the Zero in a turning fight. The lightweight design also gave the airplane an operating range that approached an almost unbelievable 1,300 miles. Indeed, early in the war, land-based Zeroes showed up in places so far from known bases that it was thought certain they were carrier-launched.

Armed with a 20-millimeter cannon in each wing and two 7.7-millimeter cowl-mounted machineguns, the Zero packed a respectable punch. One technique the Zero pilots used with good effect was to their aim and get hits with their machineguns, then open fire with the heavy-hitting 20-millimeter cannon, which had only a small supply of ammunition.

The Zero also had a long greenhouse canopy that provided excellent all-round visibility. This was critical in the whirling, twisting gunfights in which the Zero excelled. But all of these attributes came at a cost. Japanese pilots prized speed and maneuverability above all else, so the airplane's manufacturers put little emphasis on protection. Without self-sealing fuel tanks and armor protection, the Zero often caught fire and exploded after absorbing only a short burst of gunfire. This was the case with the Zero I had shot down. Moreover, the thin aluminum skin and delicately engineered airframe could not withstand rough use in the same manner that the far heavier American designs could. In fact, Zeroes were known to come apart in some maneuvers, even though they had not been fired on.

This elegant but somewhat delicate—even flimsy—design also made the Zero difficult to fly at high speeds, particularly in a dive. We learned later that we could escape the Zero by going into a high-speed dive and turning to the right. This was because the torque of the Zero's engine, combined with the higher control forces and the lack of hydraulically boosted flight controls, made it impossible for the Japanese pilots to physically move their controls quickly enough to follow us.

These shortcomings weren't enough to keep the Zero from dominating most of the aircraft it encountered early in the war. But the inability of the Japanese to modify the airplane to meet our newer aircraft on equal terms, starting in 1943, heralded the Zero's long slide into obsolescence. It was a long slide from which Japanese naval aviation never recovered.

***

During the rest of that day and the following day, October 6, 1943, I flew two more strikes against Wake Island. But the defending Japanese air contingent was nearly demolished and I encountered no more enemy aircraft. And while the antiaircraft fire continued to be heavy, we lost no more aircraft. By the time we left Wake late on October 6, the enemy installations there were in a shambles.

On the return trip to Hawaii a memorial service was held for John McGann and two bomber crews. Unfortunately, these services became an increasingly common occurrence as the war heated up for VF-9 and the *Essex*.

Chapter 16

Once back in Hawaii we were turned loose for a few days of rest and relaxation. One of the best things about returning to Hawaii was the huge backlog of mail that was waiting for us. Letters from home were lifesavers, huge morale builders as we didn't receive mail while transiting to and from a strike. Consequently, following the missions to Marcus and Wake, there were huge mail calls. Afterward, everyone scurried off alone to read their mail and open packages.

Louise and I had agreed to write to each other every day. So far, during the six months I had been gone, we had kept our promises. But because of the way the war impacted the movement of mail, even when I was in Hawaii, her letters didn't arrive daily; they came in batches. I took them to my room, arranged them in chronological order, then read each one several times over, wishing that I could hear her speaking the words I was reading. Of course, this just made me miss her even more.

About this time, we started to receive Victory mail, or V-mail. These were one-page letters that were copied to microfilm, transported to the appropriate destination, reproduced on lightweight paper, then delivered to the addressee. The government encouraged the nation to use V-mail because it saved weight and space. About half the letters I received were V-mail, and they were just as welcome as the more conventional kind.

I also received letters from friends and family. My parents sent letters from home telling me all about the local news. They often enclosed newspaper clippings that recounted our exploits in the Pacific and what was going on in Europe. Every time the local newspaper printed something about me, the publishers took great pride in pointing out that I had once been a delivery boy for their paper.

***

After we got back from the Wake Island strike on October 11, the air group organized a huge "survival party" at the Moana Hotel on Waikiki Beach. The big ballroom on the second floor was contracted for the event, and we all looked forward to the opportunity to relax, reflect, and enjoy ourselves.

The party went off pretty well and we were all feeling very good as the evening wore on. Toward the end of the night, Jack Raby decided that he needed some fresh air. Unfortunately for him, as the commander of Air Group 9, he was no longer entitled to the services of Lieutenant Junior Grade Hamilton McWhorter, USNR, of Fighting Squadron 9, handler of commanding officers. Raby was feeling no pain when he decided to step out onto the balcony. Instead, he stepped right out of a floor-to-ceiling window and fell 15 feet to the ground, breaking his leg.

Heeding his shouts, a contingent of partygoers scrambled down the stairs, rushed outside, and packed him off to the hospital. A few minutes later the party was back in full swing. On October 20, 1943, Commander Paul Emrick, the VT-9 commanding officer, relieved Raby as commander of Air Group 9.

***

We went back to Barbers Point after the Wake strike. The isolation didn't have much of an effect on our rest and recreation plans; we weren't there very long, and training occupied most of that time. My logbook shows eight flights between October 15 and October 19, 1943. On October 21, we flew back out to the *Essex* and, in company with the *Independence* (CVL-22) and *Bunker Hill* (CV-17), headed south.

As we crossed the equator, the ship's crew made preparations to initiate those of us who had never made the transition—the pollywogs. In time-honored tradition, King Neptune's Court was set up on the flight deck and the pollywogs were put through various tests to ensure that they were worthy of becoming veteran shellbacks. We had to crawl through a target sleeve while shellbacks motivated us with paddles to our back ends. Then we had to crawl on our bellies through a large trough filled with some sort of slimy liquid. This brought us to the Royal Baby—a fat, crusty, sailor whose exposed belly was smeared with some sort of icky-looking stuff. To complete our initiation, we had to kiss him right on the belly.

The non-aviators also suffered the indignity of having their hair cut into all sorts of imaginative styles. The captain forbade the shellbacks to do the same to the flyers. He was concerned that if we went down at sea, our shorn skulls wouldn't fare well in the tropical sun.

After the initiations were complete, the number-one elevator was partially raised from the hangar deck so that it formed a stage of sorts. All types of hilarious skits were performed by the different squadrons and by the ship's company. The one I remember most was put on by a flight surgeon. He gave a very convincing demonstration of how to perform a circumcision, using a very large bologna as a prop.

***

Although we didn't know it at the time, our destination was Rabaul. Located on the eastern coast of New Britain Island, which lies just northeast of New Guinea, Rabaul harbor was captured from Australian forces by the Japanese in January 1942. It had since been developed into the principal Japanese air and naval base in the region. As long as the Japanese were able to maintain effective air and naval forces at Rabaul, American forces in the Solomon Islands and New Guinea were in jeopardy. The Japanese at Rabaul had to be neutralized.

On November 5, 1943, we arrived at Pallikulo Bay, Espiritu Santo, in the New Hebrides Islands. We were not allowed to go ashore. While anchored there we

Japanese Zeroes at Rabaul. McWhorter was caught up in a great, whirling dogfight there on November 11, 1943. Although his aircraft was stitched by enemy machinegun fire, he downed two Zeroes. (Wikimedia Commons)

heard rumors that the *Saratoga* (CV-3) and the *Princeton* (CVL-23) had conducted raids against Rabaul that day and had taken significant losses. By this time most of us had guessed that the *Essex* was going to be in the thick of it very soon.

We weren't wrong. We departed Espiritu Santo on November 7, but for some unexplained reason returned again on November 8. Later that day, we departed for good as part of Task Group 50.3 under the command of Rear Admiral Alfred E. Montgomery. Our principal targets were the warships in Rabaul's Simpson Harbor. If they could be sunk while at anchor, they could not threaten the recent Marine landings at Bougainville.

There was some concern on the ship. Rabaul was known to be a heavily defended base, and our losses were expected to be heavy. In addition to the ever-present, shore-based antiaircraft batteries, the warships in the harbor could be expected to contribute to the defensive firestorm. And there were fighters based at five different airfields in the area. Rabaul was a target not to be taken lightly.

They sent us airborne just after dawn on November 11, 1943. After rendezvousing and climbing to about 12,000 feet, our strike group started for Simpson Harbor, about 160 miles to the northwest. We cruised at 180 knots and about 2,000 feet over the clouds.

The ingress was uneventful until we got to a point about 50 miles from the harbor. It was then that we picked up another escort—a dozen or so Zeroes. We were in our standard formation—SBDs and TBFs in the center, protected by F6Fs above and on each side. The Zeroes took up position a couple of thousand feet above us and farther off on either side.

The enemy fighters weren't particularly aggressive. Occasionally, one or two of them feinted toward us to draw us out of the formation. We responded with our Thach Weave tactics: the closest section to the incoming side of the attack turned away—across the bombers—and the section on the opposite side of the formation turned toward the enemy fighters. The Zeroes broke off their attacks every time. There was a strong temptation to chase them, but we were a well-disciplined air group by then and everyone stayed put. To have done otherwise would very likely have been fatal.

The enemy pilots were also hopeless show-offs. Every once in a while, one of the Zeroes zoomed out of formation, picked up a little speed, and went into a series of aerobatics—loops, rolls, Immelmanns, or whatever. I'm not sure what that was about. Perhaps they were trying to intimidate us. It seemed very incongruous; we were supposed to be killing each other, yet they were putting on air shows.

In due course we were surprised by the appearance of big, white, explosive bursts above us. They didn't look like typical antiaircraft fire. Instead of the smudgy gray or black of bursting antiaircraft shells, these were white with smoky white tendrils. We learned later from intelligence debriefs that the explosions were from phosphorous bombs with timed fuses. The bombs had been dropped by Zeroes flying high overhead. Fortunately, the fuse settings were a bit off and no damage was done.

The formation of Zeroes turned away as we neared the harbor. A moment or two later we came under traditional antiaircraft fire, which roared up through the clouds and started popping all around us. As I weaved above the formation I couldn't help feeling sorry for the torpedo and dive bomber pilots holding steady below me. In my nimble fighter I could turn away from danger—or run away if required. But the brave bomber pilots had to keep their slower, less maneuverable airplanes in formation. With Zeroes taunting the strike, bombs exploding overhead, and antiaircraft fire rocketing up from below, I am sure they were very anxious. The Zeroes flying alongside our formation certainly made me apprehensive.

Just as we arrived over the target area the clouds below us began to open. It was almost as if it was planned. Immediately, the long white wakes of Japanese warships caught my attention. They were steaming at top speed, exiting the harbor to the northwest.

We stayed at altitude with the bombers until they pushed over into their dives—careful to guard them in case the formation of Zeroes picked this moment to attack. Once the bombers were in their dives, we headed down—by now from the northeast—and passed them as planned at more than 400 miles per hour.

I could feel the G forces push me down into my seat as I leveled off about 100 feet above the water. The harbor was full of ships—and enemy fire. I maneuvered for a broadside run against a line of big Japanese warships steaming out of the harbor. For some insane reason I set myself up to fire on the biggest ship in the bunch—a 600-foot-long *Mogami*-class heavy cruiser with the classic pagoda-style superstructure.

The ship bristled with guns, and it looked like every one of them was firing at me; there was smoke and gun flashes from stem to stern. The ship was even firing its big eight-inch main guns! These huge shells were mesmerizing. I could actually see them as they sped toward me—each spinning slowly and trailing a stream of smoke. There was enough time to see the shell, recognize it for what it was, decide what to do, make the airplane do it, get out of the way, and pray the shell didn't explode as it went by! That sight stays with you forever.

I opened fire on the ship from about 1,500 feet. Every fifth round was an armor-piercing incendiary round, or API, which made a bright flash when it struck metal. With my combined rate of fire of about four thousand rounds per minute from my six machineguns, the superstructure of that cruiser was

At Rabaul, McWhorter dropped to wavetop level and, at great peril, made a strafing run against a heavy cruiser similar to this one. (U.S. Navy).

sparkling from the impacts. And I appreciated the fact that for every sparkle I saw, there were four other rounds hitting the ship that I didn't see.

Somehow, I didn't get hit. I flashed over the cruiser just at masthead height and looked down onto the deck. I saw the Japanese sailors in their gun tubs, looking back up at me. There were other Japanese sailors—dead ones.

I suddenly knew exactly how a pigeon at a shooting match must feel. I wished that my airplane could somehow go faster so that I could escape the wicked fire from the ships in the harbor. I'm not certain that I didn't actually bend the throttle; I was pushing it that hard! I started to climb and when I looked back I saw a very large explosion on the far side of the cruiser. I'm not sure if it was hit by a bomb or a torpedo, but a huge column of water erupted right next to it.

I continued my climb and turned toward the rendezvous point to the southeast. I got up to 5,000 feet and saw a huge aerial melee taking place over the big Japanese air base on the southern shore of the harbor. The scene was like something out of the movies—dozens of aircraft turning and spinning and spiraling. There was an explosion here, a parachute there, and airplanes spinning down in flames everywhere. The water was dotted with three or four big, light blue rings where airplanes had crashed and churned the surface.

The temptation was much too great to resist. Without a wingman, and without giving it any thought, I barreled into the fracas as fast as my airplane would go. There were about 50 Zeroes and perhaps half as many Hellcats. I immediately saw a Hellcat ahead of me flying along straight and level. There was a Zero behind it, pouring cannon fire into him. I don't know if the Hellcat pilot was dead, wounded, or paralyzed with fright, but he wasn't fighting at all, and huge chunks of metal were being blown off by the Zero's guns.

As fast as I could, I flew into a position almost directly behind the Zero, opened fire with a short burst at about 300 feet, and flashed past just above him. I looked down into the cockpit of the dark green fighter and saw flames coming out from beneath the instrument panel. I was amazed at how readily the enemy airplane caught fire.

An instant later I saw another Zero about 1,500 feet ahead of me and just to my right, heading away. I turned for him and started closing the range. Just as I approached I received the surprise of my life.

The noise was as if I was standing inside a tin shed and someone had thrown a handful of rocks against the outside of it. It stung my ears, and I felt the airplane vibrate as machinegun bullets slammed into it. This was certainly an attention-getter! I had made a classic mistake: over-concentrating on the target ahead of me at the expense of keeping a good lookout all around. It was the same mistake made by the pilot in the Zero I had flamed just seconds before.

I looked back and caught sight of a pair of Zeroes firing at me. Their characteristic lines of red tracers flashed past. I rolled hard over and down into a vertical dive.

It seemed as if the excitement—or terror—might never end. No sooner did I start the dive than I saw another Zero about 1,000 feet in front of me, crossing from the bottom of my windscreen to the top. I was set up for a perfect overhead 90-degree deflection shot—not an easy one to make.

Automatically—because if I had thought about it, it would have been too late—I put the pipper of my gunsight ahead of the nose of the enemy fighter and squeezed the trigger. My six .50 caliber machineguns chattered again and the Zero exploded.

Anxious to get away while I was still alive, I cleared the fight, pulled out at about 3,000 feet, and headed to the rendezvous point. Climbing through 5,000 feet, I spotted a Zero about 2,000 feet above me and to my left, flying in the opposite direction. Already slow because I was climbing, and unsure how badly my F6F had been hit, I didn't want to climb up into him for a shot. With a great deal of nervous apprehension I watched, waiting for him to drop his nose and let loose at me with those 20-millimeter cannons. Amazingly, he passed close by without taking any aggressive action. I watched him until he got to my eight o'clock position. It was then that he started a left-hand descending turn toward me. *Uh-oh, here we go*, I thought, as I started a left turn back into him.

Incredibly, the Zero immediately reversed his turn and headed back toward Rabaul, even though he had both an altitude and angular advantage on me. This puzzled me. Had the tables been turned I would have dropped down and popped him good. Perhaps the Japanese were losing some of their arrogance.

I joined with the rest of the strike group at the rendezvous point and helped escort the bombers on an uneventful trip back to the carriers. After landing, I discovered about a dozen 7.7-millimeter bullet holes in each wing. They had entered vertically, neatly bracketing and barely missing the cockpit. How they missed crashing through the canopy and into me I'll never know.

What the evidence showed was that I had not been hit by the two Zeroes firing at me from behind. Instead, a Zero I never saw had hit me from an overhead run. Startled by the hits, I had naturally looked behind me. Luckily, I saw the two aircraft that were closing in from behind, intent on killing me. In effect, the Zero that had holed my plane from above had also sounded the alarm that saved my life.

I didn't have much time to dwell on my luck. By that afternoon I was airborne on combat air patrol (CAP), protecting the fleet from Rabaul-based counterstrikes. We didn't know it at the time, but during the previous few weeks well over 100 Japanese carrier aircraft were flown from Truk into Rabaul to augment its defenses. Now they were attacking our task force. A division of Corsairs from VF-17, normally land-based at New Georgia, was recovered, refueled, launched from one of our carriers, and sent to intercept the attacking enemy aircraft. When the Corsairs arrived on the scene, the fighter director aboard the ship got only this information out of the division leader: "Christ, there's a million of them!"

We had time to get most of our fighters in the air and the action was fast and furious. While 100 or so enemy airplanes made their attacks, our fighters were busy stopping them. Over the radio I heard the confusion as the ships' fighter directors tried to vector our planes onto the enemy. At the same time, more New Georgia-based F4Us and F6Fs, temporarily operating from our carriers, were also doing their best to stop the enemy planes. Adding to the commotion was the fierce antiaircraft fire our ships were putting up—in prodigious amounts!

To my frustration, I couldn't participate. Our CAP was positioned to the south of the task force and we were kept there to guard against the possibility of a separate enemy attack from that quadrant. In the distance I could see the fire and smoke of aircraft burning, and the smaller smudges of antiaircraft fire. In and among the ships, bombs and torpedoes were falling, as were burning airplanes.

Through the action the *Essex* continued to launch her aircraft. Rube Denoff, one of my cohorts, hadn't even raised his landing gear when a Japanese Val dive bomber flew right in front of him. With his gear still down, Rube shot it out of the sky.

In another, almost freakish stroke of luck and ingenuity, my friend George Blair, who had expended all his ammunition, downed a Japanese Kate by overtaking it and jettisoning his external fuel tank on it. The enemy plane came apart and spun into the water.

The Japanese were utterly routed. Nearly all the enemy bombers were downed; the aircraft that did manage to escape were mostly Zeroes. And while there were several close calls, not a single bomb or torpedo found its mark. Through it all, I could do no more than watch and listen.

By the end of the day, we tallied more than 100 Japanese aircraft destroyed. Most important, however, numerous Japanese warships and merchant ships were sunk or badly damaged, and it was patently obvious that Rabaul was no longer a safe operating base for the enemy. The complex of bases and facilities there figured less and less prominently until, by mid-February 1944, its garrison was left by Japan to fend for itself—forced to hack gardens out of the brush and the jungle to grow enough food to eat.

Not until later, however, did we appreciate what the strikes had done to the Japanese aircraft carrier force. The Imperial Japanese Navy aircraft and crews that were sent from Truk to reinforce Rabaul were largely destroyed. It took several months for the Japanese to replace those losses. Even then, the replacement aircrews were of inferior quality.

Between the morning strike and the defense of the task force in the afternoon, VF-9 put in 55 claims for aerial victories against the loss of one pilot—Ensign Bob Kaap, Casey Childers's wingman. They were jumped by Zeroes during the morning strike and when Casey looked over his shoulder he saw Kaap's Hellcat on fire. The stricken plane pulled up, then splashed into the water. Kaap was never heard from again.

***

That evening VF-9 received the finest compliment a group of fighter pilots could ever hope for. The pilots and crews of the dive bomber and torpedo bomber squadrons paraded into our ready room carrying a big card table loaded down with all sorts of booty—candy, cigarettes, chewing gum, that sort of thing. With the gift was a commendation signed by all of them citing the protection we had given them. We had taken them all the way to Rabaul and back, through all the enemy defenses, and they had lost only one SBD to antiaircraft fire.

That felt pretty good.

Chapter 17

About this time, the *Essex* lost a torpedo bomber and its crew to sheer foolhardiness. And in the process, the *Essex* was placed in serious jeopardy. In VT-9 there was a frustrated, would-be fighter pilot known as Red. As with many of the bomber pilots, he would rather have been flying fighters, but the needs of the Navy dictated that he do otherwise. Still, he liked to show off as much as the performance limitations of the heavy TBF torpedo bomber allowed.

One of his favorite tricks was to pull up sharply after takeoff and make a quick cut to the left, just as we did in the Hellcat. But the TBF wasn't built for that type of maneuvering, and he was called on the carpet for endangering his airplane, his crew of two, and himself. That didn't stop Red. Soon after, loaded down with depth charges for an antisubmarine patrol, he tried the same trick.

This time he wasn't able to pull it off. He pulled up a little too sharply, and the heavy airplane stalled and smashed into the water before he could regain control. He and his crew went down with the airplane, which began sinking almost immediately. There followed several anxious moments when the ship overran the sinking airplane. When the depth charges reached their preset depth, they exploded with a ferocity that severely rattled the ship and sent the engineering crews deep down toward the keel to check on the extent of the damage. Other than some minor leaks and popped rivets, the *Essex* was fine. But it was a stupid, tragic incident that should never have occurred.

***

After the strike against Rabaul the task group returned to Espiritu Santo, refueled, and set out again. This time we headed for the Gilbert Islands. We were to support Marines landing at Betio Island in Tarawa Atoll. It wasn't long before we came within range and operations commenced on November 18, 1943. Our objective—in advance of the Marine assault landing on November 20—was to eliminate enemy aerial opposition, and to destroy as many as possible of the Japanese troops who were dug in on the island.

On November 18, I was part of a strike returning from Betio. It had been a fairly uneventful mission with only moderate antiaircraft fire and no enemy aircraft. I was back toward the rear of the formation, which was flying at only about two or three thousand feet, when I looked across the bombers to my left and saw a float biplane at about five thousand feet, flying on an opposite course parallel to the bombers.

This was where all that time spent in aircraft recognition classes paid off. I instantly recognized it as a Mitsubishi F1M2, codenamed "Pete" by the Allies. It was designed for reconnaissance and observation. The Japanese pilot had stumbled unluckily onto more stuff to observe and reconnoiter than he could handle.

For whatever reason—perhaps because they thought it was a friendly aircraft—no one in the front of our formation had gone after it. I immediately went to full power and pulled toward the enemy floatplane. By any analysis the coming encounter was going to be a duck shoot. My F6F outclassed the enemy biplane in every respect. Spotting me, the Pete's pilot started about

At Tarawa, McWhorter bagged an odd duck, when he shot down a Mitsubishi F1M2 floatplane, codenamed "Pete," in thick clouds on November 18, 1943.

a 45-degree dive. By now there were four or five other Hellcats behind me, hoping to beat me to the shot.

As I approached firing range, I was set up for a shot into his left rear from above. Before I could get there, though, he rolled over into a hard right-hand turn and increased the angle of his dive, heading for a large cloud. I rolled right, keeping him in my gunsight, and dove to follow him.

As I pulled within range again, I was set up for a perfect overhead shot—right into the top of his plane—when he disappeared into the large cumulus cloud. I thought, *Hell, I've lost him,* but I continued on the flight path I had set up prior to losing him and followed him into the cloud.

I was just about to abort the run when the cloud thinned just enough for me to see—only for an instant—the dark blur of the floatplane right in my gunsight. It disappeared just as quickly. Without hesitating I squeezed the trigger. The .50 caliber machineguns chattered and the incendiary tracers disappeared into the murk, but I couldn't see whether I had hit him or not.

I dove on through the cloud and quickly reoriented myself, got my fighter flying straight and level, and looked back over my shoulder. There beneath the cloud was the Pete spinning down in flames. When I saw the enemy airplane smash into the water, I almost couldn't help patting myself on the back—I had shot him down while flying on instruments.

I learned later that the Pete was the only plane shot down that day by our task group.

The next day, November 19, 1943, our division was on combat air patrol when we received vectors from the ship's fighter director to intercept a low-flying bogey about twenty miles away. We started a shallow descent from 12,000 feet, pushed the throttles up, and turned in the direction of the unidentified aircraft. When we were about four or five miles from where the fighter director was calling the target, I was the first to sight the bogey, low on the water. It was a Mitsubishi G4M twin-engine bomber, codenamed "Betty" by the Allies. The most widely used bomber the Japanese had, the Betty was employed in a variety of roles aside from just bombing, including reconnaissance and torpedo attack.

Having identified the airplane as hostile, I went to full power and increased the angle of my dive. The Betty carried a 20-millimeter cannon in its tail for self-protection, so I headed for a point in space about a thousand feet to its starboard beam. That way I could set up for an attack from the side without worrying about being hit by the cannon.

Looking back over my shoulder I saw our division leader, Mike Hadden. He had started his dive also but was headed straight for the tail of the enemy bomber and directly into that cannon. I wondered to myself about that. The Betty was very low—only about 10 feet above the water—so low that the propwash from its two engines churned up a wake on the ocean's surface. I closed the distance and saw muzzle flashes from the Betty's tail cannon as it fired at Hadden and his wingman, Jack Kitchen.

I was traveling much faster than Hadden and arrived perfectly set up for a full-deflection, flat-side shot on the enemy bomber, which was painted a medium blue on top with those classic big red meatballs on its wings and fuselage. I could barely see that the underside was painted a lighter color.

Coming in from the Betty's right side, I closed the range to about 400 feet and opened fire with a short burst. I learned later that my roommate and wingman, Gene Valencia, was shouting to himself, "Miss it, Mac, miss it!" He wanted that bomber for himself.

But I didn't miss. I saw my rounds strike the wing root and cockpit area. Almost instantly the far engine, the port one, caught fire. The Betty immediately yawed to the left, hit the water, skipped once, and then crumpled into the waves in a ball of fire and spray.

This aerial victory, my fifth, made me the squadron's first ace—and the world's first all-Hellcat ace. It also earned me a new nickname.

When I got back to the ship, they counted my ammunition and discovered that I had fired a total of only 86 rounds out of all 6 guns, including what

At Tarawa, McWhorter became VF-9's first ace, and the Navy's first Hellcat ace, when he shot down a Mitsubishi G4M bomber, codenamed "Betty," on November 19, 1943.

I had fired when I tested my guns. The skipper, Phil Torrey, decreed that thereafter I was to be known as "One Slug" McWhorter.

I never did use a lot of ammunition. I believe that some pilots used the six machineguns on the F6F to put out a huge curtain of fire in the hope that they would catch an enemy plane inside of it. Personally, I set up to fire my guns as if I was going to shoot down my target with a single shot. Every round that followed was gravy. I don't know if it was my Depression-era upbringing or not—certainly everybody else in my squadron had also come of age during the same period. But I never came close to using all of the 2,400 rounds of ammunition that were loaded into the Hellcat.

There were other guys, though, who clamped down on the trigger and never let up. Their gun barrels practically melted—drooping out of the wing. This type of firing necessitated that the gun barrels be changed out quite often as it wore out the rifling in the barrel. It essentially turned them into "smooth-bores" that were terribly inaccurate.

As it turned out, Gene Valencia didn't need that bomber after all. He went on to score a total of 23 aerial victories and became the Navy's third-highest ranking ace of all time.

Gene Valencia was McWhorter's squadron mate and friend. A superb pilot and leader, he excelled during a second Pacific cruise and eventually became the Navy's third-leading ace. (U.S. Navy)

***

With the Marine invasion imminent, we turned our attention to air-to-ground work. When we commenced our strikes against Betio in advance of the landing it was a classically beautiful south seas island, covered with green, swaying palm trees and ringed by beautiful beaches. By November 20, the day of the invasion, it looked like an ashtray.

The surface combatants—battleships, cruisers, and destroyers—contributed to the destruction as much or more than we did. They pulled up practically to the edge of the reef and let loose with their big guns, firing at point-blank range. On one flight, I watched a battleship fire at a concrete emplacement. The shell missed and went across the island, then hit the water and skipped like a stone for several miles across the lagoon until it finally disappeared.

By November 20, Betio had been worked over for two solid days and was still on the receiving end of more bombing and naval gunfire. It was nothing more than a smoldering, ugly spit of dirty sand. We watched the landing craft carry the Marines toward the reef, certain that our guys would have an easy time of it. No one could have survived the bombardment we had delivered during the previous two days.

Except the Japanese. We were incredulous when we learned later in the day that the Marines were taking catastrophic losses. We had done our best to kill or destroy anything that looked even remotely manmade on that island. The news was unsettling. The Pacific was full of islands like Betio. The war could go on a long time and cost a great many lives.

We turned our attention during the next week to providing close air support for the Marines. We usually made radio contact with a controller on the ground, and he talked us onto a target using a grid; we carried cards that had a map of the island overlaid with a grid. Sometimes he arranged for the target to be marked with a white phosphorous shell and talked us on to it from there. The white phosphorous—or Willy Pete—sent up a huge, easily visible plume of white smoke. Once it was on the ground the controller gave us directions, for instance, "From the Willy Pete, hit the bunker fifty yards to the north."

This was the first time we did much bombing in our Hellcats. We could carry a single bomb of up to 1,000-pounds on the centerline rack, where we normally carried our drop tanks, and one underneath the wing on either side of the fuselage. Normally we dove on the target from about 10,000 feet at a 60-degree angle, then dropped our bombs at about 3,000 feet. We were quite accurate and could generally count on getting closer than 50 feet to the target. A direct hit was not uncommon.

This use of the Hellcat as a bomber was a harbinger of things to come. We carried about the same load of bombs as the dive bomber and torpedo bombers. Plus, we were faster than the bombers, we could go almost as far, and—most important—we could protect ourselves.

During this combat tour, unless we were flying dedicated bombing missions, we always flew with 150-gallon external fuel tanks slung underneath the bellies of our airplanes. These tanks almost doubled our range and loiter time without having much impact on our performance. We normally started transferring fuel from the drop tanks after we had burned 12 gallons out of the right main tank. If we didn't make room in the main tank first, it overfilled and vented fuel overboard. By emptying our external tank first, we had as much fuel as possible onboard the airplane in the event we had to jettison the tank.

***

Because the Japanese were faring so poorly in their daytime air attacks against our carriers, they began to concentrate on night operations. We were called to general quarters so often because of these attacks that we finally just stayed topside on the flight deck. Otherwise, we were rousted out of our bunks several times a night and sent down to our general quarters station in the better-protected wardroom. But topside, we watched with excitement the fireworks in the pitch-black sky as the ships fired their antiaircraft guns against the intruders. When an enemy plane was hit it invariably flared into a huge flying torch, and a huge cheer went up from the men on the deck as we watched it—and its dead or dying crew—tumble slowly into the dark ocean.

These engagements weren't entirely one-sided. On the evening of November 20, the *Essex, Bunker Hill,* and *Independence* were attacked by a flight of Betty torpedo bombers. We were treated to the terrifying sight of a Betty screaming right over the deck of our carrier at less than 100 feet. Fortunately, the pilot's torpedo missed. The *Independence* wasn't as fortunate. She was struck, and it wasn't until December 7 that she was repaired well enough to return to Pearl Harbor for more extensive repairs.

Chapter 18

After Tarawa we headed back to Hawaii, with a short detour along the way to take a swipe at Kwajalein Atoll in the middle of the Marshall Islands group. This atoll was the center of enemy air and naval forces in the area and was scheduled for invasion in the near future. Anything that Task Force 50, with its contingent of six carriers, could do to eliminate enemy warships and merchant shipping as well as enemy aircraft, would ease follow-on operations.

Accordingly, on December 4, 1943, nearly 200 aircraft were launched against targets in the atoll. Rather than accompany the strike group, I was posted to combat air patrol over the task force. Again, as had happened while on CAP at Rabaul, I was frustrated by a lack of action. Although enemy aircraft got airborne in force to oppose our strikes, the Japanese did not try to attack the fleet.

This was just the way it was. I had had more encounters and opportunities to engage enemy aircraft than many of the other pilots. To become an ace required skill and aggressiveness, but it also involved a great deal of luck. And much of that luck dictated whether or not you were in the right place at the right time. There were several outstanding pilots in VF-9 who had never even had the opportunity to fire their guns at an enemy aircraft during the entire ten months the squadron was in the Pacific. So yes, I was disappointed that I didn't see any Japanese aircraft during the strike at Kwajalein, but not overly so.

The Kwajalein strike was not a big success. There was some confusion over the target and consequently the airfield on Roi was not hit as hard as it could have been. Additionally, our torpedo bomber and dive bomber pilots were not as polished as they would have liked and thus scored poorly against the maneuvering ships in the lagoon. Although a few small merchantmen were destroyed, as were about 55 aircraft, none of the warships was badly damaged and there remained a sizable air presence.

McWhorter in the cockpit of his Hellcat, which wears 10 Japanese flags to signify the number of aircraft he downed while flying with VF-9 during its first Pacific cruise in 1943–44. (U.S. Navy)

Skittish about the possibility of being caught by Japanese forces from any of the many surrounding bases, our task force commander canceled follow-on strikes, and we retired the same day.

***

We arrived back at Pearl Harbor on December 8, 1943. We had been at sea for 47 days but had flown combat on only 12 of those days. It was more efficient than our in-and-out strikes to Marcus and Wake Islands, but still it seemed to be an awful lot of floating without enough fighting.

VF-9 and the rest of the *Essex* crew got quite a bit of time off through the rest of December and on into January. During this time—I don't remember how or why—VF-9 was adopted by a kindly gentleman named Chris Holmes. He was a local mover and shaker and had a beautiful mansion on the beach right below Diamond Head. He gave it over to a very grateful VF-9 over the holiday season. We spent our time drinking milk punch out on the veranda or lying out on the beach. Milk punch was a drink containing milk and just about any liquor other than those from the scotch-whiskey family. It was actually quite tasty, and because we didn't get much fresh milk when we were aboard ship, it was a favorite while we were ashore.

A lot of us enjoyed simply relaxing and catching up on sleep inside the spacious house. And it didn't hurt the standings of the single guys when they swung their dates through such an impressive setup.

Not that there were many dates to be had. The competition was fierce. If Hawaii was bustling with military activity when we had arrived six months before, now, in the last days of 1943, it was absolutely bursting at the seams. The streets were crawling with soldiers, sailors, Marines, and airmen. Where the *Essex* was almost the only show in town when we had arrived in the spring, there were now several more big-deck carriers. And that's not to mention all the other battleships, cruisers, destroyers, submarines, and support ships that made up the rest of the fleet.

I was perplexed. The number of ships and airplanes and men and equipment in Hawaii alone was staggering. And more were on the way. We knew that Japan could not hope to stand against such might. Nevertheless, we had just seen a tiny speck in the Pacific—Betio—consume a vast number of men and great quantities of material. All of us tried to see into the future: where would we be months or even years from now? Or weeks?

***

We left Hawaii on January 17, 1944, on our way to hit Kwajalein again. The atoll, with its lagoon and the airfields on Kwajalein Island and Roi, was the linchpin of the Marshall Islands group. And whoever controlled the Marshalls controlled that portion of the Pacific. Accordingly, several islands of the atoll were scheduled for invasion on February 1. We were sent to eliminate enemy shipping and airpower as well as to soften up the atoll's defenses. The systematic destruction of enemy positions in the atoll was foremost in our leaders' minds. There could not be another Tarawa.

What had happened at Tarawa, only two months before, stunned the Navy and Marine Corps leadership. There, newly operational, thin-skinned amphibious vehicles were launched into strong, unpredictable tides and had been left more or less on their own. Once in the water, with their loads of Marines and supplies, they had to scrabble over a treacherous reef through some of the most wicked and lethal defenses of the entire war. Many of the vehicles were trapped against the reef, or blown out of the water, leaving hundreds of Marines—those who survived—to swim or slog their way unprotected to the beach. Many of them did not make it. More than 1,000 Marines, nearly 20 percent of the attacking force, were killed, and the whole mess was already being called "Bloody Tarawa."

But not all the problems were caused by the reefs or by the vulnerable amphibious vehicles. The Japanese defenses simply had not been hammered enough by warships or by carrier airpower. Though they had looked impressive as they fired from just offshore, the battleships and cruisers should have stood further away to bombard the Japanese defenses. This would have allowed them to fire their guns on a higher trajectory. Consequently, hitting their targets at a steeper angle, the shells would have penetrated more deeply and caused more damage. Additionally, the battleships and cruisers simply did not have time enough to fire the tons of shells required.

And the carriers basically did not deliver sufficient airpower. Despite the number of carriers and airplanes involved in the operation, there weren't enough sorties generated. And like the battleships and cruisers, the carriers weren't there long enough. Kwajalein was to be different.

***

There were nearly 100 enemy airplanes based at the airfield on Roi, on the northern side of Kwajalein Atoll. At dawn, on January 29, I was again flying in Mike Hadden's division as section leader. As part of an all-fighter sweep we were free of escort duties. Instead, our job was to clear enemy fighters from the sky ahead of the strike group.

Once joined following the launch, we test-fired our guns, as we always did prior to starting toward the target area. In the old Wildcat, charging the six, .50 caliber machineguns had involved pulling handles that were attached by steel cables to the individual guns; charging the Hellcat's guns was easier and more sophisticated. On the center console in front of the pilot were two hydraulic charging buttons—one for the three guns in each wing. Pushing these buttons released hydraulic pressure from accumulator bottles located on the engine firewall. After the guns were charged, they could be selected to fire by pairs—the two inboard guns, the two center guns, and the two outboard guns.

If a pilot wanted, he could fire just one gun by charging only the guns on one wing, then selecting only one pair. I had heard of one pilot who actually tried this. Word had apparently gotten around the fleet about my "One Slug" moniker, and there was a pilot who was intent on besting me—shooting a plane down with fewer bullets. He actually flew a combat flight with only one gun charged, hoping to run into some Japanese airplanes. Evidently, he wasn't successful since I never heard anything else about it.

Firing just one gun was a tough proposition anyway. The recoil from a gun—without the recoil from the corresponding gun in the other wing—caused the airplane to yaw and subsequently made it difficult to aim. No one with any common sense purposely went into combat with only one gun ready to fire.

Overall control of the airplane's armament was maintained through the master armament switch. This switch controlled the electrical firing impulses to the guns and bomb racks. It was provided for safety purposes so that the guns couldn't be fired accidentally. You were supposed to put it into the armed position whenever the flight entered enemy territory. Once back over friendly forces, and certainly prior to landing, you were supposed to put it back into the safe position. More than one guy messed this up, though, and sprayed the landing area with machinegun fire by accidentally coming down on the trigger with the master armament switch in the armed position. This sort of slip didn't particularly endear a person to the flightdeck crews.

***

When we arrived overhead, Kwajalein was covered by a 6,000-foot overcast. Fortunately, we had briefed a plan for this circumstance. In order to hide ourselves from enemy antiaircraft gunners, we were to climb into the overcast as we approached the island, then turn a few degrees away from each other to minimize the chances of colliding. After a certain amount of time, Mike Hadden was to make a call over the radio, whereupon we would all simultaneously dive out of the clouds. From that point, we would make our attacks on the enemy antiaircraft guns or airplanes or whatever other targets we could find.

As planned, we popped up into the clouds as we approached the island, then took our heading cuts away from each other. After a minute or so, Hadden made the call to drop out of the clouds. For some reason I hesitated a long moment before I pushed the nose of my fighter down.

I blinked twice as I dropped out of the clouds and into the clear. There, slightly below and ahead of me, at my 11 o'clock position and only about 500 feet in front of me, was a Zero. It was flying in the same direction I was—straight at Mike Hadden's section. Almost as quickly as it takes to think about it, I slid behind him, superimposed the pipper of my gunsight onto his fuselage, and pulled the trigger.

Mike and his wingman, Jack Kitchen, flushed like quail when the Zero exploded. They didn't even know he was back there. I shook my head at my good fortune. It could have just as easily been me dropping down in front of the Zero instead of the other way around.

Hadden got the division rejoined and we dropped down and strafed the airfield. It seemed to me that most of the Japanese airplanes there had already been hit and burned. There wasn't much left to destroy, so I put my rounds into the hangars. It was still not very bright and, as always, I was a bit mesmerized by the bright arc of my tracers against the dim early morning light.

I finished my strafing run and climbed away from the airfield to the southeast. As I approached the eastern edge of the atoll at about 7,000 feet with

Bud Gehoe still on my wing, I spotted another Zero ahead of me, flying in the same direction. It seemed that Fortune never ceased to smile on me. From about a half-mile, I closed the distance to 500 feet—all the while checking for enemy fighters that might be stalking me. Finally, I captured the Zero in my gunsight, placed the pipper just at the wing root, and squeezed the trigger.

I am sure that the enemy pilot never knew I was behind him. I turned away to the right to avoid the fireball that was his airplane only a few seconds earlier.

***

It was also at Kwajalein that one of our pilots made his second entry in the "It's Tough to Argue with Success" chapter of the book on aerial combat techniques. George Blair, who had knocked down a Japanese torpedo plane at Rabaul by dropping his belly tank on it when he was out of ammunition, exercised his unique brand of improvisation to down another Japanese airplane without firing a shot. Out of ammo again at Kwajalein, he maneuvered his plane to a position directly above a Japanese airplane and forced it to crash into the water!

In large part because of the preliminary poundings delivered by naval surface ships and air strikes, the invasion at Kwajalein went well, although we lost two more squadron mates. Steve Wright and John Benton were killed by antiaircraft fire.

Chapter 19

We left Kwajalein on February 4, 1944, and retired to the newly operational fleet anchorage at Majuro to take on fuel and provisions and to sneak a few days of rest. When we stopped like this, one of the most popular diversions was swimming. The ship would drop anchor, a shark watch with a rifle was set up on the flight deck, and we all took to the water, paddling around or diving off the hangar deck or the small-boat mooring boom, which was swung out perpendicular to the ship. The boom had rope ladders hanging down so that we could climb back up. It was great fun and a very welcome respite from the daily grind.

All through this combat tour we were blessed with the company of *Life* magazine photographer John Florea. Making war from the deck of an aircraft carrier was relatively new, and the magazine wanted to bring home to America a portrait of the men who were doing it. Florea was the perfect choice to compose that portrait. Not only was he an expert photographer, but he had an engaging personality and was fun to be around. Technically, he was assigned to cover the entire air group but he spent most of his time with VF-9—quite a bit of it in the ready room playing cards. John came to be considered almost part of the squadron. He demonstrated his mettle by actually flying in SBDs or TBFs on some of the air group's missions. And of course, we were fortunate to have him aboard to record on film much of what we did. Many of his photos from this period were published by *Life*, and of those that weren't, many ended up in our air group cruise book, which was similar to a school annual.

We departed Majuro on the night of February 12, 1944. We had been in the Pacific for nine months and were sure that we were finally headed to Pearl Harbor and then back to the States and home. But we weren't.

About ten days earlier, a flight of two four-engine Liberators led by Marine Major James Christensen had made a 2,000-mile round-trip from the Solomons to Truk. They spent 20 minutes over the atoll at 24,000 feet taking pictures. For whatever reason, they encountered no opposition from the Japanese. During their short picture-taking stint, which produced the only photos we had of Truk, they observed many warships and support ships anchored in the lagoon. This was too tempting a target, so the task forces were ordered to attack it.

Truk was home port to the Japanese Combined Fleet and its flagship, the super battleship *Musashi*. Additionally, it served as a base for submarines, freighters, and tankers, and as a staging point for airplanes flying from Japan to bases in the South Pacific. In fact, 173 naval airplanes were flown to Rabaul from Truk in late October. These made up many of the aircraft we had encountered during our strike there on November 11, 1943.

Truk was the devil's den as far as we were concerned. A collection of about a dozen mountainous volcanic islands and many smaller ones, ringed by a stereotypical tropical reef, it was a wonderful natural anchorage. Often called the "Gibraltar of the Pacific," Truk was reputed to be the most heavily defended Japanese base in that part of the Pacific. When we heard that we were going there someone penned a cartoon of the *Essex* with the caption: "This is the captain speaking. The *Essex* has been given the greatest privilege yet; we are going to hit Truk Island." The cartoon showed sailors and airmen diving off the deck, petrified at the thought of striking so deep into enemy territory. It wasn't too far off the mark.

***

Following a rendezvous with fleet tankers north of Eniwetok, we refueled and sailed at high speed for our launch point, about 100 miles southeast of Truk. When we were launched early on the morning of February 17, 1944, more than 350 enemy aircraft were waiting for our 3 task groups. Our first wave of 72 Hellcats from 5 carriers executed fighter sweeps—without bombers—over the enemy airfields at daybreak. They were met by approximately 80 fighters, and the Hellcats shot down more than 30 of them. After destroying or chasing off the airborne enemy fighters, they strafed and burned another 40 aircraft on the ground. The flights of carrier bombers that followed the fighter sweep were only barely harassed by enemy airplanes.

Again, as during the Japanese counterattack at Rabaul, I was stuck flying a combat air patrol over the task force, far from the action. We saw nothing. This frustrated me, but I didn't complain too much. For all I knew, the bullet with "Hamilton McWhorter" written on it could have been waiting for me at Truk during the first strike. Fate played a big role in determining who came back and who did not.

McWhorter strafed a Japanese destroyer at Truk on February 17, 1944. That action was captured by the reconnaissance cameras aboard his wingman's aircraft. (U.S. Navy)

Japanese shipping under attack by Navy aircraft at Truk on February 17, 1944.

Two of our pilots in VF-9 nearly didn't come back. After shooting down three planes during the morning sweep, Chick Smith dropped down to strafe the airfield on Eten Island. While he busily attended to his work—racing back and forth over the runways, shooting up everything in sight—his plane was hit by antiaircraft fire. Chick managed to get out to where one of our submarines was on station, ditched alongside, and was rescued.

George Blair's airplane was also hit by antiaircraft fire. Not quite as lucky as Chick, George had to ditch in the lagoon, smack in the middle of a dozen enemy-held islands. Some of our Hellcats maintained cover over him until an OS2U Kingfisher floatplane from one of the cruisers arrived. They strafed and sank a Japanese patrol boat which persisted in going after George.

Once he arrived, the Kingfisher pilot expressed some reluctance to land in the middle of Truk lagoon, but Jack Kitchen—who was flying overhead—suggested that he might shoot the man down if he failed to pick George up. When George got back, he related that the rear seat of the Kingfisher became rather crowded when he squeezed in with the observer. But then he allowed as how he really didn't mind at all and that, actually, it was the finest ride he'd ever had.

George Blair, a VF-9 squadron mate, was a resourceful pilot. He once knocked a Japanese aircraft out of the sky with his drop tank, and forced another into the water when out of ammunition. He was shot down over Truk Lagoon on February 17, 1944. (U.S. Navy)

George Blair was rescued out of Truk Lagoon by a Vought OS2U Kingfisher from the USS *Baltimore* flown by Denver Baxter. Observer Reuben Hickman stands on the wing. Baxter returned to the *Baltimore* essentially out of fuel. (U.S. Navy)

George Blair rides a bosun's chair back to the *Essex*. (U.S. Navy)

***

Later that morning I was sent with my wingman, Bud Gehoe, on a photo-reconnaissance mission. We were to overfly the lagoon and the airfields to determine the damage our morning strikes had inflicted. The intent was to provide photos for damage assessment in order to determine where follow-on strikes were required. I was finally putting to use the training I had taken with Jim Feasley almost two years earlier.

As soon as we landed from the CAP Bud and I were launched on our very first photo-reconnaissance mission. Bud was flying the photo plane, a version of the Hellcat designated F6F-3P. Although I was leading, I was actually flying cover for Bud. My task was to drop back and cover him while he made his photo runs over the target area.

Just as we arrived over the atoll, I spotted a destroyer beached on the coral reef. I thought that it was an old bombed-out hulk and paid it only passing attention until flak started popping all around us. Only then did I realize that the "old bombed-out hulk" had taken us under fire.

Almost indignant, I thought to myself that two could play at that game, and I told Bud to cover me while I went down. I double-checked that my guns were armed and rolled into a steep dive. As I dove, I could see antiaircraft fire reaching up at me from the destroyer's gun tubs. I didn't care. When I came in range, I fired my guns and watched the tracers arc down and spatter in a sparkling shower all over the deck of the grounded ship. *Take that!*

I zoomed low and fast over the destroyer, then climbed back up to altitude, where Bud was covering me. Once rejoined we set course for the enemy's anchorage and his airfields.

McWhorter strafed a Japanese destroyer at Truk on February 17, 1944. That action was captured by the reconnaissance cameras aboard his wingman's aircraft. (U.S. Navy)

It wasn't long before I spotted a three-plane formation at my nine o'clock position, about two miles away. They were headed directly at us, and for a moment or two I couldn't tell if they were Hellcats or Zeroes with drop tanks. Until that time none of the many Zeroes that I had seen had drop tanks, whereas our F6Fs carried them all the time. Still not sure what they were, I turned into them; you do not take chances in combat. A moment or two later I could tell that they were painted in a strange, mottled, orange-and-black camouflage scheme—just like Halloween. They were definitely not Hellcats.

At this point, I had no choice but to continue my head-on attack against the Zeroes. It was our .50 caliber machineguns against their twin 20-millimeter cannon. An alarm in my brain went off. This was definitely not a desirable position to be in—flying straight into six 20-millimeter cannon that had double the range and hitting power of our machineguns!

I will never understand why they never opened fire on us, but I am eternally thankful that they didn't. We closed to firing range very quickly. I put the pipper of my gunsight on the nose of the lead fighter and squeezed the trigger. My rounds flew straight into his engine, cockpit, and wing root. He started to burn and then exploded. Immediately, I put my pipper on the next Zero, and barely had time to squeeze the trigger a second time. This Zero caught fire instantly. I passed close by him almost as soon as I let off the trigger. I turned around and saw three flaming wrecks tumbling down—Bud had blasted the third. An instant before the second airplane exploded in a ball of orange fire, I saw a parachute open alongside; its pilot had jumped clear just barely in time. I had shot down two Zeroes in about five seconds, and we had knocked down all three in less than ten seconds!

From there we crisscrossed the lagoon a couple of times—taking the photos the task group needed so badly. We came under fire as we made our passes. I could see that there were definite disadvantages to this line of work.

Most of the enemy warships, tipped off by the sighting of our reconnaissance bombers a couple of weeks earlier, had left the lagoon by February 17, but there were still a few combatants at anchor as well as a large number of support ships. These had suffered severely during the morning strikes, and many lay burning or foundering.

After photographing the shipping in the lagoon, Bud and I turned our attention to the three airfields—Eten, Moen, and Param. These also had been hit hard, and many airplanes and support buildings lay in ruins. As we had over the lagoon, we received a warm reception from the antiaircraft gunners. Once we had what we needed we turned back toward the task group. And again, I spotted an enemy plane.

I am sure that my visual acuity—about 20/15—was one of the most important keys to my success. Typically, I spotted enemy airplanes long before my squadron mates. This ability enabled me to take the time I needed to properly set up my attacks. I was the predator much more often than the prey, and so I didn't have to take whatever situation was forced on me. I don't know why I was able to do it—born to it, I guess. At any rate, it was a godsend.

This Zero was ahead of us, passing left to right in a very shallow dive. I started after him, and as I closed the distance from behind he surprised me by starting a series of perfect slow rolls! I was startled. What was it with the Japanese and their penchant for doing aerobatics when they should have been trying to shoot us down?

Perhaps he was trying to shake me. Well, it didn't work. A Hellcat could do slow rolls all day long, so I just matched his rolls and followed him through his maneuvers until I was well within firing range, about 600 feet. Then I opened fire. Like every Zero I had ever shot at, this one caught fire quickly and went down in flames.

McWhorter and Lou Menard (second from left) watch as finishing touches are made to VF-9's scoreboard in early 1944. (U.S. Navy)

From there we had an uneventful flight back to the ship, where the film was immediately taken to the photo lab. That was the last we heard of it; no one ever bothered to tell us if the photos were okay or not.

***

That night we came under heavy attack from enemy torpedo bombers for about four hours. Several of them were shot down, but the *Intrepid* (CV-11) was hit and had to retire with a dozen dead sailors.

The next day, we encountered no airborne Japanese opposition and made several more strikes against enemy shipping in the lagoon. We departed the area about noon on February 18. In the end, 2 auxiliary cruisers, 2 destroyers, 2 submarine tenders, 6 tankers, and more than 40 support ships—totaling more than 200,000 tons—were sunk. To top it off, VF-9 added 36 aerial victories to its record. The Japanese had taken a beating.

Chapter 20

Once again, having completed a job well done, we were ready to go home. And once again, we were sent to pound the Japanese. This time the target for Vice Admiral Marc Mitscher's Task Force 58 was the Mariana Islands group.

Strategically located along many of the trade routes to Asia, the Marianas, composed of 11 smaller and 4 larger islands, were important stepping stones on the road to Japan. Magellan had discovered Guam, the largest island, in 1521, and since then various islands in the group had been under the control of Spain, Germany, Japan, and the United States. America won Guam from Spain in 1899 after the Spanish-American War; Japan was given a League of Nations mandate over the rest of the islands after World War I, following Germany's defeat. Two days after the attack on Pearl Harbor, Japan overran the tiny American garrison on Guam and claimed that island, too, as her own.

McWhorter (left) and Gene Valencia (center) examine a .50 caliber shell casing in a publicity shot. Note that the "9" in VF-9 on the board behind them has been whited out by a censor. (U.S. Navy)

But now we were back to argue the issue. Taking Guam and Saipan, the second largest island, was part of the strategy for closing the ring around Japan. Little was known about the Japanese defenses on the islands and it was determined that a naval air strike would shed some light on what our invasion forces would face when the time arrived to assault the islands. Our task groups were ready and at hand, and so were given the mission.

Gathering intelligence about the islands was the primary objective of the strike, as good photographs and other information were needed for the coming invasion. Because there had been no overflights since Guam was lost, there was precious little data. So important was this gathering of information, that any damage we might cause to the Japanese during our strike would just be icing on the cake.

***

On the night of February 22, 1944, the evening before the strike, an enemy airplane spotted our task group. We were under attack through the rest of that night and on into the next morning—even while we were launching airplanes. As at Tarawa, we spent most of the night on the flight deck watching the fireworks. So thick and deadly accurate was our antiaircraft fire that not a single ship was hit.

Hamilton McWhorter III, the Navy's first Hellcat ace, aboard the *Essex* (CV-9) in early 1944. (U.S. Navy)

One of the primary reasons our antiaircraft fire was so effective was our use of proximity-fused ammunition. Codenamed VT, which was just a meaningless designation, the proximity fuse was a device fitted into the nose of a projectile that emitted a radio signal. When that signal was reflected back from a target in great enough strength, it triggered the projectile to explode. This enabled an antiaircraft battery to shoot down a target without scoring a direct hit, or without the inaccurate guesswork involved with air bursts set off by timed fuses. The VT fuse was a closely held secret and was first used operationally by the Navy in January 1943. In fact, the Allies were so fearful it might be compromised that it wasn't until the British were confronted with V-1 attacks in June 1944 that it was released for use over land. In any event, neither the Germans nor the Japanese ever fielded a similar fuse.

***

The brief we received for our flight the next morning was reminiscent of what we had received prior to our first strike in North Africa. Essentially, we were told to go fly over Saipan and hunt for enemy airfields. We were told to shoot them up if and when we found them and, importantly, to mark their locations.

This operation for me was pretty much a nonevent. The weather was atrocious over the island, and I didn't see a single enemy plane in the air. Miraculously, underneath the one hole we found in the clouds was an enemy airfield. And just as miraculously, instead of a welcoming committee of enemy fighters, we found row after row of planes parked on the field. We dropped down and thoroughly strafed them. When we finished and started up through the break in the clouds toward the rendezvous point, I looked over my shoulder at the airfield one more time. Where only a few minutes before there were dozens of carefully parked aircraft, there were now nothing but burning wrecks. What had once been a neatly ordered military installation was now a smoking shambles.

Other strikes that day also did well, much better in fact than they realized. Although claims were put in for 48 aerial victories and an estimated 87 aircraft were destroyed on the ground, Japanese records indicate that they lost 168 aircraft in total. This is probably one of the few instances during the war when two big aerial forces came together and the damage done was underclaimed.

VF-9's cut of the total was eleven enemy airplanes shot down. But these successes did not come without cost. Lieutenant Junior Grade Henry Schiebler failed to return, presumably lost to antiaircraft fire. Another tragic loss was Ensign Lewis Matthews, Chick Smith's wingman. Their division was on CAP near the task force when incoming bogeys were detected. The fighter director gave them the command, "Vector base, two-seven-zero, Gate." That command meant that Chick and Lew had to fly back directly over the task force, then turn to a heading of 270 degrees; and "gate" meant to fly at full power.

They headed back to overfly the task force and as they reached it, antiaircraft fire from practically all of our ships opened up on them. To the gunners on the ships, anything moving in the sky was a threat if enemy aircraft were thought to be inbound. A five-inch shell made a direct hit on Lew's plane, which disintegrated. That particular command, which brought friendly aircraft directly over the fleet when enemy aircraft were inbound, was not used very often after that.

When we left the area later that evening, we had good photographic intelligence of the islands. This would save many lives during the coming invasion.

***

We returned to Pearl Harbor on March 3, 1944. We had been in the Pacific for 10 months and had spent 127 days at sea. During 8 separate combat engagements VF-9 had spent 21 days in combat and had lost 10 airplanes and 5 pilots to enemy action. Only one of those airplanes was shot down by enemy fliers. In exchange for our losses, we claimed 120 enemy airplanes shot down in the air and 159 destroyed on the ground. By any measure we had performed superlatively and were ready for a well-deserved trip back to the States. It was time to go home.

VF-9's pilots and officers with the scoreboard marking their successes during the squadron's first Pacific cruise in 1943–44. McWhorter stands right-center with ballcap. (U.S. Navy)

Chapter 21

After a couple of days in Hawaii, we said goodbye to our airplanes—leaving them for newly arriving units—and boarded the *Essex* for the trip home. Escorted by a pair of destroyers that had also finished their combat tours, we sped out of Pearl Harbor and pointed toward home.

We occupied our time during this trip in much the same way we always did. Of course, the knowledge that we were headed home rather than into combat made the voyage more relaxed and enjoyable. I remember that we played a lot of volleyball on the hangar deck, and as usual card games went on nearly nonstop. The war was still far from won though, and there was little talk of being able to leave the Navy. The best we could hope for was that our next assignments would keep us out of combat.

Curiously, there was no concerted effort by the upper echelons to take advantage of this downtime to poll or query us about what we had learned during combat. We had learned what worked and what didn't, but there didn't seem to be any energy spent to compile that information. Perhaps the debriefings we had conducted with the intelligence types immediately after we flew our missions had provided the needed information.

***

I experienced an incredible sense of relief when we passed under the Golden Gate Bridge on March 14, 1944, and moored in San Francisco. I had actually survived and gotten safely back, just as I had promised Louise 10 months earlier. There was a huge crowd and bands waiting on the pier as we came in. When they finally got the gangplank down, there was a mad rush by officers and enlisted men alike for the telephone booths on the pier.

I only had to wait about 30 minutes until I could make my call and hear Louise's voice for the first time in almost a year. I don't remember what we said; I think I was satisfied just to hear her voice. Since Sampson, New York, where she was staying with her parents did not have an airport we agreed to meet in Buffalo so that we could be together that much sooner. She reserved a room in one of the hotels and told me where it was when I called her the next day.

***

One unpleasant aspect of our return was the tearing asunder of VF-9. New aircraft carriers and new air groups were being commissioned at such a phenomenal rate that it was difficult to keep track of them. And these new ships and air groups needed crews with some experience. In order to provide this leavening, units that had seen combat had their ranks harvested for seasoned personnel who then formed the nucleus of the new units.

VF-9 was split almost down the middle. Half the squadron members stayed in order to bring a new cadre of youngsters up to snuff, while the other half, myself included, was assigned to form a combat team to train new pilots for a new squadron.

Although we understood and for the most part agreed with the reasoning, it was difficult to watch our unit disband. We had been together for two solid years—as long as any other squadron in the Navy—and as far as we were concerned, we were the best there was. We had fought together from Casablanca to Saipan. No other squadron in the world had done what we had.

But that was the way it was. I said goodbye to all my close friends and on March 16, 1944, left for Sampson, New York.

***

People who haven't spent a long period of time away from a loved one can't understand the emotions that precede the reunion. You can ride a roller coaster of excited anticipation sprinkled with a bit of anxiety and self-doubt. I knew that I loved Louise, certainly more than when I had left, but I was still concerned. What if she—despite what she said in her letters—had fallen out of love with me? What if, in my absence, she had built an image of me that I couldn't live up to? What if I had done the same thing? What would I say when we shared our first embrace? What if I said something stupid?

I put my doubts aside. Though we were together only three of the fourteen months since we had gotten married, I knew that we were truly in love.

I managed to get an airline ticket and departed San Francisco in a DC-3, but got only as far as Chicago. The weather to the east was awful, so we were deplaned and left to find other means of transportation. For some reason I don't remember, I couldn't get a train. Instead, after I called Louise to give her a quick update, I boarded a bus. I arrived in Buffalo at about eleven that night and went to the hotel where Louise was waiting for me. I was beyond anxious to see her.

Finally, three days after leaving San Francisco, I walked—rather, I ran—up the stairs and knocked on the door. I will never forget the beautiful sight when she opened the hotel room door. There before me was my tall, blonde, beautiful Louise in a gorgeous black negligee, something that my wildest fantasies about this moment had never included. I grabbed her in my arms and kissed her, just as I had done the first time I met her 16 months earlier. There were some tears, but they came from the joy of finally being together again. We had a lot of catching up to do and I don't think I let her out of my arms all night.

After spending a couple of days getting reacquainted in the hotel in Buffalo, we caught a bus and went on to the naval training station at Sampson, near Geneva, New York, where her father was the head chaplain. I'll admit that I experienced a bit of trepidation at my impending meeting with her parents; Louise and I had been married for 14 months and I had never met them. I knew that her mother was very worried that her daughter may have made a big mistake and fallen in love with a backwoods redneck. Then, too, her father was a captain in the Navy. In fact, he had been in the Navy longer than I had been alive. I was only a lieutenant junior grade at the time; there were three full ranks between us.

There I was, a blooded combat veteran, one of the nation's ranking aces, afraid to meet what turned out to be one of the nicest couples I have ever encountered. Our meeting turned out to be quite pleasant. My best behavior was more than enough to win over Louise's mother, also named Louise, and Captain William Edel likewise welcomed me into the family. Things couldn't have gone better.

We stayed a few days with the Edels at the Sampson Naval Training Station where they had a nice house by Lake Seneca. The captain took me around the complex at Sampson where young recruits received their initial training—boot camp—before they went on to train in their specialties. While I was there he arranged for me to speak to the recruits, and I did my best to interest them with tales of combat in the Pacific.

***

One highlight of VF-9's return to the States was our appearance in *Life* magazine. It was the May 1, 1944, issue and it was managed by John Florea. Hal Vita's picture was on the cover, and the story's opening page had a big banner, "Air Group Nine Comes Home," with a picture of one of the VB-9 pilots, John Sullivan, bounding up the steps of his home. There were seven pages of photographs of VF-9 and Air Group 9 pilots—even one picture of me looking adoringly at Louise as she played the piano. This picture was taken while Louise and I were staying at her parents' house in New York. I will note that an adoring look wasn't something that I had to practice much.

This was really something for me. When I was younger and *Life* made its debut, it was a magazine that rich people bought and read. I never dreamt that I would have my picture in it, alongside a beautiful wife.

At this time one of the top-rated shows on radio was Major Bowes *Amateur Hour*, broadcast out of New York City. Previously screened amateurs performed a wide variety of acts on the air, and if they did reasonably well Major Bowes let them finish. If they didn't, he rang a big gong and off the stage they went.

Anyway, the show found out through the Navy that I was close at hand and invited me to New York City to appear. They figured that as one of the Navy's highest scoring aces, I would be a pretty big draw. The Navy saw my appearance as a good recruiting plug. I looked at it as a perfect honeymoon opportunity for Louise and me. Everyone was going to benefit.

They treated us very well. We were given a nice sleeping car on the train to New York City and were booked in the Waldorf Astoria when we arrived. On top of that, they gave us a good bit of spending money so that we could entertain ourselves during the day. We ate out and saw a Broadway show and generally had a very nice time.

The night of the show was almost overwhelming. It was held in a huge theater with two balconies, in front of an audience of more than a thousand people. Since my more formal Navy dress-blue uniform had long ago been packed away in a box somewhere, I was dressed in my aviation greens, which were not quite so formal. Because of that I felt a little self-conscious, but I shrugged it off.

Major Bowes was very nice and asked me several questions that I managed to answer without embarrassing myself or him or the Navy. When he asked me how many airplanes I had shot down, I told him, "Ten Japanese airplanes, sir." Well, the whole theater gave me a standing ovation. That was a pretty good feeling.

We stayed in New York for another day after the show. Though the war was on, New York was still bustling and full of people and energy. Restaurants and theaters were full, and there was no lack of things to do. At night there was no blackout in effect; the city was bright with lights of all kinds and colors. And although rationing was in full swing by then, it didn't look as if anyone was suffering any ill effects. Things could be gotten if a person had connections and money. To be fair, New York was far from unique in this regard.

We returned to Sampson for a few days. It was during this period that we bought our first car, a 1941 Dodge sedan that was in pretty good shape.

Owning a car during the war was more difficult than usual. Repair parts were tough if not impossible to find, and oil, tires, and gasoline were all rationed. Because I was in the service we were able to get extra gas coupons for travel involving military orders, but for personal use, we got as many coupons as everyone else. The ration on these coupons was about five gallons a week!

After bidding farewell to my new family, Louise and I climbed into the Dodge and headed for Philadelphia to visit with her sister Mary and her husband, Frank Blaha. Frank was a submarine officer and had already completed a successful combat cruise aboard the submarine *Greenling* (SS-213). He was currently assigned as the executive officer of the *Escolar* (SS-294). The *Escolar* was only just nearing completion, and Frank was busy assembling the crew and familiarizing himself with the new ship.

We all got along really well together, and Frank and I took a special delight in teasing each other.

"Frank," I'd say, "a person would have to be out of his mind to shut himself up in a big steel tube and then go splashing around underwater. You poor guys don't stand a chance if something goes wrong."

"Mac, you're thinking like a pilot," he'd answer. "When my engine stops, I come up to the top. Then I float around and eat steak and lobster, or play pinochle until the engine gets fixed, or until someone comes to get me. Now, what do you do when your engine stops?"

I'll admit he did have a point. Nevertheless, the mere thought of service aboard a submarine made me claustrophobic.

At any rate, Frank was a fine man and he and his fellow submariners were sinking more tonnage than our airplanes and surface ships combined. Additionally, submarines serving as "lifeguards" were rescuing downed airmen regularly. Pilots and crews who were shot down and would have been captured, or who would have died in the open ocean, were returned safely to service.

After a couple of very enjoyable days with Mary and Frank, Louise and I pointed the Dodge south, toward Georgia. Our reception in Athens was marvelous. Louise was welcomed again with open arms by my family, and my father and uncles showed me around town like I was a famous movie star. The local newspaper wrote another article, and one movie house even gave me a lifetime free pass. There were lots of nice things like that.

One day I was invited to the University of Georgia campus in town to address a group of preflight naval aviation cadets. When I was about 16 or 17, I had had a job doing menial work helping to build the auditorium we were gathered in. It was kind of ironic for me—being an honored guest in a building that I had helped construct as a mere laborer. But the talk went well. After all, I was a product of their system.

After a week or so in Athens, we finally set off for Naval Air Station Melbourne, Florida, where I was to report to Experimental Group Able. This unit was the brainchild of Commander Charles Crommelin, who believed that newly commissioned pilots placed under the supervision of combat-experienced pilots could be trained faster and better.

Chapter 22

We arrived in Melbourne in early April 1944 and found a room in a local hotel. Several former VF-9 pilots were also staying there with their wives, so it was nice for Louise to have some friends to be with while I was at the air station. Because of the housing shortage, the hotel had a rule that you could only stay for seven days. Fortunately, the desk clerk was very sympathetic. Instead of kicking us out, he let us move to another room and start a new seven-day period.

At the air station, seven new students were assigned to my care, six brand-new ensigns and a lieutenant commander. The ensigns were high school graduates, only 18 or 19 years old—products of the huge training machine that the Navy had built for the war.

I may have forgotten what it was like to start out as an inexperienced youngster, or perhaps I expected more because of what I had been through, but it seemed to me that these kids were ill prepared. They were so young. Although I had only two years of college before I started training, I believed that two years makes a tremendous difference in maturity at that age. Most of these kids didn't have it yet.

The lieutenant commander, Frederick "Mike" Michaelis, was a different story. He was an Annapolis graduate and formerly a surface ship officer. He certainly had the requisite maturity, but his flying skills were still about the same as those of the younger kids. I was in the awkward position of being junior to him in rank but senior to him in the "classroom." It was going to be a tough job for Mac McWhorter—a wizened old 23-year-old, with two combat cruises under his belt! But we got on with it.

Although there was a syllabus of instruction, I pretty much set up the flying schedule the way I wanted it. We flew and flew and flew. If my students weren't catching on, then we flew some more. And after they caught on, we flew some

McWhorter, newly transferred to VF-12 in 1944, was charged with training newly assigned pilots. Standing (left to right) are Ensign Jay Finley, Ensign Eddie Ball, Ensign Lee Furse, and Lieutenant Hamilton McWhorter III. Kneeling (left to right) are Lieutenant Commander Fred Michaelis, Ensign John Gallagher, Ensign Bill Carlson, and Ensign L. C. Garrison. (U.S. Navy)

more anyway—lots of formation tactics, and air-to-air and air-to-ground gunnery, some instrument and night work, and, of course, dogfighting and the usual tail-chases on the way back to the airfield.

***

We also dropped countless practice bombs. These were heavy little iron bombs that were loaded with a smoke charge. They looked very much like cartoon bombs or the old-style bombs from World War I. We started the students out with 45-degree bomb runs. They rolled into their dives from about 6,000 feet and then released at about 3,000 feet. As they got better, we increased the dive angle to 60 degrees. Usually, we had one airplane circling to one side. The pilot of this airplane recorded the students' bomb hits.

To help critique the students' dive angles, we had wires strung on a frame so that they formed a quadrant—a 90-degree segment of a circle—with a 10-degree angle between wires. The frame was placed at a right angle to the dive path, about 2,000 feet from the target. The range crew could look through it and approximate the dive angle of an airplane. It was primitive, but it worked.

Dive-bombing using a fixed gunsight, as we were doing, is very difficult and hinges on precise mathematical calculations. For each dive angle and airspeed, there is an exact gunsight setting and release altitude. Everything must be perfect for the bomb to hit the target. If the airspeed is too fast when the gunsight is over the target, the bomb will go long; too slow, and it will fall short. Likewise, if the dive angle is too steep, the bomb will go long, but it will fall short if the angle is too shallow. And if the altitude is too high when the bomb is released, the bomb will go long; too low, and it will fall short.

Angles of bank cause the bomb to miss wide, and an untrimmed aircraft will also throw the bomb off the mark. Any kind of wind demands a calculated correction. And, of course, the pilot has to adjust the height of his release to the height of his aircraft above the ground, not the height above sea level, which is how his altimeter is read.

It wasn't easy. But after a lot of practice the students got to the point where they could consistently drop their bombs inside a 100-foot ring. Some were much better than that—bull's-eyes were not uncommon.

Generally, all aspects of the training progressed well enough. Some of the students had talent that shone through, while others caught on more slowly. But by and large I was confident that I could get them ready before we went into combat. Of course, there were other old VF-9 hands there with me, including Chick Smith, Matt Byrnes, Lane Bardeen, Robert Green, Jim Miller, James Steel, Hal Vita, Rube Denoff, Tubby Franks, Lou Menard, and Buck Toliver. We kept in touch, shared notes, and did what we could to help each other out.

Occasionally someone asked me about my combat experiences—my aerial victories and such—and I did talk to them. But I wasn't really that keen about it. I had already lost a lot of friends, so many that I couldn't keep count. With that came guilt when I couldn't remember details about them, or when their faces began to fade a little in my memory. On top of that I knew that I was probably going back to the Pacific and that I would likely see more of my friends killed. I was tired. Not physically so much as mentally. Today they call it stress.

And in the very back of my mind was the thought that I could be the friend to be killed.

***

The other side of my life revolved around Louise. It was heaven to be able to go back to the hotel each day, knowing that she was waiting for me. She was having a ball with all the other wives living in the hotel. We hit the beach on the weekends, usually just the two of us, in order to have as much time together as possible; we knew that another deployment to the Pacific was not too far off for me. As before, we tried our best not to think about it, but it was always there, hanging over our heads.

***

The training went quickly. Only a couple months after we started, we received orders to San Diego. Louise and I loaded up the Dodge again and drove out of Melbourne on June 7, 1944. For our cross-country trip, the Navy issued me gas ration coupons for 206 gallons and paid me 8 cents per mile.

But first, we drove up to Athens to spend a few days with my family and friends. The visit went well, although the town was practically empty of men my age. The war had been going on long enough that several of my high school classmates had already been killed. This fact weighed heavily on my parents, who were sending their son into combat for the third time. The goodbye was especially strained. My father did a pretty good job of keeping a stiff upper lip, but my mother did not. Consequently, our departure was a heartbreaking, tearful affair.

We headed west on U.S. 80. This was before the days of the interstate highway system, and U.S. 80 was a curving two-lane asphalt road that pretty much followed the contour of the land. Because of gas rationing there wasn't too much traffic. The most frustrating traffic we dealt with were the large, slow military convoys. They were often several miles long and thus very difficult to get past.

Everything went well for the first couple of days. There was no problem getting gasoline since all the little towns had gas stations. Lodging was scarce, though. Generally, we stopped early in the evening, as we didn't want to be out late looking for a place to stay. The motels we stayed in were quite spartan by today's standards. Our lodging was usually nothing more than a small cabin or a room with a bed and some worn furniture. But for the most part they were clean, and best of all they cost only a couple of dollars per night.

On the third day out from Athens we were somewhere near the Louisiana–Texas border when the engine began making a loud rattling noise. I pulled the car over to the side of the road and opened the hood to look at the engine. From what I could see, there was nothing obviously wrong. While Louise and I stood there wondering what to do, the first motorist that came along stopped to offer help. I guess he saw me standing there in my uniform. After taking a look at the engine, he offered to drive me into the next town—only two or three miles away. I shudder now when I remember that I left Louise alone with the car. But that was a different era, and at the time neither one of us thought anything of it.

The other driver dropped me off at a small garage. When I explained my problem to the mechanic working there, he stopped what he was doing and piled me into his tow truck. Within an hour we were back at the Dodge. Louise reported that two or three other motorists had stopped to offer help while I was gone.

The mechanic put us all into the cab of his truck and towed our car back to his garage, where he set to work on it right away. He found that a valve had failed and punched a hole into one of the pistons. He wasn't able to find a ready replacement part, so he tore down another engine that he had in the garage in order to get the parts he needed to fix *our* engine. It was getting late, and he told us to go to a nearby motel and come back the next morning, a Sunday. He promised us the car would be repaired.

He was as good as his word. When we showed up the next morning, the car was ready and in good running condition. The bill he presented me was ridiculously low—even for that time and place. After thanking him profusely, Louise and I continued west to California.

***

We arrived in San Diego intact in both body and spirit only to immediately receive orders to Naval Air Station Astoria, in Oregon. Louise and I broke camp again and headed up the Pacific Coast. On U.S. Highway 1, near San Luis Obispo, California, the Dodge blew a tire. I changed it, and we went into town to get a replacement. To do so, I had to go before the ration board. They initially seemed reluctant to give me—an out-of-towner—one of their tire allotments. But after I produced my orders, they immediately issued me a coupon for a new tire.

By and large, people were friendly and helpful everywhere we traveled. The strict rationing of almost everything meant that you could not always get exactly what you wanted, when you wanted it. But almost everyone accepted this minor hardship without a lot of grousing.

We arrived in Astoria on July 4 but couldn't find a place to stay. Every hotel and motel we stopped at was booked for the holiday. Frustrated, we went down to the beach and watched some very hardy souls try the 50-degree water; then we went searching again for a room.

No luck. Finally, after dark, we parked on a side road and spent the night in the car. When we woke up in the morning, we found that we had spent the night in a cemetery. Feeling as refreshed as we could feel after a night in the car—as the unwitting guests of hobgoblins and ghosts and such—we set out in search of a room again and at last met with success.

After showering, shaving, and putting on a uniform, I went to check in at the naval air station so that I could get started helping to form the new squadron—VF-12. Actually, we were re-forming the squadron. The original VF-12 had been on the *Saratoga* with the famous "Jumpin' Joe" Clifton as skipper. It had then been land-based for a time in the South Pacific before being decommissioned just the month before—June 1944.

The air station was just big enough to hold our still-forming squadron. But the size of fighter squadrons in the Navy was changing dramatically at this time. VF-12 had already begun to receive what ultimately turned out to be 72 new F6F-5s, not the traditional 36.

The new F6F-5s differed very little from the F6F-3s we had flown previously. The engine was upgraded a bit, which increased our top airspeed by 10 knots or so. There were also provisions to carry rockets—three per wing—beyond the wingfold. But most of the improvements were simply refinements, such as better cockpit lighting and things of that nature. I didn't notice that it flew much differently at all. That major improvements weren't needed spoke well of the original design.

By now the F6F had demonstrated not only that it excelled in its original role as a fighter, but that it could carry and deliver bombs about as effectively as the dive bomber. It was also cheaper to produce, was smaller and easier to handle on the deck than the bombers, and needed only a one-man crew. All these factors influenced the decision to change the mix of the air groups on the big aircraft carriers. The standard air group composition aboard the *Essex*-class ships was ultimately changed to 72 F6F Hellcats, 12 SB2C Helldivers, and 12 TBM Avengers.

Carrier Air Group 12 was commissioned on July 20, 1944, under Commander Charles Crommelin, with VF-12 under Commander Noel A. M. Gayler. Commander Gayler had five kills to his credit and was the first Navy officer ever to receive three Navy Crosses. He had been assigned to VF-3, then VF-2, aboard the first *Lexington* until that ship was lost at the battle of the Coral Sea in May 1942.

His early successes were all the more remarkable because he had achieved them while flying the old Wildcat. He knew his business and was a good fit for the job, though his leadership style was more standoffish than what I was used to. All the other combat veterans—12 of us—came from VF-9.

The rest of Air Group 12 was scattered at various other bases along the West Coast. Charlie Crommelin was one of five brothers who were all officers in the Navy. He was a fighter pilot's fighter pilot—an aggressive, hard-flying, smart-fighting, tough individual. The previous year at Mille Atoll, during the

Noel Gaylor was the commanding officer of VF-12 when McWhorter joined. Already an ace while flying Wildcats during the early days of the war, he rose quickly in rank, eventually commanding all U.S. forces in the Pacific during the 1970s. (U.S. Navy)

Tarawa invasion, his airplane had taken a 20-millimeter cannon round in the cockpit. Wounded and bleeding badly, and only able to see out of one eye, he managed to bring his badly stricken aircraft back aboard the *Yorktown*. He went so far as to park his airplane before he collapsed unconscious in the cockpit. He set a good example.

Because the air group's composition changed we received 18 dive bomber pilots from VB-12 on September 9 for retraining as fighter pilots. One of these was my good friend Norm Sandler, who was with me through flight school and with VB-9 on the *Essex*. He had been transferred to VB-12 and now was being transferred again, this time to VF-12. He became the section leader, number three, in my division. By this time, I was the fourth-ranking officer in the squadron and was assigned as a division leader.

For many dive bomber pilots the transition was not particularly difficult, but others had a tough time. There were positive and negative aspects to these transition pilots. On the plus side, they had a lot of experience and savvy in the air. On the minus side, their dive bomber expertise wasn't always what was needed to make a good fighter pilot. They were accustomed to the stable flying required in bomber formations and were not used to the abrupt maneuvers often required in flying a fighter. It was often difficult to convince a guy who had as much combat time as you—and who often outranked you—that he didn't know what he was doing. But we pressed on with our training and made it work.

I'm not certain why Astoria was selected as a location for a naval air station. It certainly wasn't because of the good weather. During the time we were there the coast was almost always blanketed by a shroud of wet, gray, low-hanging clouds. Typically, we took off in two-plane sections and, upon starting our climb, almost immediately become enveloped in the thick, wet gloom. It wasn't long before we became very good instrument flyers.

Fortunately, the overcast layer usually reached to only three or four thousand feet. There was a perceptible lightening as we climbed through the murk and neared the top of the cloud layer, then a blinding brightness as we popped out into the stunningly clear blue sky. Instead of the depressing grayness below, the clouds on top reflected the sunlight in a dazzling brightness that hurt the eyes. Tears pooled in my eyes, and I had to squint for a moment or two until they adjusted to the glare.

Once rendezvoused above the clouds, we trained as we always had—air-to-air gunnery, tactical formations, dogfighting, and so on. I often became apprehensive when we fired live ammunition at a towed banner above the clouds. Although we always practiced this over the ocean, we had no way of knowing if there were any boats on the water beneath the clouds. I guess we never hit anything; I'm sure we have heard about it otherwise.

The air-to-air gunnery pattern didn't really differ from what we had practiced in the F6F-3—or even in the old Wildcat. A pilot started his gunnery run from a perch position about 1,000 feet abeam and above the tow aircraft, on a course parallel to it. He turned in, putting his aircraft in a dive and at a 90-degree angle to the target; then the pilot gradually reversed his turn to arrive in a firing position about 1,000 feet behind and about 20 degrees off the target banner. Even in a slight dive, the pilot had only a few seconds to properly align his aircraft and fire his guns before he overtook the target banner and had to recover from his dive.

Flying this pattern as a single airplane was not too difficult. But when several other airplanes were thrown into the mix—each one at a different position—things could get quite interesting. Especially when we were loaded with live ammunition.

Scoring our hits after gunnery flights was a big deal. A crowd always gathered around the target banner, and there was lots of pointing and arguing about who shot what, and how much. The bullet tips in each aircraft were all painted a distinct color. For instance, all the bullets in one airplane were painted orange, while all those in another were painted green or blue or any of a number of other colors. The idea was that when the bullet struck the hard mesh of the target banner, it would leave behind a small bit of paint, making it possible to score the hits.

The problem was, several of the paint colors could be mistaken for others, particularly after having been fired through a machinegun. Black often looked like blue or green or brown, and vice versa. Orange, red, and yellow were also easily confused. And the lucky guy whose airplane was loaded with purple bullets could claim just about all the hits. Often, the pilot who was credited with the most hits was the one with the biggest mouth or the highest rank. Having already proven myself in combat, I didn't get as wound up about the hits as some of the other guys. Nevertheless, it was amusing to watch them—especially the new pilots—argue among themselves.

***

An innovation that significantly improved our air-to-air gunnery was introduced during this period—the Mark 23 gyro-stabilized gunsight. Gyroscopic devices that sensed the firing airplane's motion were used to compute the amount of lead—rhymes with speed—that was required to hit the enemy airplane. An illuminated ring with a center dot was projected on the glass gunsight. Rather than being fixed in place as on previous gunsights, the ring on the gyroscopic gunsight moved around as the airplane moved. The size of the ring could be adjusted by rotating the throttle grip.

It was easy to use. The pilot simply had to adjust the size of the ring until it matched the wingspan of the target. Then he had only to maneuver to put the pipper that was in the center of the ring over the target and squeeze the trigger when he came within range. If the enemy airplane was not maneuvering dramatically, the gunsight was *deadly* accurate. If the target was maneuvering, the pilot could twist the throttle grip to the stop. This nullified the gyroscopic function and the moving reticle defaulted to a fixed position.

***

The social life in VF-12 was vastly different from what we had known in VF-9. It was impossible to get closely acquainted with all 98 pilots in the squadron. There were some I barely knew at all.

Squadron events were seldom held, so we mainly went around with our old friends from Air Group 9 days. Norm Sandler and his wife, Jerry, were particularly close friends. We often went out in the evenings with them and we enjoyed playing golf on the weekends. But Louise and I mostly enjoyed just being together and walking along the beach or through the nearby woods. We did it even though the woods were always so wet and dripping from the ever-present fog that it was impossible to keep dry. The beach was more rocky than sandy, and occasionally we found a big Dungeness crab or two trapped in one of the small pools left behind by the receding tide. These made for a wonderful meal.

Because the weather was so poor at Astoria, we often moved our operations east, flying from Naval Auxiliary Air Station Pasco over the semidesert near Walla Walla, Washington. Here the weather was nearly always conducive to flying, and we were able to maintain a high tempo of operations.

One of the new features of the F6F-5 was its ability to fire aerial rockets, which had recently been introduced as a practical and very accurate weapon. The Navy standard was the HVAR, or high-velocity aerial rocket. It used a five-inch warhead similar to those fired from a ship's five-inch guns. This warhead was mated to a high-velocity rocket that could be mounted underneath our wings. The F6F-5 could carry three HVARs under each wing and fire all six in one pass. In effect, we could deliver the equivalent firepower of a broadside from a destroyer.

We really liked these new rockets. They were very accurate and much easier to employ than a bomb. Whereas dive-bombing required extremely disciplined and accurate flying, the HVARs were almost a point-and-shoot weapon. To shoot the HVARs we adapted the same patterns that we used for dive-bombing.

Although we did practice with full-sized HVARs, most of our training was done with SCARs, or sub-caliber aerial rockets. These were smaller, lighter, and less-expensive versions of the HVAR. The SCAR had no warhead; instead, it carried a smoke charge so that we could see where the rocket had hit.

We also did a lot of night flying at Pasco. The Navy was beginning to operate its airplanes more and more at night, and the accident rate was too high. Just the previous June, during the first battle of the Philippine Sea, dozens of aircraft were lost during a disastrous night recovery.

My recollections of clawing around in the dark following the predawn launch against Marcus a year earlier were enough to send tingles up my spine. And the youngsters I was working with were far less experienced than I had been. The only way to get better was to practice.

I remember one night in particular; it was very dark, with no moon, no visible horizon, and very little man-made lighting below us. I had Norm Sandler on my wing for some night navigation work. Just a short time into the flight I looked over to my right and was surprised to see the belly of his airplane. He was in a near-vertical bank, turning away from me.

"Norm, level your wings," I called at him.

"They are level! You level your wings!"

It was obvious to me that because it was so black outside—no visual cues whatsoever—Norm was suffering from vertigo. His body was trying to tell him that a 90-degree angle of bank was straight and level. And he was buying it. The only way for him to recover and get back to a wings-level flight attitude was to ignore his tactile senses and to do what his flight instruments told him to do.

I called over the radio again, "Norm, get on your instruments now and level your wings. You've got vertigo." Vertigo had killed a lot of pilots and I didn't want Norm to be another victim.

"I said, get on your instruments, Norm!"

After an anxious moment or two, his airplane, now several hundred feet away, began to right itself. A short time later we sorted things out and continued on to finish our training mission. The funny thing was, after we landed, my dear friend Norm tried to make me out to be the bad guy. Said that I had turned or rolled or something and that I had been the one with vertigo!

***

During October and into November, heavy fog very often compounded the low-hanging clouds. When the weather got too bad it was impossible to fly. We didn't mind when the airfield was socked in, as we pretty much had the day off. But we were losing valuable training time, so they decided to send us back down to the San Diego area.

The weekend before we were to leave, we had a huge farewell party—104 officers in one squadron makes for a *very* big party! There were several skits put on, one by Dave DeVere, our personnel officer. He demonstrated with very exaggerated motions, to the great amusement of all, how women manage to squeeze into girdles. Another skit had several of the biggest pilots, me included, on the stage with tiny, doll-sized baby bottles of milk. We were pitted against each other to see who could empty his bottle the fastest—quite a sight! A great time was had by all.

Chapter 23

On November 9, 1944, VF-12 moved to Naval Auxiliary Air Station Ream Field in San Ysidro, California, between San Diego and the Mexican border. This was to be our final training base before we left for the Pacific. Unfortunately, the foul weather we had battled so long claimed a final victim from VF-12 during the trip to Ream Field. Ensign Bill Murray became lost in clouds and was never heard from again—presumed lost at sea. It's a good bet that he fell victim to vertigo in the featureless gray of the clouds.

I did not fly down to Ream; the skipper was kind enough to let me drive with Louise, and we took Bill "Stoney" Carlson and his wife with us. When we arrived, we were lucky to find a Quonset hut available. We shared it with the Carlsons, hanging a blanket between the two single beds for a bit of privacy. So much for wartime housing. A week or so later, we found a room in the Maryland Hotel in San Diego, where several other squadron mates were living. The arrangement was very similar to what we had had in our hotel back in Melbourne. Once more, we had to change rooms, this time, every five days. Louise didn't seem to mind the move, though. She had enjoyed living in San Diego as a young girl and still had friends there.

Air group exercises and carrier qualifications occupied much of our time. The weather was so much better than it was at Astoria, and we were all able to get in our field carrier practice and get carrier-qualified. Ironically, the carrier we trained on was the old *Ranger*—the same ship that I had fought from in North Africa. If she had looked old to me in 1942, now, after my combat tour on the *Essex* she looked like an absolute antique. Her deck seemed so narrow and those silly swinging smokestacks looked so strange. But she worked just fine as a training platform, and we spent a good part of November on her in order to get everyone qualified in daytime landings.

On November 27 we were sent to Naval Auxiliary Air Station Holtville near El Centro, California, for night flying and night field carrier practice in preparation for night carrier qualifications. The days around Holtville were always hot and clear, and the nights as pitch-black as they were at Walla Walla—difficult for seeing but excellent for night flying practice. We got through the night field carrier landing training with little difficulty, although I'm sure we put a scare into many of the jackrabbits when we got too low in the pattern.

One black night we were taxiing out to the runway for takeoff when Tom Northcutt suddenly called over the radio that his plane was on fire. We saw him stop, shut off his engine, and jump to the ground. After the plane was checked and nothing was found to be wrong, we discovered the "problem." The exhaust from all eighteen cylinders of the big R-2800 engine collects in a circular manifold that runs around the back of the engine, and it gets rather hot—exceedingly so if the cowl flaps are inadvertently left closed when taxiing. In fact, it gets so hot that it emits a bright red glow that radiates out from under the engine cowling at night. That is what compelled Tom to "bail out" on the taxiway. To this day, he's known as "Hot Stacks" Northcutt.

Early one morning at the end of November, Louise and I received a heartbreaking shock. I was asleep when Louise took phone call from her father, who gave her the news that the submarine *Escolar* and all her crew—including Mary's husband, Frank Blaha—were declared lost. Louise was so distressed that when she turned to me and saw that I was still asleep, she vented her rage at the war by slapping me on the arm with all her strength. It was the only time she ever did anything like that. We spent the rest of the morning holding each other.

The *Escolar* had last been heard from on October 17, as she was transiting the Yellow Sea, south of Japan. By mid-November she was overdue to return from patrol; on November 27, she was officially declared lost. No trace or record of the *Escolar* was ever found, and it is believed that she may have hit a mine.

When I heard the news, I couldn't help thinking of the good-natured ribbing I had given Frank about the perils of submarine service. Now I felt awful. Frank and the crew of the *Escolar* must have suffered an agonizing death. Poor Mary was left alone to take care of Frank, Jr., and was only days away from giving birth to their second child. Louise was stunned. I'm sure that Frank's loss must have intensified her own fears for my safety.

***

We returned to Ream Field on December 4 and went back aboard the *Ranger* on December 15 for nighttime carrier qualifications, completing them on Christmas Eve 1944. But no matter how much we prepared, carrier aviation—as always—exacted its price. Ensign Fred Nittel was killed during a night landing on December 20. Another ensign, Walter Brock, crashed into the barricade on deck and the canopy of his aircraft slammed shut on his hand, injuring it so badly that he had to be detached.

Ever since the squadron was re-formed, new pilots and enlisted personnel continued to join and swell the ranks. On December 10, 23 additional pilots reported aboard from VF-5. By early January 1945, the squadron had become so large that it was too unwieldy to administer effectively. There were 104 pilots, 4 nonflying officers, 32 enlisted men, and 72 airplanes. I didn't even know the names of many of the pilots in my own squadron.

When I compared the situation with VF-12 in 1945 to my early days with VF-9, the differences were remarkable. In the spring of 1942, VF-9 under the command of Jack Raby had seemed like an extended family. Everyone knew everyone else, as well as their girlfriends or wives, their likes and dislikes, their strengths and weaknesses. In contrast, VF-12, although manned by wonderful people, was so big that it sometimes seemed like a huge processing plant for Navy fighter pilots. People were coming and going every week. I couldn't keep track of all the moves.

But a huge number of fighters was needed now, more than ever. During the second battle of the Philippine Sea, the previous October, our fleet had lost several ships to the new kamikaze threat. These fanatical suicide attacks were expected to intensify as we closed on Japan. Large numbers of fighters, and the pilots to man them, were essential to the defense of the fleet.

The solution for our huge, unwieldy squadron was a simple one and was implemented throughout the Navy. The squadron was split in half on January 2, 1945. Half the personnel—including me—stayed with VF-12 and its original commander, Noel Gayler. The other half was re-formed and renamed VBF-12 (Fighter-Bomber Squadron 12), commanded by the former VF-12 executive officer, Lieutenant Commander Edward Pawka. My former student at Melbourne, Lieutenant Commander Frederick Michaelis, became VF-12's new executive officer.

In practice the split was almost purely administrative since both squadrons flew exactly the same types of missions despite their different designations. We even flew each other's airplanes on a regular basis. What this change really did was give the commanding officers a reasonably sized group of men to administer, control, and lead.

During the next 10 days or so, the entire air group—VF-12, VBF-12, VT-12, and VB-12—flew coordinated simulated attacks on friendly shipping in the area. One of our targets was the newly commissioned *Essex*-class aircraft carrier *Randolph* (CV-15), which had just arrived in the Pacific and was passing San Diego on her way to San Francisco. These exercises served as a final examination for us as well as for the ships we attacked. To facilitate training for the warships, some airplanes executed kamikaze-style attacks, diving down from 35,000 feet, while others ran separate attacks from masthead height.

We also worked closely with the dive bomber and torpedo bombers in large-scale exercises against ground targets. Because the Imperial Japanese Navy was largely destroyed by this time, the Navy used TBMs more for conventional bombing than for torpedo bombing. They also carried 5-inch rockets as well as the new Tiny Tim rockets, which had a 150-pound warhead, and weighed more than 1,200 pounds. As long as there were no enemy fighters about, or there was adequate protection, the TBM was a quite capable bomber.

That the exercises went well was fortunate. In a very short time we were to board two CVEs, the *Attu* and the *Breton*. They would take us from San Diego to Guam, where we were to replace a yet-to-be-determined air group on one of the *Essex*-class ships.

But, as so often happens in wartime, plans changed at the last minute. On January 14, 1945, the entire air group received orders to move to Naval Air Station Alameda, California, in order to embark aboard the *Randolph*—one of the ships we had practiced aerial attacks against earlier that month. We were to replace Air Group 87, which had been relieved upon the *Randolph*'s arrival in San Francisco following her shakedown cruise. Evidently that air group was not yet ready for combat, and Air Group 12 was selected to take its place.

I'm not sure if Charlie Crommelin, the Air Group 12 commander, had a hand in the change or not. He had close ties to some powerful people in Washington, and the change seemed to suit his aggressive style. He had an air group that he had trained to fight, that he knew was ready to fight, and by God he wanted to take it where it could do some fighting.

The timing couldn't have been worse for Louise and me. The air group was scheduled to leave Ream on January 16, our second wedding anniversary. Again, we agreed to write each other every day, and we made the kinds of promises that people in love make. Just as I had when I left for the Pacific the first time, I gave her my solemn word that I would return to her safe and sound. I prayed—and I know she did, too—that I would be able to honor that commitment.

Chapter 24

The first elements of Air Group 12 began moving out on January 16, when we flew our planes up to Alameda. The nearby Golden Gate Bridge exercised its siren call, which proved too much for Lou Menard and his division. They got themselves into a bit of trouble by flying under it.

We completed the move to Alameda in record time. By January 20, all required personnel and equipment, including the airplanes, which had to be craned aboard, were embarked aboard ship and under way for Pearl Harbor. On January 29, after only two days in Hawaii, where we picked up a night-fighter team of six pilots, four planes, and their maintenance crews, the *Randolph* departed Pearl Harbor in company with other ships of the Pacific Fleet. The destination was the huge Navy anchorage at Ulithi Atoll in the Western Carolines.

The anchorage at Ulithi atoll hosted the largest and most powerful naval forces in history. (U.S. Navy)

The situation in the Pacific had changed dramatically in the 20 months since I had arrived in May 1943 with VF-9 aboard the *Essex*. In successive stages the Japanese had been pushed farther and farther back toward their home islands. Without a single failure, our Marines and soldiers had seized bases whenever and wherever they were needed. Once-fearsome and powerful bastions of enemy power such as Rabaul and Truk were pounded, strangled, and bypassed along with countless smaller islands whose names have been forgotten. Japanese soldiers, sailors, and airmen—hundreds of thousands—were cut off from their homeland, helpless to strike at our forces. Indeed, so wretched was their situation that many of them were starving to death.

There remained only a few major campaigns until American forces were at the empire's doorstep, ready to invade the Japanese home islands. Army forces under General Douglas MacArthur, already engaged in the Philippines since October 1944, would need several months to finish that campaign. Marine forces were scheduled to take the tiny volcanic island of Iwo Jima sometime in February. We needed Iwo as an emergency and escort base for Army Air Forces B-29s on their operations over Japan. Finally, once our forces secured Iwo Jima, they would invade the island of Okinawa—only 350 miles south of Japan—and prepare it as the jump-off point for the anticipated Japan itself. The Navy's mission was to cover and support all of these campaigns. We had come a long way.

***

We arrived at the anchorage in Ulithi Atoll on February 7. The next day, our skipper, Commander Noel Gayler, received orders to report to Pearl Harbor for a new assignment on the staff of Vice Admiral John McCain, commander of Fleet Air Pacific. Gayler's association with our squadron was over but he eventually earned four stars by the end of the Vietnam War, nearly thirty years later.

So, on the eve of our young squadron's introduction to combat, we found ourselves with a new commanding officer. Actually, he was not new to the squadron, just new to the assignment. It was my former student, Frederick "Mike" Michaelis.

I had a few private reservations. Mike was a good man, with enough rank and maturity for the job, but he was charged with leading a 36-airplane squadron into what was anticipated to be some of the toughest fighting of the war. He was far from being a seasoned hand; he had not been flying much longer than our average ensigns, and none of his flight time was in combat. I could only hope that he had the savvy to recognize his limitations and the courage to ask for help when and where he needed it.

A Naval Academy graduate several years senior to McWhorter, Fred Michaelis was nevertheless a green pilot. Under McWhorter's tutelage, Michaelis learned quickly. He eventually became the commander of VF-12 and an ace. (U.S. Navy)

Mike did make some changes along those lines, and one of them caught me quite by surprise. Although I was the fourth-senior pilot in the squadron, Michaelis made me second-in-command in the air. I was to head the 18 planes that made up the second half of the squadron.

***

On February 10, 1945, the *Randolph* weighed anchor and sailed from Ulithi as part of what the VF-12 history describes as "the largest and most potent aggregation of naval power ever assembled." We had received several intelligence briefings and guessed that we might be enroute to Iwo Jima in support of the Marine invasion. Instead, we were surprised when Commander Charlie Crommelin announced that Task Force 58—the Fast Carrier Task Force—was going to attack targets in and around Tokyo, the very heart and soul of Japan.

The size of our armada absolutely staggered the senses. Task Force 58 was made up of 11 big-deck fleet carriers, 5 light carriers, 8 battleships, 13 cruisers of various sizes, and no fewer than 77 destroyers. The catalog of auxiliary ships steaming in support was impressive as well. Even when airborne, I could look in every direction and not see all the ships of the task force. Together, the various ships carried nearly 1,500 airplanes. It made the little force that had attacked Marcus Island in 1943 seem laughable.

After air-support rehearsals with the Marines on Tinian on February 12, we turned toward Japan. The farther north we went, the colder it became. And with the cold came dreary skies and storms. As we neared Japan we encountered low clouds, squalls, sleet, and even some blowing snow. Having come from tropical Ulithi, it felt ridiculous to bundle up against the cold only a few days later.

Nevertheless, the miserable weather cloaking our forces worked to our advantage. As large and powerful as the fleet was, we took great care to keep our approach a secret. There was no sense giving the Japanese time to mount a concerted spoiling attack. Our route was scouted and cleared by various bomber and observation patrols as well as destroyer picket lines. We sank several small Japanese picket ships as our fleet neared the launch point, only 50 miles off the eastern coast of the main island of Honshu. In the end, all our precautions and a good bit of luck worked to our favor. Task Force 58 arrived unmolested.

I made my way topside on the morning of February 16, 1945, to man my airplane for the first strike of the day, and the first for Air Group 12. The activity on the flight deck had taken on a strange look. The enlisted airplane handlers

Aside from his flying skills, McWhorter's leadership was a key element of VF-12's success during its 1945 combat cruise. (U.S. Navy)

and other maintenance types—armorers, fueling personnel, mechanics, and such—were all bundled up against the freezing wet. The low-hanging clouds—at times the ceiling was as low as 200 feet—were spitting a mixture of sleet, snow, and freezing rain. And 30 knots or so of wind that the ship's speed whipped up made it especially cold. For someone like me, who had gotten used to fighting his war in the tropics, this was quite a change.

I wasted no time climbing into my airplane and getting it started. Soon I was as warm as toast behind the 18 cylinders of my F6F's Pratt & Whitney engine. Once airborne I turned to the northwest and climbed to rendezvous with the rest of the squadron. This too was different from what I was accustomed to. I had the canopy pulled shut against the icy wind, and I shivered instinctively as blowing rain and sleet spattered noisily against my airplane. The white-capped waves, only a few hundred feet below, had a steely gray, angry look to them—inhospitably cold. Inside my cockpit, I felt I was in a snug cocoon. It would have taken quite an emergency to make me ditch or bail out from the warmth of my fighter.

VF-12 Hellcats ready to launch from the deck of the *Randolph*. (U.S. Navy)

After our squadron was joined, we started our climb through the clouds. As a full-fledged division leader, I had Jay Finley on my wing; Norm Sandler and Stoney Carlson made up my second section. We were part of a 47-plane fighter sweep led by the air group commander, Charlie Crommelin. This was when our training at Astoria, where the weather was so miserable, really paid off. We were able to maintain formation through 18,000 feet of the icy, freezing gray. Above the overcast, we adjusted our speed and altitude to assemble into one large strike package.

Tokyo lay northwest, only 100 miles distant. Southwest of the city, I could just make out the snow-capped cone of Mount Fuji. As we approached the coast, the weather began to break, and through the breaks we caught sight of the Empire of Japan for the very first time. The ground was covered with snow and the landscape looked deceptively serene.

But this wasn't some far-flung Pacific atoll, a newly seized piece in Japan's imperialistic expansion. This was the enemy's homeland. Serene landscape or not, we were taking the war not just to his doorstep, but right into his living room.

But I didn't have much time to reflect. I looked over my left shoulder and spotted a Zero about a mile away at our seven o'clock position. He was in a slight dive, pointed right at us. I immediately turned hard into him. As I did so, he steepened his dive, intent on escaping into the clouds below us. But by doing that, he gave up his chance to outgun me with his two powerful 20-millimeter cannon, and instead served himself up as a target.

Just before the Zero passed below me, I rolled inverted and pulled down toward it in a vertical dive. I double-checked that my guns were charged and armed, then put my gunsight pipper on his nose and twisted the throttle to adjust the size of the circular reticle of the new Mark 23 gunsight. I adjusted it so that his wings fit just inside the circle.

I was set up for a perfect, overhead, 90-degree deflection shot at the top of his airplane. The black of his engine cowling and the bright red meatball insignia set against the dark green of the rest of his airplane stood out in sharp contrast to the white clouds below us. I held the pipper on the nose of his airplane, kept his wings framed inside the reticle, and squeezed the trigger as I reached firing range.

The new gunsight performed perfectly. I saw the bright flashes of my incendiary rounds striking exactly where I was aiming—his engine, cockpit, and wing roots. Surprisingly, he did not catch fire immediately. I kept firing, and the Zero finally began to trail a long streak of flame just before it reached the clouds. I pulled off and gave up the chase as the fighter disappeared into the murk, still trailing fire.

As I climbed back up to altitude, I collected the rest of my division. No sooner had we gotten back together than it was time to drop down on our targets. Air Group 12, untested in combat up to this time, was assigned to attack some of the more innocuous targets in the quadrant northeast of Tokyo—assumed to be less heavily defended than targets elsewhere in the city. Our orders directed us to attack airborne aircraft, aircraft on the ground, and aircraft manufacturing and servicing facilities, in that order of priority. I had shot down the only enemy airplane we had seen up to that point.

We dove down through the clouds unmolested to strafe and fire our 5-inch HVARs at airplanes parked at a number of different airfields. We strafed and rocketed one airfield, popped up, set a new course for a moment or two, and dropped down on another. There were so many airfields in such close proximity that our squadron alone strafed nine of them on that strike: Mito, Mito South, Konoike, Hokoda, Kasumigaura, Mawatari, Iitomi, Hitachi, and Hyakurigahara.

We hit so many airfields that I would be lying if I said that I strafed them all, or that I remembered which was which. However, they all had one feature in common, and that was intense antiaircraft protection. We were attacking the very heart of the Japanese homeland, and they were defending it with a vengeance—at least from the ground.

Their parked aircraft drew most of our attention, and we shot up and hit quite a few of them with rockets. At low altitudes—sometimes 10 feet or less—we raced back and forth, guns chattering. I often joke when people ask if I have ever set foot in Japan. "No," I tell them, "But I've come within ten feet of doing so."

With so many airplanes parked on the ground, it puzzled me that so few were airborne trying to knock us out of the sky. Perhaps we had caught the Japanese by surprise, or perhaps they lacked enough fuel to get them all into the air. Our submarines and other forces were making it almost impossible for them to bring in oil from the East Indies. I did spot a single enemy fighter over one of the airfields, but when I turned to give chase, it slipped immediately into the clouds and was gone.

That isn't to say that other VF-12 pilots didn't engage the enemy. Lieutenant (JG) Sabe Legatos shot down one Zero and made a head-on pass with another. Both he and the Zero pilot were observed firing when both aircraft caught fire and crashed in flames. In all, VF-12 pilots put in claims for fourteen aerial victories on February 16, 1945.

Miraculously, especially considering the vile weather, the squadron returned to the *Randolph*, descended through the clouds, and recovered without incident. It made me think that the poor weather at Astoria wasn't such a bad thing after all. It was excellent preparation for a day like this.

***

Navigating to and from the ship is talked about almost as an afterthought. But it should be remembered that flying to the target and then returning across a fairly large expanse of ocean was a navigational challenge. Much of it was done by dead reckoning—flying by time, heading, and distance. We had rudimentary radio navigation as well, in the form of a system commonly called YE/ZB. The YE was the transmitting equipment on the ship, while the ZB was a receiver in the airplane. The low-frequency YE equipment transmitted a different Morse code letter in each of twelve 30-degree sectors measured from magnetic north. Aboard our airplanes, we tuned our ZB receiver to pick up the signals from the YE.

Every day, the letters that identified each sector were changed. For instance, the identifying letter for the sector 000-030 degrees might be B one day and L the next. When a pilot got within range of the signal he could identify which sector he was in, but wouldn't know for sure whether he was heading toward or away from the ship. He would then turn down the volume until it was barely audible. If the volume of the signal increased he knew he was heading toward the ship; if it decreased, he was heading away. It was primitive, but it worked.

***

Generally there were anywhere from 10 to 12 fleet carriers in the task force—3 to 4 carriers to a task group and several groups to a task force. The carriers in each task group sailed in a box formation, 2,000 yards apart. Since the carriers looked so similar from the air, except for the identifying hull numbers painted on the bow and on the forward end of the flight deck, a pilot had to be aware of the position of his own ship within the formation.

One carrier out of the four was designated the "open-deck" carrier, and airplanes from other carriers could land on it if they were low on fuel or if their ship had a fouled deck. Many pilots did, but woe to the poor slob who unwittingly landed on the wrong carrier.

One foul-weather day, a pilot from the carrier ahead of us turned downwind and must not have realized how much wind there was. He must also have had his head down in the cockpit, because he flew right through his own carrier's downwind pattern and into ours. It wasn't until he crawled out of his airplane that the very startled ensign realized he was on the wrong carrier! Needless to say, when he was launched to go back to his own ship, his airplane was well decorated with hand-painted comments on his inability to find his way home.

My good friend Lou Menard nearly died during one of these first strikes on Tokyo. His airplane was badly shot up—so badly that it couldn't sustain controlled flight below about 175 miles per hour. He nursed his wounded fighter back over the task group, cinched his harness down tight, threw back the canopy, and bailed out over the cold and crashing waves. Unfortunately, he had tightened his harness so much that he wasn't able to release it when he hit the water. The 35-knot wind quickly reinflated his parachute and started dragging him through the swells. Within seconds he was bouncing across the waves like a giant fishing lure gone crazy. Exhausted by the brutal beating he was taking against the icy whitecaps, Lou very shortly lost consciousness.

That would have been the end of my friend, but a quick-thinking destroyer skipper saw what was happening and, despite the heavy seas, was able to maneuver his ship downwind of Lou and the rogue parachute. With an expertise that I hope earned him a medal, he timed his speed so that the parachute blew into his ship directly amidships and deflated. The destroyer crew managed to fish Lou out of the water—there are few things as heavy as a wet, unconscious man—thinking that he was dead. Working against the odds, they performed mouth-to-mouth resuscitation. Lou began to puke out buckets of water and miraculously came sputtering back to life.

Badly shaken and traumatized, Lou eventually made a complete recovery, but the accident debilitated him long enough that it earned him a ticket home. I was happy to see my friend rescued and sent safely out of harm's way.

Shortly after I landed from that first strike I learned the fate of the Zero I had sent flaming into the clouds. It had come tumbling out below, right through another formation of our fighters. The pilots mentioned that it had startled them quite a bit—but it was positively confirmed as destroyed. I also learned much later that the Zeroes produced at that stage of the war were equipped with self-sealing fuel tanks. This explained why that particular airplane had not flamed immediately upon being hit, unlike the Zeroes I had shot down earlier in the war.

News also came that Phil Torrey, our beloved skipper of VF-9 during our first Pacific combat tour, was killed that day. Then we were informed of the death of the commander of Air Group 9; he was leading his air group on a strike from the Lexington when he was hit by an Imperial Army Nakajima Ki-44 Tojo fighter. His loss was a mean blow.

***

Although it didn't seem possible at the time, the weather continued to worsen. On February 17, the one-year anniversary of the big Truk raid, we managed only one strike of the several that were planned. We strafed and fired rockets at some of the same airfields we had attacked the previous day, and again we lost another good man.

Buck Toliver, who was a squadron mate all through my time with VF-9 and VF-12, was hit in the engine by medium-caliber antiaircraft fire. He managed to come out of his strafing attack, gain some altitude, and glide out over the water, where he ditched his Hellcat about five miles off the coast. The rest of his division circled overhead and watched him climb out of his airplane and into his tiny life raft. He struggled against the waves and the wind as he tried to paddle himself away from the coast. Tragically, the water was too shallow for either a submarine or a destroyer to pick him up, and the task force was already steaming too far out of range to launch a rescue floatplane. Ultimately, he was lost. Whether he succumbed to the sea or was captured and killed, we never learned.

Ensign Eddie Ball was one of the fresh-caught ensigns among my students at Melbourne in April 1944. He was a tall, lanky, affable young kid who looked as though he should have still been in the high school lunch line rather than in combat. He had done well in training, on a par with his peers, and had developed into a solid pilot. On February 16, the day of his first combat flight, he had spotted a Zero and given chase. He blasted away, firing all 2,400 rounds of ammunition to no effect other than inflicting grievous wear-and-tear on his gun barrels. That evening he took quite a bit of good-natured ribbing for his "marksmanship."

The very next day, Eddie got airborne, intent on earning back some respect. Instead, he earned a new nickname. He did his part strafing airfields with the rest of the air group, but after the flight he was disgruntled at the lack of aerial opposition and the opportunity to redeem his reputation as a marksman. He pointed out that he hadn't seen a single enemy plane in the air. Nevertheless, when his gun camera film was developed, it clearly showed a Zero crossing right in front of him while he was in a strafing run. He hadn't even seen it! Thereafter he was known as "Bogey Ball."

In the end, though, Eddie Ball proved his mettle and finished the combat cruise with a Nakajima Ki-43 Oscar fighter to his credit.

One form of amusement that we enjoyed as we approached Japan was listening to Radio Tokyo piped over the ship's public address system. The ship's crew knew exactly when our first strike reached Tokyo; the infamous Tokyo Rose suddenly started screaming and abruptly went off the air! When we finally left the area, she came back on the air boasting that we were driven off with the loss of 142 planes and 20 ships, including one aircraft carrier. The truth was that no Japanese planes had gotten to the task force. We got an even greater chuckle later, when we heard her say that the *Randolph* was sunk.

By this point in the war, our airpower was absolutely dominant; we had achieved air supremacy. Each fleet carrier—and our task force had 12—embarked an air group that was composed of nearly 100 aircraft. Outside their home islands, the Japanese didn't have a single airfield in the entire Pacific that could muster 100 aircraft. The Japanese were helpless against us.

We left the area on February 17 and headed south toward Iwo Jima. On February 18, as we passed the Bonin Islands, we launched a strike against Chichi Jima, an island north of Iwo that was to be bypassed. Its garrison commander was notoriously cruel; he beheaded captured American flyers and ate their livers.

No enemy airplanes were seen on the strike, but the intense antiaircraft fire shot down two of our torpedo planes, and both crews were lost. Many of our other airplanes were also damaged by the severe antiaircraft fire but managed to return safely.

Chapter 25

We were in position to support the landings by the Marines on the sands of Iwo Jima on February 19, 1945. Volumes and volumes have been written about the terror, chaos, and ruin that characterized this battle. And although we suspected it then, we did not know for sure how rough a time the Marines were having.

I was on combat air patrol over the fleet on the first morning of the battle. From high above I watched as landing craft emerged from their parent ships, then formed into moving circles, one following another as they waited for the signal to turn toward the beach. Once the signal came, the small landing craft swung out into neat lines parallel to the beach and started in—at a crawl, it seemed to me. Almost immediately Japanese artillery fire began to rain down among them. The smaller-caliber shells peppered the sea around the landing craft, while the large ones made huge geysers. I knew it was only a matter of time before the inevitable occurred.

When it did, it struck with a terrifying suddenness that stunned me, detached as I was by distance and altitude. One of the landing craft took a direct hit and exploded into fire and smoke and spray. When the wind cleared the scene, there was nothing but a dirty smudge on the water where a boat full of men had been. It made me sad for the Marines, but also selfishly thankful to be where I was.

The Navy had learned its lessons earlier in the war; too many Marines were killed when enemy positions weren't hit hard enough prior to invasion day. This had been tragically illustrated at Tarawa. As a result, the Navy was placing special emphasis on ground-support missions for the Marines at Iwo Jima.

I was part of a strike mission later in the day on February 19. The strike included 16 F6Fs, 8 SB2Cs, and 8 TBMs. The airplanes in my division each carried six, five-inch, high velocity aerial rockets (HVARs) and a centerline drop tank loaded with napalm. This was the first time we carried napalm.

The task force lay about 75 miles west of Iwo Jima, so the island came into view only a few minutes after we launched. Iwo was just an ugly gray nothing of an island—only about five miles by two—marked by its one prominent feature, Mount Suribachi. This volcanic peak rose almost 600 feet and provided the Japanese with superb firing positions.

Charlie Crommelin was leading the strike and he checked in with an orbiting aircraft that was tasked with coordinating strikes for the Commander Air Support Control Unit (CASCU). Crommelin passed our position, our composition, and our ordnance loads, then anchored us in an orbit to await instructions.

While we orbited, we watched boats moving back and forth from the invasion fleet to the beach. Smoke and dust from the detonation of large-caliber shells obscured parts of the island. It was obvious that the Marines were having a difficult time.

After a few minutes we received our targeting assignments. Targets were referenced from a map overlaid with a grid. This grid defined numbered sectors, which in turn were subdivided into 25 much smaller lettered sectors. Thus, a target assignment for "an artillery position in sector 135A" defined a very precise position.

Our assigned target was a group of gun emplacements near the top of Mount Suribachi. Crommelin directed the bombers to drop one bomb each. The first two divisions of F6Fs were ordered to fire rockets; the second two divisions of F6Fs, to drop napalm. My division was one of those assigned to drop napalm.

From about 5,000 feet and a couple miles offshore, Crommelin pushed over into a shallow dive, and the rest of the strike airplanes followed him down. I looked over to make certain that Jay Finley and the rest of my division was in position, then went to full power to build up as much speed as possible. Not too far ahead of us, antiaircraft fire was already exploding.

As we neared Suribachi I could clearly make out the guns in cave-like emplacements. At about 2,000 feet I squeezed the trigger and watched my tracers arc down into one of the emplacements. When I got so close that I had no choice but to pull up or smash into the mountain, I released the napalm and yanked back on the stick. The G forces from the abrupt maneuver pushed me down into my seat and caused my face to sag. I felt particularly vulnerable exposing the belly of my airplane to the gunners below.

Luckily, I didn't get hit. I craned my head around as I cleared the island, but I couldn't see where my napalm had struck. As we rendezvoused back out over the water, the air coordinator reported good hits with the rockets and bombs, but said that only two of the eight napalm-filled centerline tanks had exploded. This frustrated me greatly; it was stupid to expose ourselves to enemy fire, only to deliver weapons that didn't function.

The air coordinator sent us back to hit more targets in the same area. On three more runs we fired our rockets with good effect. The antiaircraft fire continued to lash up at us, but probably just as dangerous was the very real possibility of a midair collision with one of the other strike airplanes over the target.

Next, the air coordinator moved us to targets north of Suribachi, where we strafed troop concentrations. Finally, our ammunition nearly expended, we returned to the *Randolph*. Although the antiaircraft fire had been heavy, none of the airplanes from my division was hit.

The problem with napalm persisted throughout the campaign at Iwo Jima. It was estimated that only one out of three weapons dropped actually ignited. The Navy finally solved the problem by adding a second fuse to the tank. This fix was in place before the invasion of Okinawa. When put to the test on the battlefields there, it worked quite well.

***

On the afternoon of February 21, I was sitting in an airplane waiting to take off and was looking over at the *Saratoga*, about 2,000 yards off our port side, slightly aft of abeam. Suddenly I caught sight of airplanes—kamikazes—diving on her. One of them struck the aft part of the ship and another hit just behind the forward elevator. The second airplane apparently went through the flight deck and the bomb it was carrying must have exploded right under the forward elevator, because that 20- or 30-ton aircraft elevator went flying hundreds of feet into the sky, flipping like a champagne cork. But instead of champagne, the *Saratoga* was belching fire, smoke, and debris. And bodies. I was dumbstruck.

The *Randolph* came under attack at the same time and responded with her five-inch guns. It just so happened that we had received delivery of five brand-new F6F-5s from a jeep carrier; they were parked aft of the island next to the five-inch gun mounts. Unfortunately, the kamikazes attacked from such a direction that the guns had to fire right over the top of those beautiful new airplanes. The concussion from the blasts popped nearly every rivet on every one of those Hellcats, turning them into total wrecks. The deck crews simply pulled the clocks—prized for some odd reason as souvenirs—from the instrument panels, and pushed the aircraft overboard. It was a shame to lose the new airplanes, but at least the *Randolph* wasn't hit.

The kamikaze was a new and puzzling phenomenon to me. By now the Japanese leaders realized they were not going to win the war. Their only chance of holding on to what remained of their empire—which in China,

McWhorter was in the cockpit of his F6F aboard the USS *Randolph* near Iwo Jima on February 21, 1945, when he saw a kamikaze hit the USS *Saratoga*, pictured here. (U.S. Navy)

if not the Pacific, was still considerable—was to negotiate an armistice. The only way they could hope to press an armistice on us was by exacting hellish numbers of casualties, beyond what we as a nation were prepared to bear. The only way they felt that they could inflict these casualties was through the use of suicide bombers, more popularly known as kamikazes.

To deliver a bomb in the conventional way took a great deal of training and skill. Targeting and hitting a moving ship with a bomb was difficult for even the most experienced aircrews. But after several years of war without an adequate training scheme for replacement personnel, Japan had precious few skilled pilots left.

What it had was plenty of airmen and would-be airmen willing to sacrifice their lives by flying their airplanes directly into ships—a much easier task than bombing. From October 1944, during the invasion of Leyte in the Philippines, the Japanese had hurled suicide bombers at our ships in an organized, premeditated fashion. The threat had our higher-ups scrambling for solutions.

But it wasn't just the physical threat of the kamikazes that was frightening. It was also the idea that the Japanese were recruiting and organizing whole

The kamikaze concept was desperate and ultimately ineffective. (U.S. Navy)

units of men—ultimately, thousands of men—who would purposely sacrifice their lives against us. To even contemplate the idea required a complete shift in our way of thinking. Even though we were also deep in the business of war, the sacrifice of our lives was not a deliberate act *ordered* by the highest levels of our government. (Several years later my faith in humankind was restored somewhat when I learned that there were many in the Japanese military who also found the idea horrifying and repugnant.)

One of the many changes caused by the increased kamikaze threat hit close to home. The squadron ready rooms were consolidated and moved from directly underneath the flight deck into the big wardroom beneath the armored hangar deck. Where before the wardroom was a refreshing and clean refuge from the grunge of the daily grind, it quickly became cluttered with a big status board and piles of worn and sweaty flight equipment. It made for quite a mess, but we were much safer.

We stayed in support of the landings at Iwo Jima until February 22. During those three days, we pounded the Japanese positions on Mount Suribachi with bombs, rockets, machinegun fire, and napalm. The deck crews made the napalm—essentially jellied gasoline—right on the flight deck. As they filled our 150-gallon centerline drop tanks with gasoline, they simultaneously added a substance that turned it into a gel. After the tank was filled, they screwed an omnidirectional fuse into the fuel filler opening. The tanks were not originally intended to be accurate weapons and consequently tumbled through the air and hit the ground at all sorts of weird angles which necessitated the use of the omnidirectional fuse to ensure detonation.

To guarantee the best possible accuracy, we dropped the napalm tanks on Japanese positions from very low altitude—50 to 150 feet. When the tank hit, it ruptured and the fuse ignited, splashing an area about 50 feet by 100 feet with the fiery substance. Although we used napalm a great deal against enemy-held caves in an effort to kill the Japanese by suffocating them—burning up all the oxygen—we also directed it against whatever other targets we could find. The whooshing blast and fire and smoke it created made it a terrifying weapon that I'm sure had as much of a psychological effect as a physically destructive one.

***

When foul weather at Iwo Jima caused the cancellation of our planned support strikes on the afternoon of February 22, we left again for the Japanese home islands. As it had been during the strikes of February 16 and 17, the weather was awful. On February 24 we ran into a terrible storm. Huge waves crashed over the bow and ripped off about 100 feet of the catwalk around the forward part of the deck, damaged 7 planes on the flight deck, and wrecked the two 40-millimeter gun mounts on the bow.

The *Randolph* rolled and pitched worse than I had ever experienced. Plates and items on the wardroom table slid back and forth; when the carrier plowed into one of the huge waves, the impact jolted the whole ship. Nevertheless, we had it easy compared to the smaller ships. The destroyers pitched up so far that their entire bows came out of the water, and at other times their sterns were exposed enough for us to see the propellers. They rolled so far over that we could almost see their keels. The sailors aboard those ships had to be miserable. In fact, the seas were so rough that—even though our speed was reduced to 16 knots—a destroyer's bow was crushed by the waves.

We were off the coast of Japan again on February 25. The weather was somewhat better, but still bad, with low clouds and poor visibility. We were launched that morning on fighter sweeps to hit Hyakurigahara, Hokoda, and Mawatari air bases. Jay Finley was my wingman and Norm Sandler and Stoney Carlson made up my second section.

The catapult officer was Lieutenant Commander Sam Humphries. We called him "Slinging Sam." He did a commendable job getting our planes off that morning. The seas were very heavy, and it was unnerving to be sitting on the catapult, ready to go, only to see nothing but a huge wall of water directly ahead as the bow pitched down. Sam timed the catapult shots just right, launching us when the bow neared the top of its rise. It sure made for some anxious moments, though!

Some of our airplanes experienced an unanticipated problem as they climbed up through the freezing clouds. It was so cold that the engine oil circulating in the propeller domes, which controlled the pitch of the constant-speed propellers, congealed into a semisolid. The pilots of these planes, including Commander Charlie Crommelin, were left with fixed-pitch props—not a good thing in a combat situation.

As we neared Hyakurigahara airfield I led my four-ship division down through a scattered undercast and set up for a strafing run on several single-engine airplanes parked on the main ramp. I had not seen any Japanese planes in the air. As always, the antiaircraft fire was heavy and accurate, and I flinched reflexively when several bursts came particularly close to my airplane.

I lined up on the first of the enemy airplanes, and as the illuminated pipper of my gunsight settled onto the center of its fuselage, I squeezed the trigger. My rounds slammed home and I moved my aim onto the next airplane in line. Again, my bullets found their mark. Just before I reached the point where I had to pull up to avoid crashing into the ground, I sprayed a quick burst into the center of the rest of the airplanes.

A second or two later Stoney Carlson called out that Norm Sandler's plane had disintegrated as it pulled out from the strafing run. I looked back but could not see where Norm had crashed. We made more strafing runs during which I tried to spot Norm's airplane, but I could not find it. Finally, I corralled the rest of my flight and headed back. Along the way I kept hoping that somehow Stoney had made a mistake and that Norm hadn't crashed, but rather that he had become separated from the rest of us and would show up back at the *Randolph*.

Somehow, we managed to find our way out to the carrier through the rapidly deteriorating weather. Lieutenant Fred Kidd was the air group LSO for this strike and he worked miracles getting us back aboard. The weather had turned really foul, and the stern was pitching up and down 20 feet or more. Fred managed to get us aboard without an excessive number of wave-offs by very competently judging the deck motion and giving cuts only when the deck was pitching down. This ensured that a descending airplane wouldn't get damaged by rapidly meeting up with a rising flight deck. Only one F6F was damaged; it suffered two blown tires when it did not get down to the deck soon enough after the cut.

After I parked my airplane, Jay Finley and Stoney Carlson got aboard. I caught up with Stoney on the cold, rainy flight deck.

"Stoney," I said, "what happened to Norm?"

The expression on Stoney's face telegraphed bad news. "I don't know what happened for sure, Mac. I saw him as he started his pullout. I'm not sure if he got hit or what, but the tail of his plane came completely off."

I imagined what it must have been like at the end for Norm—helpless, the ground rushing up. "Did he hit hard?" I asked.

Again, Stoney's expression answered the question before he spoke. "It was bad, Mac. He's gone."

***

Although my division hadn't encountered any Japanese in the air, some of our air group had more business than they wanted. Our skipper, Charlie Crommelin, whose airplane was one of those with a frozen-pitch propeller, shot down two planes! But he almost paid for it with his life. After he landed his bullet-riddled plane back aboard, more than 50 holes were counted in just one wing. The whole plane looked like a sieve.

The bad weather caused the cancellation of any more strikes, and the task force withdrew and headed south.

***

The loss of Norm Sandler hit me very hard. Not only was he the section leader in my division, he was my very close friend. I had known him since flight training at Pensacola in 1941, and we were together on the *Essex*—training together afterward at Astoria and San Diego. There, he and his wife, Jerry, and Louise and I had spent a lot of evenings and weekends together. On this cruise, Norm and I had shared a stateroom.

Back in our stateroom—mine alone now—I couldn't help thinking of Jerry while I went through the unpleasant task of inventorying and packing Norm's personal belongings. At that moment she was probably doing mundane things, with no idea that her husband was gone. I felt sorry for Louise, too. She would inevitably help to console Jerry, and would raise her own fears about my well-being. I hated the hurt that this would cause Louise and felt that, somehow, because of the nature of what I was doing, I was partly to blame.

It is very hard to lose a close friend like that. But in order to keep going your mind somehow blocks out the grief and nearly everything else about him, almost as if he had never existed. It sounds like a cruel thing to do, but it is necessary to survive in combat—to keep your mind in sharp focus—when so many of your close friends do not come back.

Chapter 26

We returned to the anchorage at Ulithi for some rest and refit time before our next operation. We got ashore several times to have big parties at the little officers club on Mog Mog Island. We played softball and such, but mostly we drank a lot of warm Acme beer. I will never forget that name. In honor of where we were—and because we were sailors—we called it "Grog Grog." One day, after quite a few beers, the junior officers decided that it would be the greatest idea in the world to toss the senior officers into the lagoon. What fun! And so they did. Even Charlie Crommelin got a good dunking. It was a great break in the action and helped to relieve a lot of tension.

On March 9 and 10 we went back out to sea for some simulated combat operations, making attacks on a sled towed behind the carrier. The sled simulated a surface vessel. Although it was relatively small, it was designed to kick up quite a wake, which made it more visible from the air. And because it was moving at the same speed as the carrier, we had to adjust our aim point—putting in some lead—just as we would for a real warship. We got quite a bit of practice with this sled with strafing, firing rockets, and bombing.

Even this practice proved costly, though. One of the TBMs crashed into the water near the sled and the crew was lost. The pilot had probably fixated on the sled during his bombing run and pulled out of his dive too late.

On the evening of March 11, 1945, I was sitting in the squadron office tending to some paperwork when a tremendous explosion rocked me out of my chair. Dazed, I hesitated a moment as I collected my wits, then picked myself up and threw open the hatch to the gangway that ran along the side of the ship just below the flight deck. Rushing outside, I pulled myself up a ladder and saw a tremendous conflagration on the aft portion of the flight deck. I scrambled back down to the gangway and ran down to the hangar deck to find out what had happened and to see what I could do to help.

Jay Finley, McWhorter and Stoney Carlson were the remaining members of McWhorter's four-plane division after Norm Sandler was killed on February 25, 1945. Here they are at Mog Mog Island in March. (McWhorter Family)

Mog-Mog Island, part of Ulithi Atoll, included sports and beach and other facilities to meet the rest and recreation needs of many thousands of sailors, to include these VF-12 pilots. Drinking beer was popular. Note the beer cans are camouflaged olive green. (McWhorter Family)

Kamikaze damage to the *Randolph* (CV-15) cause by single Yokusuka P1Y1 medium bomber, codenamed "Frances." (U.S. Navy)

The aft end of the hangar deck was absolute mayhem. Flaming pieces of the kamikaze that had hit us were strewn all over. Worse, its bomb had also exploded, and bits and pieces of bodies were spattered everywhere. Sailors were running all over the place, some in panic, others in a hurry to get to their damage-control stations. The noise from the screams and shouts and the explosions from the ammunition stored in the area was deafening.

The best thing I could do was get out of the way. I worked clear of the smoke and heat and carnage until I got as far forward on the forecastle as I could. I stayed there until Charlie Crommelin passed the word for all pilots to report to the wardroom for a head count. Fortunately, we had lost no pilots.

The damage-control parties did a marvelous job. Within minutes, the initial panic had subsided and the sailors turned to the task of saving the ship. In only an hour, the fires were contained and the ship was no longer in any mortal danger.

The kamikaze that had hit us was an Imperial Navy Yokosuka P1Y1 twin-engine light bomber, codenamed "Frances." It had carried a single 1,750-pound

The repair ship *Jason* pulls alongside *Randolph* to begin making repairs to the kamikaze damage. (U.S. Navy)

bomb. With a flight of 19 others, it had left Kanoya, Japan, earlier that day with the ships at Ulithi as its primary target. During the 1,300-mile, 10-hour flight, half the would-be kamikazes got lost in poor weather and darkness, 4 crash-landed on Yap, and only 2 actually made it to Ulithi. The airplane that crashed into us hit near the stern on the starboard side of the ship, at hangar-deck level. It exploded as it traveled through the hangar deck, blowing a 40-foot-by-40-foot hole in the starboard side that went up through the flight deck. Thirty-five of the *Randolph's* sailors were killed and more than 100 were wounded. The remains of three Japanese airmen were found in the wreckage.

In a strange way, we were largely saved by the movies. Whenever the ship was at anchor, movies were shown forward on the hangar deck, but because the ship's crew was so large—more than 2,600 of us—there had to be two showings. When the kamikaze hit, just after eight o'clock, the first showing had just ended, and the audience was trying to exit through the crowd of sailors who were waiting at the rear to get seats for the second showing. Had

A Yokusuka P1Y1 medium bomber, codenamed "Frances." (USAAF)

the kamikaze struck at any other time, many more men would have been in the aft section of the ship, and our losses would have been much higher.

The other kamikaze that reached Ulithi mistook a small island for a ship and crashed into a lighted baseball diamond. It injured no one, but the wreckage made covering second base a bit dicey.

The repair ship *Jason* pulled alongside the morning after and commenced repair work. On March 15, we catapulted 25 airplanes off, along with a contingent of bombers, and flew to the nearby Marine airstrip—codenamed "Topaz Base"—on Falalop, one of the islands that made up Ulithi Atoll. In keeping with our tendency to rename things at Ulithi, Falalop Island inevitably became "Flop Flop." The new name seemed to work better with Mog Mog Island and Grog-Grog beer.

We flew daily combat air patrols over the anchorage and drank a lot of warm beer, something that wasn't readily available—or permitted—onboard ship. The Marines had a small officers' club—a well-appointed shack, really—that attracted every sort of vagabond in that part of the Pacific. There was always a crowd and the evenings could get quite raucous.

While we were waiting for the *Randolph* to be repaired, we flew strikes against the Japanese garrison at Yap which wasn't much more than a rock about

McWhorter, in Rayban sunglasses, enjoys time at Mog Mog Island with VF-12 squadron mates. (McWhorter Family)

four miles wide and seven miles long, with an airstrip and lots of antiaircraft guns. The higher-ups wanted to make certain that we didn't lose our keen edge as well as ensure that we kept our heads in the game. Yap lay only about 90 miles west of Ulithi. It was one of the many enemy-held islands that was bypassed, and we were pounding it into nothingness. That this Japanese base was allowed to exist so close to the powerful fleet anchorage at Ulithi was an indicator of how impotent the Navy had rendered its garrison. Nevertheless, since kamikazes might still be staged through Yap, we mounted several preemptive strikes against it, just to make sure that it remained unusable.

But if Yap's offensive punch—its airplanes—had been destroyed, it still possessed a potent defensive sting. It was common for strikes to the island to come back with airplanes missing—victims of antiaircraft fire. We were briefed accordingly.

I was airborne as part of a strike force against Yap on March 21, 1945. As we approached the island, I couldn't make out anything that warranted our

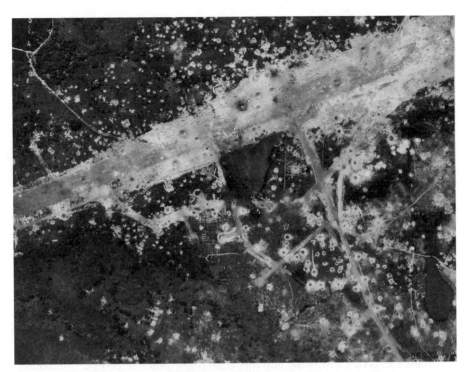

The Japanese airfield at Yap Island where McWhorter was nearly shot down was already in ruins even before VF-12's attack on March 21, 1945. (USAAF)

attention. The airfield appeared to be in ruins—hangars and other buildings were bombed-out hulks—and the rest of the installations were a shambles as well. As we came in range the enemy gunners started putting out antiaircraft fire. From my position ahead of the bombers, I pushed over into a dive to strafe one of the antiaircraft positions.

Through my gunsight, I saw dirt and other debris kicked into the air by my machinegun rounds. The Japanese gunners had disappeared, gone to ground in an effort to escape the hail of thumb-sized bullets I was spraying down on them. As I pulled out of my dive at about 50 feet, I heard and felt a thump, and a sudden flash on my right wing caught my attention.

Not all the enemy gunners had gone to ground! About four feet from the cockpit, my right wing was engulfed in flames that reached all the way back past my tail. Thinking that the wing was about to depart the rest of the airplane, I felt I had to get out. My body reacted faster than my mind, and before I had time to think about it, my hands had thrown back the canopy and released my shoulder and lap harness.

As I stood up to bail out over the island I was surprised at the force of the slipstream, which pushed me back into the cockpit. At that moment, common sense began to prevail over panic. First of all, I noted that my airplane was still flying and gaining altitude. Second, although the midsection of the wing was still on fire, the portion of the wing that joined the fuselage was still sound. If I bailed out over the island, I was certain to be captured by a very angry and cruel enemy whom I had just finished strafing. My chances of survival would be slim-to-none.

I settled back into the seat and continued to climb my airplane out over the water. In a minute or so—it seemed like forever—the fire burned itself out. Soon after that I was joined by my wingman, Jay Finley. He looked my plane over and reported that he saw no damage other than a hole burned through the top of my right wing.

I stayed with the strike formation for the rest of the trip back to Falalop, but off to the side with Finley. I was still flying unstrapped and with the canopy open. If the wing fell off, I wanted to be sure that I wouldn't run into any other planes and that I'd be able to make a quick exit. I got a call from Mike Michaelis, who suggested that I join up, but I told him what my problem was and opted to stay put.

Thanks to Mr. Grumman and his trademark practice of overengineering everything he built, the wing stayed attached. When I got back, we discovered that an enemy round had penetrated the gun boxes and ammunition trays. It had also ruptured the gun-charging lines, igniting the flammable hydraulic fluid. The burning hydraulic fluid had in turn cooked off the ammunition in the gun trays. Fortunately, most of the fire had burned aft of the load-bearing main spar.

Ensign Delbert "Snuffy" Martin, who had scored the squadron's first aerial victory during the first strike at Tokyo, had not been so lucky. He was seen to crash straight into the ground, probably killed in flight by antiaircraft fire.

Privately, I questioned the wisdom of these strikes on an island that posed so little danger to our fleet. We had paid for this one with Snuffy Martin's life—and nearly my own. It didn't seem like a fair trade.

We returned to the ship on March 22, and VBF-12 replaced us at Falalop.

***

The crew of the *Jason* made remarkable progress in repairing the ship. We put to sea on April 1 for a brief shakedown cruise and returned on April 3. The next day, six replacement pilots reported aboard. One of them, Ensign Bill Townsend, joined my division as wingman for Stoney Carlson, who replaced Norm Sandler as my section leader.

Chapter 27

If Japan couldn't be made to surrender, it would have to be invaded. But an invasion of the home islands would require a maritime logistical effort of a magnitude never before attempted—an effort that would dwarf the landings at Normandy in June 1944. To support such an undertaking, the Navy needed a base to stage from. Ulithi, the closest anchorage, lay almost 1,600 miles south of Kyushu, the southernmost of the Japanese main islands—too far for effective sustainable operations.

The island of Okinawa, however, fit the bill perfectly for the required bases. Largest of the Ryukyu Island group, Okinawa is centrally located about 340 miles south of Kyushu, 360 miles southeast of the Chinese mainland, and 360 miles northeast of Formosa (present-day Taiwan). Some 55 miles long and from 2 to 7 miles wide, Okinawa—like its surrounding islands—is volcanic in origin and surrounded by coral reefs. In 1945 Okinawa's population stood just short of 1,000,000, making the island one of the most densely populated places on earth.

The Okinawan people themselves were a mixture of Malayan, Chinese, and ancient Japanese who practiced their own animistic religion. Administered by a single, native dynasty from 1187 until they were invaded and subjugated by the Japanese in 1875, the Okinawans were gentle people who had no history of warfare or arms. Mostly they were peasant farmers who worked small fields they had carved out of the hilly countryside.

Traditionally the Okinawans had served as intermediaries for affairs between Japan and China although they had stronger ties with China. Regardless, they paid tribute to both nations. Seen as a mongrel, inferior, and lazy race by the Japanese, the Okinawans were disdained and treated poorly. Unfortunately for them, they would suffer more casualties in the upcoming campaign than either of the combatants.

On April 1, 1945, after months of preparatory bombings and naval shelling, our forces launched their invasion of Okinawa from a fleet of more than 1,300 ships. Our forces were puzzled at the initial resistance to the landings, which was uncharacteristically weak. Unknown to us the Japanese had retreated to highly defensible positions inland. Nevertheless, the Japanese reaction from the air was immediate.

If the island's proximity to China, Formosa, and Japan made it attractive as a staging point for our follow-on operations, it also worked to our disadvantage. Scores of Japanese airfields were within kamikaze range of Okinawa, and heavy attacks on our warships and support shipping began even before the landings.

After our brief trial run following the repairs from the kamikaze attack of March 11, the *Randolph* sortied from Ulithi for Okinawa on April 5, 1945. It was during this time that those of us in Air Group 12 lost our commander, Charlie Crommelin. While the *Randolph* was laid up by the kamikaze, Charlie had thrashed about, looking for a way to get into the action; he couldn't stand to be idle. He pulled some strings and hired himself out to the task group commander as an air strike coordinator aboard the fleet carrier *Hornet* (CV-12). As such, he was responsible for directing aircraft onto ground targets on Okinawa prior to the landings. During one of these missions, on March 28, he and a young ensign in an F6F-5P collided head-on. They were both killed. When we heard the news we almost didn't believe it. Of all people, this aggressively talented leader of ours was among the very last we expected to lose.

Commander Ralph Embree, the VB-12 commanding officer, replaced him. I had known Embree from our days aboard the *Ranger* at Casablanca, when he was in VB-41 and had scored a hit on the battleship *Jean Bart* with a 1,000-pound bomb. Embree did not have Charlie Crommelin's charisma, but he was a good, steady man and was well-liked by all. His wife and Louise were good friends as well.

We began operations immediately upon our arrival in the waters southeast of Okinawa on April 8. The *Randolph* was assigned to Task Group 58.2 along with the *Enterprise* (CV-6) and the *Independence* (CVL-22). Three other task groups—58.1, 58.3, and 58.4—rounded out Task Force 58. In total, the fast carrier task force consisted of 11 fast fleet carriers, 6 light carriers, and more than 80 battleships, cruisers, and destroyers.

***

My first sortie of the campaign was a target combat air patrol (TARCAP) over the Amami Gunto area, about 75 miles north of Okinawa. The Japanese were marshaling airplanes through Wan Airdrome on Kikai Shima prior to launching them on attacks against our warships. We were sent to keep that from happening.

VF-12 Hellcats launching from the deck of the *Randolph*, likely off the coast of Okinawa. The linear object is a barrel from one of the ship's five-inch gun turrets. (U.S. Navy)

After about two hours of seeing nothing, it was time to return to the *Randolph*. Prior to the flight, I had briefed the flight that we would strafe the airfield after our patrol period was over—give the Japanese a little "howdy" from VF-12. The area was cloudy, with an overcast cloud base at about 10,000 feet and some lower scattered clouds—perfect for strafing attacks. In our preflight brief I explained how we would execute our attacks from the overcast. As Mike Hadden had us do at Kwajalein during my first Pacific combat tour, we would climb into the base of the clouds, then after a certain amount of time we would push over into our dives. This would minimize the time we would be exposed to the antiaircraft gunners.

Pointed on the appropriate course, I led the flight up into the clouds, held us on heading for a certain amount of time, then made the call, "Pushing over."

I pushed forward on the control stick and quickly popped out of the clouds with the airfield almost directly in front of and below me, less than two miles away. Already, smudgy gray puffs of antiaircraft fire were bursting below me. The orange flashes of the detonating rounds contrasted surrealistically with the gloomy daylight below the clouds. The same was true of the bright, arcing tracers of the rapid-fire 20-millimeter guns.

From a 60-degree dive, I plunged through the enemy fire, picked out a particularly large gun emplacement, and sprayed it thoroughly with machine-gun fire. The armor-piercing incendiaries, or API rounds, sparkled brightly as they hit the metal surfaces of the gun, while those rounds that didn't strike the gun itself plowed up the surrounding dirt and sand into a dusty cloud.

I pulled out of my dive at about 50 feet and flashed by the gun emplacement, just off my left wing. It was the biggest gun I had ever seen and had a barrel about 20 feet long. I later learned that it was a Type 88 antiaircraft gun, which fired 88mm rounds. Looking over at it, I could see several Japanese huddled behind its armored shield. Some of them looked at me, but most were looking up behind me for the airplanes that were sure to follow.

As I climbed, I glanced back over my shoulder to look for the rest of my division. And I looked and looked. I finally realized that I had just made a solo strafing run!

Mad as could be, I raised hell with the rest of my flight over the radio while I finished climbing back up and corralling them. They had essentially refused a lawful order—had refused combat! Not only that, they had left me on my own. Right then and there I threatened them with bodily harm if they ever did the same thing again. I could understand Bill Townsend's reluctance, since this was his first combat flight, but the others had no such excuse.

I finally got them all joined up and again we climbed into the clouds. This time when I called "Pushing over," they all followed me down. We made two or three more strafing runs. On the last run, I felt a solid thump as I pulled out, and my airplane pitched a bit, as if nudged by a giant hand. I knew that I had been hit.

My airplane was still flying reasonably well, so I headed for the rendezvous point and called for the rest of the flight to join me. Instead of three other planes, though, only two showed up. My wingman, Jay Finley, was missing.

No one had seen what happened to him, and I feared the worst. During earlier strikes, Jay had a bad habit of following me too closely during strafing runs, and I had schooled him more than once against doing so. Not only might he accidentally shoot me down, it was actually more dangerous for him. Antiaircraft gunners generally miss *behind* a target. If they fired at me and missed, they could quite possibly hit Jay. I feared that this might have happened to him.

We flew around the airfield looking for him until low fuel reserves forced us back to the *Randolph*. Back on board we found a three-foot-diameter hole

McWhorter was shot up by ground fire at Amami, north of Okinawa on April 8, 1945. His wingman, Jay Finley, was shot down on this same mission and was recovered five days later. (U.S. Navy)

in my right elevator. Had the round hit a few inches further inboard it would have blown the tail off. Much too close!

I felt awful; first Norm Sandler was killed and now I had lost my wingman. Several other flights looked for Jay over the next few days, but nothing was found.

The loss of Jay Finley was a complicated and hurtful blow. It meant more than just losing a close friend. When he disappeared, I also lost a trusted wingman, a man who had flown with me since he was one of my fledgling students in Melbourne, Florida. I was his leader, but he was my protector. I could always count on him to be on my wing, protecting me from attacks from the rear. I would get a new wingman, but it would take time for him to get from me the same level of trust and confidence that Jay had earned.

***

We were fighting a completely different kind of war than on my previous combat cruise. Air Group 12 had been in combat barely two months; but we had been to Tokyo twice, supported the Iwo Jima invasion, flown strikes against Chi-chi Jima, Yap, and Okinawa, had our carrier almost blown up by a kamikaze, and had lost 4 pilots in only 13 days of combat. This differed so dramatically from the 10 months of my combat cruise in 1943–44. During that entire period, we were involved in just 8 separate actions and flew only 21 days of actual combat. Our losses to enemy action during the entire 10-month period were 5 pilots.

Many of our missions during this period were combat air patrols over the airfields on Kikai and Amami islands and over the task force. We also flew patrols over the radar picket destroyers which had the job of detecting enemy raids on their radar scopes and providing an early warning to the fleet. Typically, the pickets were stationed 40 to 100 miles from the task force in the direction from which most raids originated. The normal drill was for a flight of fighters to establish radio contact with the radar officer aboard a designated picket ship. Upon establishing contact, the flight orbited overhead until the radar officer sent it on a vector to intercept incoming bogeys. These picket destroyers took a real beating because they were the first ships that enemy raids encountered.

Occasionally we flew rescue combat air patrol missions, known as RCAPs. On these missions we orbited at a designated point between the ship and the target. The flight leader and the section leader each carried a life raft mounted on a bomb rack under his wing. If a plane had to ditch, the flight leader was vectored to the location. Upon establishing visual contact with the downed flier, he dropped the raft. Fortunately, my services were never needed during my few RCAP missions.

As at Iwo Jima, our most important missions were the close air support missions we flew for our ground troops. From the air the combat on the ground looked like a grinding, messy affair against a well-entrenched enemy in difficult-to-see, heavily fortified positions. As always, I thanked God that I was high above it all.

***

Flying day after day over the enormous numbers of warships and support vessels that made up the invasion fleet filled me with a certain sense of awe. I was fascinated not so much by how such an enormous force was commanded and controlled, but rather by how our nation was able to sustain it.

The size and herculean effort of the logistics fleet supporting the invasion far surpassed anything that had ever been created. Just the sheer variety of the ships servicing the fleet was amazing. There were several water tankers assigned to the forces ashore since they could not drink from the island's contaminated water sources. Four escort carriers served exclusively to ferry replacement aircraft and pilots into the battle. There were oilers, repair and salvage ships, refrigerator ships, hospital ships, dry-goods ships, and ammunition ships—among others.

Together they delivered an astounding diversity of material, ranging from fresh fruit to diesel fuel to airplane engines. That our nation had become the dominant combatant in the conflict was illustrated by the fact that we had the resources—and caprice—to deliver more than a million candy bars and almost three million packs of cigarettes to our forces at Okinawa, during just the first two-and-a-half months of operations.

As astounding as the volume and diversity of material and supplies were, the methods by which they were delivered were even more so. Ships got replenished almost exclusively at sea while under way, and it was an amazing sight to watch. We pulled alongside one of the many supply ships, and lines were fired out of special guns from the replenishment ship to ours in order to bring over heavy manila lines. The crew used slings to pass supplies and equipment—everything from chow to ammo, including airplane engines at 3,500 pounds apiece! Even personnel traveled back and forth on special slings called bosun chairs. Naturally, a resupply operation was a big event, and sailors crowded the gangways to see what goodies were being brought aboard. Mail, of course, was the big favorite.

After taking leave of the supply ships, the *Randolph* would then marry up with another ship for refueling. Again, lines were fired from ship to ship in order to snake across the appropriate fueling hoses. All types of fuel were supplied to the fleet, including fuel oil, diesel fuel, and aviation gasoline. By May 27, almost 22 million gallons of aviation gasoline alone was transferred to the carriers.

For all this effort, it seemed to me that the quality of the food delivered to the *Randolph* in this period was not up to the standard we had enjoyed during 1943–44 aboard the *Essex*. Rather than fresh, much of it was canned, processed, or otherwise prepared to endure a long shelf life. Perhaps because we were almost the only game in town during our time aboard the *Essex*, we had received preferential treatment. Or maybe I had just become jaded. But I can tell you with certainty that green eggs are not a product of someone's imagination. And to this day, I will not touch Spam.

***

We lost our president on April 13, 1945 (on our side of the International Date Line). I was sitting in the cockpit on the flight deck, getting ready for a strike, when an announcement came over the loudspeaker: "Attention, all hands. President Roosevelt has died. I say again, President Roosevelt has died. Our supreme commander is dead." Roosevelt was the only president I could really remember. While his loss was a bit unsettling, I was too busy with other things to think much about it. Looking at everything that was going on around me, it hardly seemed plausible that the loss of one man would change what was happening to me on that day or anytime soon.

But there was also good news on April 13. We learned that Jay Finley had been found and rescued! A Martin PBM Mariner flying boat had spotted a mirror flash and discovered Finley drifting in the ocean in his life raft. The big plane landed and picked him up. He was safe at the seaplane base on Kerama Retto, a group of outlying islands, and would be returned in a few days. On April 16, I got word that I was to escort a TBM Avenger to Yontan airfield on Okinawa the following morning to pick him up.

At dawn the next morning, I had just climbed up onto the flight deck to man my airplane when I heard the steady booming of 20-millimeter cannon fire coming from aft of the ship. I turned and was shocked to see huge glowing tracers arcing up from below flight-deck level, parallel to and just outboard of the port edge of the flight deck—and only about 40 feet from me. I immediately dropped to the deck, wishing I could somehow dig a hole. An instant later the Zero that was firing roared up from below the edge of the flight deck. Then it pulled up into a climb with its cannon still putting out rounds. When it reached an altitude about 50 feet above the ship, it pushed over and turned in, obviously intent on crashing into the flight deck.

Very fortunately, this kamikaze pilot was not well trained. Instead of crashing into the ship, he missed and plunged into the water just ahead of the bow. When he hit, his airplane and the bomb he was carrying exploded with a concussion that jolted the entire ship and sent a shock wave through my already shaking body. A few seconds later I hunkered down further as chunks of his airplane and shrapnel from the bomb rained down. No one had seen him coming and no one had fired a shot. Fortunately, there were no injuries.

After the commotion subsided, I was launched with my division and the TBM, and we flew the short distance to Yontan airfield. Yontan was taken from the Japanese on the first day of the invasion and was now being used by our forces. It was particularly valuable for our carrier-based airplanes as an emergency field, and as such had already saved us quite a few planes that were damaged or had experienced engine trouble and would not have made it back to the ship. Although the field had been under our control for two weeks, there was still fighting very close by, and when I shut down my engine I was surprised to hear the boom of artillery and rifle fire. Veteran that I was, it was the first time I had heard the sounds of a land battle.

While we were waiting for Jay, we wandered through some nearby caves that the Japanese had used as workshops. There was aircraft wreckage and 20-millimeter and 7.7-millimeter ammo strewn all around, but we found no worthwhile souvenirs to take back. What we did find, after we were back aboard the *Randolph*, was that we had brought back a lot of fleas. We were stripped and dusted with DDT by a very disdainful corpsman, and our clothes and flying gear were put into an autoclave to be sanitized. When I got mine back, much of it had shrunk to a size that was just about right for an eight-year-old junior birdman.

Jay finally arrived, tired-looking, sunburned, and a few pounds lighter but otherwise in great shape considering that he had been floating around in the Pacific for five days. Sure enough, just as I had feared, he told us that he was hit on the last strafing run. He was over the water at about 300 feet when the rear end of his airplane parted company with the front end. Amazingly, he pushed himself clear of the careening blue wreck and pulled the ripcord to his parachute. He was sure that his parachute wouldn't open in time and he braced himself for the impact with the water, which almost certainly would kill him.

Just before he smashed into the waves, there came a tremendous crack and a jolt as the canopy of his parachute snapped open, jerking him like a rag doll in his harness. Almost simultaneously, he hit the water hard, but not hard enough to injure him badly. Fortunately, his survival gear was undamaged. After he collected his wits and cleared his "bilges," he inflated his life raft. The raft was painted blue on the bottom for just this type of situation. He tipped it over and hid under it until the wind and tide carried him far enough from the island to be safe from capture. Whether the garrison on Kikai Shima didn't see him go down or was fearful of being strafed if they launched a boat to get him, he didn't know.

Jay said that he had watched as we flew overhead looking for him, and that no sooner had we departed for the ship than a flight of 15 Zeroes zoomed in low, almost directly over him, and landed on the island. They must have been monitoring us and had stayed out of harm's way until we were gone.

Jay floated in that tiny raft for the next five days—bruised, tired, thirsty, and hungry. A man has a lot of time for thinking in that sort of situation, and I'm sure he did his share. That he had survived up to that point was a miracle.

It seems incredible, with as much surface and aerial activity as there was in the area, that it took so long to find him. He had started to give up hope when finally, he was able to use his signal mirror to attract the attention of the PBM crew that rescued him.

The same afternoon that we picked Jay up, I was part of a target combat air patrol over Amami and Kikai. The TARCAPs over Kikai Shima were beefed up to 12 planes and Mike Michaelis, the squadron skipper, was leading the flight with his division. Hal Vita's division rounded out the flight along with mine. After treating Wan Airdrome to a dose of machinegun medicine, we were vectored onto a flight of about 15 bogeys approaching from the north. Mike quickly took in the situation and gave orders for his and Hal's division to attack. He directed me to take my flight up to 20,000 feet to provide high cover.

This was a sound tactical decision. There was a chance that the enemy airplanes we had spotted might be covered by a higher flight of fighters. Mike was putting me in position to protect against that.

The only problem was, the high flight of protecting fighters never materialized. And from where I was perched, all I could do was watch the now-raging dogfight. I felt like the family dog at Thanksgiving dinner, watching everyone eat while I sat and licked my chops. Enemy planes were falling in flames everywhere. I called over the radio several times that the sky above was clear and that my flight was ready to lend a hand. Each time, Mike told me to maintain my position.

In the end, the pilots in Mike and Hal's divisions shot down 14 enemy airplanes while my division safeguarded them from nonexistent enemy fighters. Mike and Hal got three apiece. I held a grudge for a while after that. I was mad as hell and I let Mike know it. After all, there were plenty of enemy airplanes to go around. But Mike's tactics were sound and I had little room to argue. Perhaps I should have been proud that my former student had performed so well.

***

Once back aboard the ship, Jay Finley took a day or two to recover from his ordeals, then declared that he was ready to fly combat again. We were scheduled for a ready CAP alert. For these alerts, which were designed as quick-reaction measures against inbound kamikazes, we each manned a fighter that had been warmed up and readied for launch and was harnessed to one of the two catapults on the bow.

After about a half-hour of just sitting there, a call came to "start 'em up." There was an inbound bogey. I started the engine on my airplane and looked over at Jay. He was going through the motions and finally got his airplane started and ready for launch. We sat there for a few moments checking our switches and gauges to be sure we were ready to go, monitoring the radio at the same time. The catapult officer signaled me to go to full power for launch, and I was just about to give him a salute indicating that I was ready to go when he suddenly waved his level palm across his throat, which meant "Cut 'em." The inbound bogey had turned out to be friendly.

Jay and I finished the three-hour alert period, then crawled out of the airplanes and made our way down to the wardroom. On the way down, I could sense he was agitated.

"How are you feeling, Jay?" I asked.

"Not so good, Mac. I was ready to go when the bogey was still unidentified, but I think that the call to cut our engines was a signal of some sort for me. I don't think I can do this anymore."

I waited a bit before I said anything. I didn't blame him at all. What he had gone through, floating alone in the Pacific for five days, was beyond traumatic; it was enough to challenge any man. Finley was only 19 or 20 years old and, like any young man that age, had a lot going on inside.

I told him so. "Jay, don't feel bad about it. I don't blame you, and there's no one on the ship who will blame you for the way you feel. You need a rest. Maybe you'll feel different afterward. Maybe you won't, but you've at least earned some time off."

I sent him to the flight surgeon. He agreed that Jay was not ready to fly yet. Jay was transferred to another ship and was soon back in the States. Ensign Bill Wolfe became Stoney Carlson's new wingman, and Bill Townsend replaced Jay as mine.

Chapter 28

The Japanese launched their first missions using the manned flying bomb, the Ohka, on March 21, 1945. From that date—with their focus on the fleet assembled at Okinawa—they tried to shape the war to their favor with this strange, desperate weapon. The Ohka was essentially a 2,600-pound bomb mounted into the nose of a cigar-shaped fuselage with stubby wings and three small rocket motors fixed into the tail. Capable of speeds of more than 500 miles per hour, the bomb was small, only 20 feet long with a wingspan of just over 16 feet. What made it unique was its guidance system: a live pilot. The concept was fantastically morbid to us, and we quickly dubbed the weapon *baka*, which was Japanese for foolish or crazy.

Unable to take off on its own, and obviously not designed with the capability to land, the Ohka had to be slung underneath a mother plane, usually a Betty bomber. The mother plane then carried the flying bomb to within range of our fleet—about 15 miles—before releasing it. Upon release, the Ohka pilot had to fire the rockets, which weren't very reliable, spot a target and fly through our antiaircraft fire and into a ship.

While plausible—although grotesque—in concept, the actual deployment posed formidable problems. First, the weight and drag of the Ohka drastically limited the speed of the mother planes, making them more vulnerable than ever to interception by our fighters. Protection of the mother planes with fighter escorts sounded feasible, but the Japanese fighter pilots of the day generally lacked expertise. Combine that with their inferior equipment and it all but negated their effectiveness. In most cases, enemy escorts proved nothing more than a distraction to our hordes of well-trained, well-equipped, and aggressive fighter pilots.

Another problem the Japanese faced stemmed from the characteristics of the flying bomb itself. Its construction was rudimentary at best, and reliability suffered because of it. The pilots had very little training with it, and because of the nature of the mission there was no way to bring back any lessons from its employment in combat. In other words, once the *baka* bomb was released from its mother ship, the pilot was going to die one way or another. And dead men tell no tales.

Moreover, the pilots, if they were actually launched within range of our ships, had to find a target and then fly the aircraft into it. No one alive knows for sure, but it couldn't have been easy. Finally, to be effective against a fleet our size, the flying bombs needed to be deployed in huge numbers, and the Japanese simply didn't possess enough mother planes—or enough Ohkas themselves.

Of the many attempts made against our fleet, at best only a few dozen of these flying suicide bombs were ever carried close enough to be launched. Typically, the mother planes—with or without fighter escort—were set upon by our fighters and sent down in flames long before they could get close enough to launch their payloads. And of those few Ohkas that actually made their way through our antiaircraft fire and managed to strike a ship, none was given sole credit for destroying even a single surface combatant.

Considering how few of these manned bombs were actually launched, it is probably unusual that I personally witnessed two Ohka attacks on two separate days. I was on a radar picket combat air patrol on the afternoon of April 12, when my attention was caught by a small, dark shape streaking downward at very high speed. Off to my left side and below me, this thing was making a

The purpose-built Ohka (Cherry Blossom) suicide aircraft was a flawed concept and an operational failure. McWhorter encountered these piloted, rocket-powered bombs during the battle of Okinawa. (Wikimedia Commons)

line straight for a destroyer on the picket line. We had already been briefed on the existence of Ohkas, and because of its odd shape and the high speed at which it was moving, I instantly knew what it was.

The Japanese pilot must have known what he was doing, because only a few seconds later he crashed himself and the bomb directly into the bow of the destroyer. The entire ship seemed to be engulfed in the huge explosion, which sent a plume of fire, smoke, and spray hundreds of feet into the sky. Shock waves rippled out from the stricken ship, sending more rings of spray into the air. I felt certain that the ship and her crew were finished.

But we Americans build a sturdy boat. When the smoke cleared, the ship was still floating, though her bow looked to be almost completely blown off. Almost immediately, my division was given a vector, and we left the ship behind in a vain search for bombers that might be carrying other Ohkas.

I didn't expect the ship to stay afloat. I later learned that the ship was the destroyer *Stanly*, and not only did she stay afloat but she never stopped making way. In fact, she took several more kamikaze hits that day and suffered only three men wounded.

A couple of weeks later I was again on station above a radar picket destroyer when, in almost an exact repeat of what had happened to the *Stanly*, another *baka* attacked a destroyer. This bomb either missed the ship or smashed clear through it without exploding, because it didn't detonate until it struck the water on the other side.

***

Manned flying bombs aside, the Japanese were contesting Okinawa with as many aircraft as they could muster. In fact, during the entire campaign, they expended more than 2,000 kamikaze sorties alone. Thousands more sorties were flown in more conventional attacks against our fleet, and quite often our combat air patrols were overwhelmed by the sheer number of enemy aircraft that suddenly appeared, mostly from airfields in southern Japan. But by this point in the war, fortunately, most of the enemy pilots were so poorly trained that only rarely were they able to shoot down an American pilot. More often than not, the Japanese tried to escape rather than engage in aerial combat.

Aside from having little training, the enemy—particularly the kamikaze corps—was reduced to using obsolete equipment. Because their factories just couldn't produce the numbers of airplanes they needed, the Japanese were forced to throw into the air whatever they could collect from their far-flung airfields. Indeed, it was not uncommon for our pilots to encounter older types of aircraft with fixed, nonretractable, landing gear—something we never saw during our combat tour in 1943–44.

All this translated into an incredibly lopsided tally of aerial combat in favor of our forces. Many pilots scored in the double digits, and there were quite a few ace-in-a-day pilots. In short, enemy airplanes were everywhere, and they were easy to shoot down.

I just couldn't seem to find them. Except for the big fight on April 17—the one in which Mike Michaelis wouldn't let me play—I hadn't seen an enemy airplane in the sky for weeks. If there was big action over the fleet, it was the same day that I was moving mud with bombs on Okinawa. If enemy aircraft managed to make it to the island some other day, then I was probably in some quiet sector over the fleet. I didn't know what the problem was. Perhaps it had something to do with which side of the bunk I crawled out on, or the way I held my tongue when I flew, or maybe I was unwittingly paying my dues for having seen so much aerial combat early on in the war. At any rate, it was frustrating. If there were enemy airplanes around, it was almost a certainty that I was nowhere nearby.

As we continued to grind out sorties, Okinawa quickly became a gruesome consumer of our men and equipment. On April 14, Ensign Eddie Jindra went over the side as he attempted to take off during an enemy attack. Luckily, he survived the plunge and was later rescued by a destroyer that had returned to look for him after the attack. Not so lucky was Ensign Bill Mason, who was killed in a landing accident on April 17. As the action intensified over the next several weeks and we all became worn out, these types of operational accidents became nearly as deadly a hazard as the Japanese.

And the pilots weren't the only ones at risk. Even without kamikaze attacks, the deck of an aircraft carrier was one of the most hostile workplaces in the world, keeping our deck crews and mechanics always at tremendous risk. One accident I remember involved a sailor who accidentally drove an aircraft tug off the edge. He was never found. There was another incident when a plane captain servicing a torpedo bomber walked into a spinning propeller—a gruesome accident that every one of us had imagined but hoped never to see.

The heavy, dangerous workload and the threat of kamikaze attacks began to wear on everyone, and our cramped wardroom arrangement didn't help the matter. The situation was ripe for an incident, and what happened—in retrospect—is quite humorous. At the time, however, it was rather hair-raising.

As a result of the kamikaze attacks at Iwo Jima, we had moved our squadron ready rooms down to the officers' wardroom, which was just below the armored hangar deck. But since the wardroom wasn't designed for such

The tempo of operations during the fight for Okinawa was exhausting and mistakes were common. Ensign William Mason was killed when his aircraft went off the deck in a landing accident on May 17, 1945. (U.S. Navy)

use, there was nowhere to hang our flight gear; we just piled it on the deck along the bulkheads. Our flight gear included Smith & Wesson .38 Special revolvers that we carried in shoulder holsters when we flew. Loaded with tracer ammunition, they were to be used primarily as signal guns during rescue, rather than for self-protection.

Anyway, one day in late April, two of the wardroom stewards got into a rather heated argument. One of them reached down into a pile of flight gear, grabbed one of the .38 pistols, and went after the other. The steward who was the intended target recognized what was about to happen and desperately scrambled toward the hatch, intent on a record-breaking exit.

Six incredibly loud shots rang out, and .38-caliber tracers began ricocheting around the wardroom. The pilots in the room immediately made a mass dive under the tables and did not emerge until the shooting had stopped. Fortunately, the mess attendant was a lousy shot and no one was hurt. It was bad enough to go out and get shot at by the Japanese, but to be shot at in your own wardroom was beyond too much!

***

During one of our standard target combat air patrols over Amami on April 18, we found nothing at the airfield except the usual antiaircraft gun sites. Thinking that we might try something new, I decided to patrol the coastline to see if we could find any of the small suicide boats that our intelligence people told us might be hiding in the coves and inlets.

We were flying at about 1,000 feet, just offshore and about a mile from the airfield, when I spotted a propeller protruding out of the thick vegetation. I wheeled my division back around and, sure enough, there was a very well hidden Zero, all covered with tree branches except for part of its propeller. I set myself up for a gunnery run and strafed it, but it did not burn. It probably had no fuel. Nevertheless, I don't think that it did any flying after that.

Excited by our find, we snooped around some more and found about a dozen other Zeroes, similarly hidden. We all strafed them a couple of times over, but again none of them burned even though we filled them with bullets. I'm certain that few, if any, of them, ever flew again, and I'm also certain that we saved the fleet from a dozen or so kamikazes.

***

On April 19 we were airborne, loaded for ground support, when we were called up by the airborne strike coordinator and told to report to the forward air controller (FAC) on the ground. The troops were using large colored panels and red smoke to define the front lines for us. Once we established contact with the FAC, he gave us coordinates for our target which was a series of caves on a ridge that ran down the center of the island. The Japanese had apparently been rolling their artillery pieces out of the caves—just barely into the open—firing them, and then rapidly pushing them back into the caves.

We had to take time to visually identify the targets, because by now the Japanese had caught on to our trick of marking targets with white phosphorous artillery rounds or mortar shells. As soon as they saw a white phosphorous round on the ground, they fired their own white phosphorous rounds back behind our lines to confuse us. It worked pretty well.

On this mission, we each carried six high-velocity aerial rockets and a load of napalm. Once in the area, I double-checked the coordinates with the caves I could see on the ridge. I told my division that we would drop the napalm first, then come back around to deliver the rockets. I selected a large, easily discernible cave and told the others to each choose one of several caves to the right of it.

I went to full power and rolled in from 6,000 feet. I knew that every Japanese soldier in sight would take potshots at us as we flew over their lines at low altitude, and I wanted to be going as fast as possible. The initial part of my dive was at about a 45-degree angle. At about 2,000 feet I started strafing just before I pulled back on the stick to reduce my dive angle to about 20 degrees. With my gunsight pipper over the mouth of the cave I released my drop tank from about 150 feet, then pulled up sharply to climb out of the range of small-arms fire. I looked back and saw that the napalm had hit just below the cave and had splashed up into the mouth, engulfing it in a huge fireball. I watched the other three planes in my division and was pleased to see that every cave they targeted received a good dose of napalm.

We came back around and made rocket attacks on other caves on the ridge, firing two rockets on each run from an altitude of about 3,000 feet. The rockets were our favorite air-to-ground weapons as they were very accurate. We put them right into the mouths of the caves.

After we had expended all of our ordnance, the FAC called and congratulated us on our nice hits, then released us to return to the ship. Surprisingly, considering how many enemy troops were on the ground, none of us was hit by ground fire. This mission, with variations such as bombs instead of rockets, was typical of the many, many ground-support missions we flew.

***

We had another bad accident aboard the *Randolph* on April 22. Ensign Lowell Rund experienced engine problems shortly after takeoff and had to

Lowell Rund landed with a belly tank and engine trouble. The tank detached and the fuel exploded. This is the aftermath. Rund survived with third-degree burns to his face. (U.S. Navy)

come back aboard. Unfortunately, he failed to jettison his full 150-gallon drop tank, and when his plane engaged the arresting wire, the tank broke loose and went through the propeller and immediately burst into flames. The fire crews quickly put out the fire and pulled Rund from the cockpit, but he was out of action for some time with third-degree burns on his face and arms.

The same thing happened on April 24, when one of our ensigns had an emergency shortly after takeoff and had to land immediately. He was directed to land on the *Yorktown*, as she had an open deck. He made two serious mistakes: he not only forgot to jettison his full drop tank, but he also forgot to safe his guns. When he engaged the arresting wire on the *Yorktown*, his drop tank tore loose and burst into flames when it hit the whirling propeller. At the same time, the ensign squeezed the trigger and sprayed the deck with machinegun fire—injuring seven deck crewmen and punching holes in several airplanes. He was not badly injured himself, but neither was he a very welcome guest.

Chapter 29

The last year of the war saw the Navy's night-fighter concept reach operational maturity. Attached to VF-12 aboard the *Randolph* was a detachment of eight night-fighter pilots and six of the new F6F-5Ns—essentially standard F6F-5s with the addition of the APS-6 radar. The small radar—it weighed only about 250 pounds—was mounted on the starboard wing and was the distinctive external difference between the standard Hellcat and the night version. Though the pod looked a bit ungainly mounted out on the wing, it penalized performance by only about 10 knots or so.

Our night-fighter pilots were viewed as the "redheaded stepchildren" onboard the ship—as night-fighter pilots were aboard almost all aircraft carriers. They were on duty during the hours of darkness, when the bulk of the crew was at rest, and launching and recovering them often seemed more trouble than it was worth. (Balancing that, however, they were often called on to fly normal missions during the day, when there weren't enough regular airplanes or pilots to meet demand.)

They were skilled and invaluable airmen. They could do what none of the rest of us could—find enemy airplanes in the dark and kill them. When there were kamikazes about at night, the ship's crew somehow didn't seem to mind so much the inconvenience of launching and recovering our contingent of night fighters. Their training, 29 weeks beyond what the normal fighter pilot received, made them particularly valuable in experience alone, if nothing else.

When they talked night fighter tactics around the rest of us, it was almost a foreign language. We could only shut up or ask questions; we had little to contribute. The nature of their specialized flying made their job much more dangerous and demanding than normal flight operations.

Typically launched for a four-hour shift over the fleet, the night-fighters operated under the control of shipborne radar. When enemy aircraft came within range of the ship's radar, the F6F-5Ns were vectored into a position behind the contact and within range of the APS-6 radar—about five miles. Once the night-fighter pilot established radar contact he drove into a position—usually inside a couple hundred feet—from which he could confirm that the bogey was an enemy airplane. Then, if he hadn't been seen, he dropped back into a firing position and shot the enemy airplane down in flames. If the enemy airplane maneuvered at all, intentionally or not, the process became more difficult by orders of magnitude. It required more than the ordinary dose of precision, nerves, and situational awareness.

Our detachment of night-fighters scored their first kill early in the morning on April 14, when Lieutenant Donald Hypes splashed a snooping Paul—an Aichi E16A1 long-range reconnaissance floatplane—just beyond the task group's screen of destroyers. The detachment continued to score, but like us they suffered losses. In fact, their loss rate was the highest in the air group—a reflection of the danger inherent in that type of flying.

***

Personnel replacements arrived for all of our losses. By now—despite the incredible numbers of aircraft carriers we had in the fleet and despite our losses—the Navy was actually producing more pilots than it could use. Where there were fewer than 3,000 pilots in the Navy when I joined in 1941, there were now 60,000! The war had become, for better or worse, more impersonal.

This impersonality extended even to the airplanes we flew. Painted a dark, glossy, navy blue with stark white insignia and identification codes, they seemed sullen and unromantic compared with the brighter, tricolor blue aircraft we had flown from the *Essex* during 1943 and 1944. What's more, it was forbidden in Air Group 12 to personalize our aircraft in any manner—including the painting of Japanese flags below the canopy rail when we scored aerial victories.

***

It was around May 10 that we learned of the surrender of Nazi Germany. I remember that I was in the wardroom briefing a mission when the word was passed. The war in Europe had been a world away from me. It was a war that other friends fought and died in. It hadn't been a less important war than mine, it was just a different war. I was happy it was over, of course—and even happier that we had won—but I wasn't sure what it would mean to the Navy's part in the war against Japan.

After all, it wouldn't free up many carriers for the fight in the Pacific. Most of the carriers the Navy had used in the war against Germany were the smaller escort types. Though they were useful, the little jeeps weren't nearly as capable as the big, fast fleet carriers.

I guessed that what the end of the war in Europe really meant to those of us still fighting in the Pacific was that the entirety of our nation's effort would now be focused on finishing the war against Japan. Although it would certainly be bloody—and perhaps a year or two in coming—the outcome could hardly be in doubt.

***

The tragedies never stopped at Okinawa. On May 12, Commander Ralph Embree, the still-new commander of Air Group 12, was killed. While flying an F6F and serving as a strike coordinator directing attacks against an enemy ground position, he made the mistake of flying a consistent, predictable, racetrack pattern. His plane was hit by a single burst of heavy antiaircraft fire and began to disintegrate immediately. Falling from 3,500 feet, his airplane shed its wings, and the remaining wreckage was engulfed in flame. At about 300 feet, a parachute was seen to blossom partially—but not fully—before it hit the ground. Accompanying airplanes searched the area, which unfortunately was well behind enemy lines. The parachute was spotted draped across a hilltop, but no sign of Ralph was found. He was never heard from again. It had been less than two months since he had taken over from Charlie Crommelin.

Again, I dreaded what Ralph's death would do to my Louise. She was very close to Ralph's wife, Eleanor.

Ed Pawka—who only five months before was just a squadron executive officer—became the new commander of Air Group 12.

Chapter 30

Through the first month of our operations at Okinawa, I still hadn't engaged any enemy airplanes in aerial combat. But my turn was coming. And it was about time. My friend Hal Vita—we had been together since our early days in VF-9—had shot down five enemy fighters since I had last scored on February 16.

During the night of May 12, we left the Okinawa area and headed north for a two-day attack against the airfields on Kyushu, the southernmost of the Japanese home islands. In the hopes of reducing the number of kamikazes getting through to the fleet at Okinawa, we aimed to destroy as many airplanes and airfield facilities as possible.

On May 13, for the first flight of the day, I was on combat air patrol near the task force and was vectored to intercept a high bogey. I turned to comply with the vector and really poured on the coals. It's a good thing I did, because when I looked behind me, I saw about a dozen other Hellcats struggling to catch up and shoot *my* bogey down before I could get there.

After about five minutes, as I led my division up through 20,000 feet, I spotted the bogey. It was a single engine Nakajima C6N reconnaissance airplane—codenamed "Myrt." It was up at about 25,000 feet, 3 miles in front of us, and traveling away. During a brief tail chase I was able to close to about 500 feet. From directly behind and slightly below, I put a burst into the enemy's rear fuselage and belly.

The Myrt immediately flamed, then exploded. I was so close behind it that engine oil from the burning airplane covered my canopy and windscreen. Two parachutes opened alongside the Myrt after it exploded, and a moment later—when I was sure there were no other Japanese airplanes nearby—I circled around to take a look at them. To my surprise, neither parachute had anyone in it. To add to the mystery, we hadn't seen anyone

McWhorter's final aerial victory of the war was a fast and high-flying Nakajima C6N reconnaissance aircraft, codenamed "Myrt." He downed it near Kyushu on May 13, 1945. (Wikimedia Commons)

fall from either the airplane or the parachutes. Instead, in the seat straps were boxes about the combined size and shape of our own seat cushions and the attached survival gear. But they were very heavy and solid. One of my ensigns found this out when he got too close to one of the parachutes and smashed into its box with the wing. Sometimes I felt like I was leading small children. It left a very deep dent in his wing's leading edge, all the way to the main spar.

After we got back to the ship and debriefed with intelligence, we learned very little more. To this day I can only guess that the boxes may have been some sort of beaconing devices.

This was one of the few aerial victories I scored that actually yielded decent gun-camera footage. After the film was developed, you could easily identify the aircraft type from the footage, and the flames coming out of the fuselage made it obvious that the airplane was mortally damaged. The quality of this footage was by far the exception. We had been carrying gun cameras and film ever since we started flying the Hellcat, but we typically had lousy luck with it. Mounted in the leading edge of the port wing, the lens typically got gummed up with oil, dirt, and salt spray, or rolled itself out of focus. On top of that, vibrations from the engine and the firing of the machineguns often rattled the camera so badly that it captured nothing at all discernible. Besides, with everything that was required to get the airplane ready for combat—regular maintenance, fueling, arming, and such—the care and feeding of the gun camera placed fairly low on the list of priorities. The results were consistently poor. Targeted airplanes usually showed up as shapeless gray blobs—consumed with a bright flash if they exploded.

***

I had just returned from a sweep against Omura airfield in northwestern Kyushu on May 14 when I got orders to get my division ready for another mission. Ensign John Morris and his gunner, ARM3 Phegley, had gotten their VB-12 SB2C dive bomber shot up on a strike against Usa Airdrome in northern Kyushu. They had ditched about five miles offshore in the Inland Sea and were in the water, awaiting rescue. My division was to escort two Kingfisher floatplanes from the cruiser *Astoria* for the pickup.

Soon after we were airborne we joined formation with the floatplanes. Initially I put the division in a normal escort position, about 1,000 feet above the Kingfishers, and set up a weaving pattern with our airspeed at about 250 knots. I wanted to keep our airspeed high enough so that we could engage enemy fighters if we were attacked. Otherwise, we were little better than the floatplanes we were assigned to protect. Traveling as they were at only about 80 to 85 knots, the Kingfishers were sitting ducks.

Unfortunately, the situation just didn't allow us to keep our airspeed up. The downed fliers were 180 miles away, and at the speed the rescue planes were traveling the mission would clearly last five or six hours. If we stayed at 250 knots, we would be out of gas before we got back to the *Randolph*. Reluctantly I pulled the power back until the engine was producing only 1,200 rpm. The F6F propeller had two-to-one reduction gearing, so it was turning at only 600 rpm—slow enough that I could see the individual blades as they passed in front of me.

Even then, we still were traveling at about 110 knots and had to continue our weave pattern in order to keep from outrunning the Kingfishers. With the hair on the back of my neck standing almost straight up—I was fearful of being caught by enemy fighters—I settled down for the long trip to the Inland Sea.

Sitting still in a small, cramped space for any length of time becomes uncomfortable for anyone. In the F6F it became uncomfortable very quickly and stayed that way. We sat on top of our survival pack, and right at the top of that pack was a can of water. It was positioned in just such a spot that it dug a divot smack in the middle of your right rear cheek. After several hours, it became so painful that it was actually a distraction. Pilots tried all sorts of tricks to relieve the pain—extra cushions, extra underwear, whatever. Nothing seemed to work very well. Always, beneath whatever extra padding you had between your buttocks and that seat, you could still feel the edge of that can; it was like the Navy version of the fable about "The Princess and the Pea." Today, more than a half-century later, I think I'm still walking around with a dimple in my backside.

After about two hours we reached the entrance of the strait leading to the Inland Sea, only to be greeted by flak popping nearby. Someone came up on the radio and asked if anyone could see where it was coming from. Someone else answered—in a squeaky voice—that he didn't care where the hell it was coming from. He just wanted to know where it was going!

About this time Lieutenant Lane Bardeen, whose division was providing cover for the downed SB2C crew, advised that he had to leave because of low fuel. Earlier, Bardeen and his wingmen had strafed and driven off two destroyers that had poked their noses too close to the downed fliers. I advised him that we were approaching the area, and soon after I spotted the bright yellow dye marker that the fliers were trailing from their raft.

As the Kingfishers dropped down to set up for their water landings, I detached my division and we increased speed and climbed to establish top cover. Though we were in the heart of the enemy's home, my anxiety decreased as my airspeed and altitude increased. From high above I watched the floatplanes touch down. The first Kingfisher water-taxied to the raft and picked up the first crewman with no difficulty.

Next, I watched the pilot of the second floatplane jockey into position; I was concerned because I could tell that his engine was idling very slowly. But I was absolutely astonished when I saw his propeller stop ticking altogether. He had cut his engine in the middle of Indian country! This seemed foolhardy to me in the extreme, particularly since the Japanese airbase at Usa was only 15 miles away.

After the floatplane fished the second flier out of the raft, I saw a puff of white smoke come out of the second floatplane's engine as the pilot fired his starter cartridge. These were gunpowder cartridges—similar to shotgun shells—that turned the engine over fast enough to let the ignition sequence take place. The engine didn't start. I watched anxiously as the pilot attempted another start. Another puff, and again the engine failed to start.

I turned and scanned the sky and sea for any sign of the enemy. The coast was clear. For the moment, I had even forgotten the pain from the water can that was biting into my fanny. The Kingfisher pilot tried again to start his engine. And again. Still no luck.

I rechecked my fuel gauges and wondered how many starter cartridges the Kingfisher had.

Finally, the engine caught. When that propeller started spinning, I think there was a big sigh of relief from every man in every plane. We learned later that the engine had started on the very last cartridge.

The return flight was still slow, but thankfully uneventful. After a total of five hours and 36 minutes we dropped the Kingfishers off at the *Astoria* and landed back aboard the *Randolph*. Our bomber crew was back with us by late that afternoon. This was the longest sortie I flew during the war.

Sadly, we lost another squadron mate this day, during a fighter sweep over Sodohara Airdrome on Kyushu. Ensign Robert Welty was hit, probably by ground fire. He failed to recover from a strafing run and crashed into the ground.

***

On May 18, we launched a long-range sweep against Tokuno Airdrome on Yaku Shima, just south of Kyushu and almost 250 miles from the task group. Armed with 5-inch HVARs, I rolled in from 10,000 feet and lined up on a pair of Zeroes parked in a double horseshoe-shaped revetment. The antiaircraft fire rising from the gun emplacements on the airfield was, as always, incredibly intense. It made my firing run seem particularly long.

Finally within range, I fired two rockets, one from each wing, and watched as they streaked downward. I started to become concerned when the rockets veered toward each other on a collision course and then crossed paths. I thought to myself there was no way they were going to be on target. Incredibly, they both hit home; the rocket from my left wing exploded into the Zero parked on the right side of the revetment, and my right rocket hit the Zero parked on the left.

As I pulled out of my dive, I couldn't help but feel a little pleased with myself. Ignoring the streams of enemy tracers that were reaching for my airplane, I lined up on a third Zero parked across the airfield and filled it full of machinegun fire. It didn't burn, despite the volume of fire I poured into it. I believe that it had no fuel onboard.

After we completed our strafing runs I gathered my division and turned toward the air group's rendezvous point. As we made our way through a corridor of towering cumulus clouds I spotted a Nakajima J1N twin engine reconnaissance aircraft—codenamed "Irving"—about half a mile away at my one o'clock position. It was coming toward us.

I turned into it, and it immediately banked away and started a shallow dive for the clouds. Even though I was at full power I was not gaining appreciably on the Irving. I considered jettisoning my centerline tank in order to gain some speed, but it still had fuel in it and we were well over 200 miles from the carrier. The idea of dumping fuel didn't really appeal. I started to go to war emergency power, but I remembered my experience at Barbers Point when my engine had quit and the plane had turned into a big blue glider. I decided I wasn't too keen on that option either. In the end, the Irving simply outpaced my F6F, and disappeared into the clouds before I could reach firing range. The rest of the flight proved uneventful.

Sadly, we lost a pilot at Tokuno. Ensign Charlie White crashed and was killed. Although the actual cause of the crash was not known, it is possible that he shot himself down. He was recovering from a strafing run when he fired one of his 5-inch HVARs from very low level—only about 100 feet above the ground. Fired from such a low altitude the rocket would have hit its target almost immediately, and Charlie's plane could well have been within lethal range of the exploding warhead.

**

It was on this day that the *Randolph* set a new record. While engaged in combat operations she launched a total of 199 airplanes. She recovered 197—two were lost. Such was the tempo of our operations during the Okinawa campaign.

**

As the war progressed, the operations of the big fleet carriers were augmented more and more by jeep carriers, CVEs. These were small ships converted from a freighter-type designs, generally about 500 feet in length. While they were useful, they could make only about 16 knots. This affected their ability to keep up with the faster fleet carriers, which could make 30-plus knots. It also limited when and how they could launch their airplanes.

The CVEs, with a much smaller deck, also presented challenges to their pilots, who flew FM Wildcats— an improved four-gun model of the venerable F4F built under license by General Motors—and TBMs. I remember getting airborne one day off the coast of Okinawa just before dawn. There was no wind and the Pacific was like a millpond—as still as I had ever seen it. Climbing to altitude, I was startled by a bright flash out on the horizon. I didn't learn until later that the explosion had occurred when a fully loaded TBM crashed after being launched, without enough wind over the deck, from one of the escort carriers.

Our losses continued to grow. We had already lost more than half the airplanes we started with, although with constant replacements being flown aboard from the escort carriers, we were never lacking for aircraft. In fact, since the time we had picked up the very first Hellcats for VF-9, just more than two years earlier, Grumman had produced more than 10,000 of the new fighters. And Grumman wasn't the only manufacturer churning out airplanes. The Navy, which had fewer than 2,500 aircraft when Pearl Harbor was attacked, had accepted nearly 60,000 new airplanes from a number of manufacturers. A telling example of America's industrial prowess at this point in the war involves Navy airplane losses at Okinawa. During the campaign, we lost approximately 550 airplanes of all types. Where it would have taken eight months to replace that many airplanes in 1941, by 1945 the country could do it in only 12 production days. We weren't just outfighting the Japanese, we were burying them with equipment.

***

Almost all of the missions we flew took us into antiaircraft fire, and while a flier could take certain measures to decrease his chances of being hit, it was a matter of luck whether his "number" came up. We started to joke grimly among ourselves about how we were playing a long, strung-out game of Russian roulette. Typically, we spent four or five days "on the line," flying combat air patrol or support missions, and then took a day off to refuel and resupply the ship. Even then, the pace of operations was such that we occasionally flew missions on our nominal day off.

As in previous battles, the Japanese launched night attacks. Calls to general quarters in the middle of the night became almost routine as flights of enemy airplanes—real or imagined—made their way toward our task group. There was no way to sleep during these raids, so we spent much of our time either in the wardroom beneath the armored hangar deck or up on the flight deck watching the fireworks. The greatest achievement of these enemy forays was probably that they deprived us of so much sleep. After a while, it became telling.

The horrors that could befall us were well understood—more than 700 men, including a large number of the pilots in Air Group 5, were killed when an enemy plane bombed the aircraft carrier *Franklin* on March 19. Ironically, 23 very fortunate—and thankful—pilots in VF-12 had transferred in from VF-5 shortly before we had left the States.

The *Franklin* incident showed that, aside from kamikazes, the Japanese were still able to score with conventional bombing attacks despite the woeful condition of their air forces. The threat of death or injury aboard our ship was very real, and the crew, quite naturally, responded in different ways. Some men adopted a cavalier, devil-may-care attitude. Others withdrew into themselves, speaking little or not at all. Some were openly fearful and made no pretense about putting themselves into the safest compartments of the ship.

Others took unusual precautions. I still remember Jim Whiting, a bomber pilot who was desperately fearful of being burned. He had gotten hold of a quantity of the heavy, white, zinc oxide anti-flash burn cream that the antiaircraft gunners put on their exposed skin. Whenever general quarters was sounded, Jim showed up in the wardroom all bundled up in his flight suit and flying gloves, his face covered with cream. We all huddled in the wardroom, and in the middle of the crowd, sitting nonchalantly, was Jim with his stark-white face. For some reason, the incongruity of it struck me as hilarious. He took a lot of good-natured ribbing from us because of that cream.

There were so many attacks during this time that it seemed as if general quarters was sounded whenever we turned around. Quite often, we just stayed at general quarters for hours at a time. We actually started to become conditioned to it—just like lab rats. It got to the point that as long as the *Randolph* was firing just her five-inch guns, we pretty much conducted business as usual, figuring that the bogey was still four or five miles away. When the 40-millimeter guns opened up, we became a bit more concerned, because that meant the bogey had closed to maybe just a couple of miles. If the 20-millimeter guns started firing there was a mad rush to get down to the wardroom, below the armored deck.

The stress started to manifest itself among all of us, including me. On May 28, 1945, our last full day at Okinawa, I returned from a mission just at dusk. Flying up the ship's wake, I arrived overhead, then turned hard into a left downwind to set up for landing. As I came around the corner in a left-hand turn, just prior to setting up in the groove—the final approach—I scanned over to where the LSO was perched on the port side of the stern. To my surprise, he had his paddles well above his head, the signal indicating that I was high.

Now, if I wasn't the most experienced pilot on that entire ship, I was certainly in the top four or five. And I knew that the LSO was wrong. I could fly the landing pattern in my sleep. For that matter, the Hellcat without a pilot could just about fly the pattern. So, I disregarded the signals the LSO was giving me and continued my approach. As I did, he kept waving his paddles above his head, trying to communicate to me that I was much too high. I knew I was right in the groove, so I ignored him.

I was also beginning to get a bit frustrated with this confused LSO, and I made a note to myself to debrief him after the flight. His was a role that was critical to safe and efficient operations. If he couldn't perform it properly, he had no business being at the back end of the ship.

It wasn't until I got over the ramp that I finally realized—in fact, was completely astounded by the realization—that I was 60 or more feet above the deck. I should have been at 20 feet. It dawned on me then that the LSO wasn't the player in this game who needed a little bit of counseling. As quick as I could, I poured on the power to execute the wave-off that he was frantically signaling me to take. There was no way I'd be able to safely salvage the approach. Once I was away from the deck of the ship, I flew the pattern by the numbers, just as if I was a brand-new ensign, and I finally got aboard.

I know that it was the stress of the months-long combat tour that had nearly killed me, and I mentally kicked myself. Losing my life in combat would have been tragic enough, but to die—and maybe kill others in the process—because I fouled up a routine landing would have put an ugly stain on what I hoped was an otherwise worthy career.

Chapter 31

At noon on May 29, we finally got the break we needed. The *Randolph* departed the waters off Okinawa with orders to transport Admiral Marc Mitscher and his staff to Guam. Admiral Mitscher had transferred his flag to the *Randolph* on May 14, after a kamikaze hit the *Enterprise*. Just a few days earlier Mitscher had had his flag aboard the *Bunker Hill*, and she also was hit. The admiral wasn't exactly a good-luck charm, and so we kept our fingers crossed, hoping that the kamikazes wouldn't follow him to the *Randolph*.

Since April 8, we had been in combat for 51 consecutive days. During that time, I logged more than 196 combat flight hours, an average of almost 4 hours per day! Many of my squadron mates had flown as much. We were all well overdue for a rest.

We did not return to Okinawa. We had flown through the fiercest of the fighting, but the island would not be declared secure until July 2, 1945, more than a month later. Ultimately, the Okinawa campaign was the costliest in the history of the United States Navy. Thirty-two ships were sunk—although none was larger than a destroyer—and another 368 ships and other craft were damaged. More than 4,900 sailors died, more than in any other battle of the war. In fact, the loss of lives suffered by the Navy at Okinawa exceeded the Navy's total losses from all previous wars combined.

I was relieved to have gotten out with my life, but saddened that so many others had not.

After dropping Admiral Mitscher and his staff at Apra Harbor, Guam, on May 31, we made ready to press on to the Philippines, where we were to get some much-needed R&R. But Apra Harbor is not large enough to easily maneuver a ship the size of the *Randolph*. On that occasion there were no tugboats available. We were more or less stuck in the harbor, pointed the wrong way.

A view from the *Randolph* as the aircraft carrier *Bunker Hill* (CV-17) burns in the distance after being hit by a pair of kamikaze aircraft off the coast of Okinawa on May 11, 1945. (U.S. Navy)

To get out of the harbor required a bit of ingenuity on the part of the *Randolph*'s skipper, Captain Felix Baker. He had the deck crews tie our aircraft securely to each side of the flight deck—fore and aft—with their tails pointing outward. The planes on the starboard side forward and the port side aft were directed to crank up to full power. The thrust they generated slowly rotated the ship, turning it 180 degrees. As the bow approached the proper direction to exit the harbor, the first group of planes powered back and the planes on the port side forward and starboard side aft turned up their engines, thus stopping the rotation. We dubbed the maneuver, "Operation *Pinwheel*."

The *Randolph* arrived at San Pedro Bay, Leyte, in the Philippines, on June 4. Even though there were boats going ashore, I think most of us stayed onboard for the next couple days in order to enjoy the respite from gunfire and calls to general quarters.

On June 7, a big party was scheduled for a day of liberty at the Seventh Fleet's recreational facilities on the island of Samar. Along with the bases at Guam,

Ulithi, and Manus, the port complexes in and around Leyte were developing into some of the Navy's biggest anchorages in the Pacific. At midmorning a big landing craft dumped several hundred of us on the beach where we found the usual entertainment—softball diamonds, volleyball nets, and horseshoe pits. Also, an area of the beach was cordoned off for swimming. There was plenty of food—hot dogs and hamburgers being the main attractions. It was the standard formula for entertaining young military men who were far from home, and it never really changed during the nearly three decades that I spent in the service.

Of course, there was plenty of warm Acme beer. No base in the Pacific was without it.

We spent the next few hours amusing ourselves with various sports—playing hard, as young men do when they still believe they can make it in the Big Leagues. Between games, during which we endeavored to prove that we really *were* the best athletes in the world, we ate too much food and drank too much beer. Old sea stories were told and retold, embellished at each new telling, and everyone shared their plans for "after the war."

But the fun eventually began to wind down, as it always does. The near-equatorial sun was blistering, and people were sweaty, sticky, and sunburned. Sand that had found its way into clothes and crevices worked its discomfort, and too much beer and not enough water proved a perfect recipe for afternoon headaches. All of this, and the ache of muscles unused to exertion, made for cranky sailors. By midafternoon we were ready to get back aboard the ship.

But our ride didn't arrive at the appointed time. We waited, increasingly more impatient, in the heat. Someone pointed out a plume of black smoke on the horizon which had been curling skyward for a while and we speculated on its source as we waited. We guessed that one of the ships at anchor was conducting some sort of fire-fighting practice. After all, enemy aircraft had long since been chased out of the area, and it was unlikely that a Japanese submarine could have approached the ships anchored offshore.

Still, we waited. And waited. And waited. Finally, hours after it should have arrived, the landing craft nudged itself onto the beach and we clambered aboard, anxious to get back to the *Randolph* where we could shower and get a clean change of clothes. When we pressed them about their tardiness, the crew of the landing craft told us what had happened.

Two Army F-5Es, the photoreconnaissance version of the P-38 Lightning fighter, had dived on the anchored *Randolph*, no doubt intent on "showing the Navy how *real* aviators flew." One of the aircraft, piloted by Lewis Gillespie of the 6th Photo Group, zoomed down, just barely above the water, approaching the bow of the ship from a 90-degree angle. Just as the airplane neared the ship, the pilot started a slow victory roll—that he never finished.

With a deafening roar, the Army aircraft smashed into a pack of F6Fs parked on the bow of the ship, killing the pilot instantly. The Navy airplanes caught fire while pieces of the F-5E crashed through the flight deck and started fires below. By the time the crew brought the fires under control, 11 men were dead and 14 injured. Nine airplanes were completely destroyed.

Poor Eddie Jindra—who had tumbled off the flight deck in his airplane during an attack on the *Randolph* at Okinawa—was sunbathing on the deck when the Army pilot crashed. He suffered third-degree burns from the blast and was transferred to the hospital ship *Refuge*.

When Hal Vita finally was able to make his way to his stateroom, he found that his bed was already occupied—by one of the F-5E's still-smoldering Allison engines!

The *Randolph* seemed to be unlucky at anchor. Since I had come aboard the ship in January, she had been anchored only five times. On two of those

The *Randolph* as seen from a distance after an Army pilot smashed into it. The pilot, flying an F-5E, the reconnaissance version of the P-38, was showing off . . . poorly. The foolhardy man was killed, as were 11 sailors. Nine aircraft on the *Randolph*'s deck were destroyed. (U.S. Navy)

occasions, she was smashed into by airplanes—once Japanese and once American. Lives were lost both times. It wasn't a very good record.

We were very fortunate that the Army pilot had hit well forward on the flight deck, because the hangar deck was covered with bombs and ammunition that had been unloaded from an ammo barge tied alongside. Even so, there were anxious moments when blazing gasoline from the damaged planes dripped down through the hole in the flight deck to the hangar deck. Fortunately, the damage-control parties managed to extinguish the flames before any of the ammunition caught fire.

Once again, the repair ship *Jason*, which had done such a fine job restoring the *Randolph* at Ulithi, pulled alongside and was able to fix the damage in about four days.

Chapter 32

Fate works in funny ways. A typhoon wreaked havoc upon the ships of Task Force 38 on June 5. Among others, the aircraft carrier *Hornet* was badly damaged. The storm battered the carrier, crumpling the forward 25 feet of her flight deck and greatly weakening the rest of it. Consequently, the men of Air Group 16, who were waiting to replace Air Group 17 aboard the *Hornet*, found themselves without a ship. Fortunately for us, the *Randolph* had not been too badly damaged during the tragic P-38 accident of June 7. Consequently, the decision was made to transfer Air Group 16 to the *Randolph*—and to send Air Group 12 home. We could hardly believe our good fortune.

On June 17, we boarded the escort carrier *Makassar Strait*. We arrived at Guam on June 23, and disembarked to await further transportation. The wait at Guam was hardly considered R&R since there wasn't much to do. The quarters were rather sad and the chow lines a mile long. The island teemed with restless Marines, sailors, soldiers, and airmen who spent a lavish amount of time making life difficult for each other. Aside from exploring a bit around Guam, which had been recaptured only a year earlier, we didn't do very much.

A couple of the other pilots and I got restless, so we wandered over to one of the Army camps to see if we could pick up some souvenirs. For bartering purposes I brought along a couple of parachute bags. These were big, heavy-duty canvas bags with a strong zipper and snaps. We used them to carry our flight gear. When we got onto the Army base I ran into a sergeant who traded me an M1 carbine for one of the bags. It seemed like a great deal to me—a bag for a carbine. I still have that weapon.

On June 30, a week after we arrived, we boarded the escort carrier *Kalinin Bay* and headed east, rocketing across the Pacific at an excruciatingly slow 12 knots. Although we were headed home, this was an almost agonizing trip for me. There was little to do, and our snail's pace made it seem as if we were stopped in time. The air group was much too big for the ship, and people had to spread out and sleep everywhere. You could hardly turn around without bumping into someone else, and the crowded quarters made for short tempers. Being more senior officers, my peers and I got decent quarters and were able to eat in the wardroom. But the junior officers had to sleep in bunkrooms or on cots on the hangar deck, and had to stand in the chow lines with the rest of the crew, who were crammed into whatever spaces were available.

After 12 miserable days at sea, we arrived at Pearl Harbor on July 11, and without wasting any time at all, departed the next day for the States. We reached San Diego on the evening of July 19, but were told, to the accompaniment of a chorus of groans and general bitching, that the U.S. Customs Service had to inspect all our baggage before we would be allowed off the ship. Customs officials were concerned about what we may have picked up in the Philippines and Guam. Next morning, we dutifully threw our bags into one huge pile on the hangar deck. Shortly after we docked at Naval Air Station North Island, a customs agent came aboard, took one look at the enormous pile of bags and another at the sea of glowering faces—the faces of war-weary veterans—then shook his head and signed off without checking a thing.

While we all milled about, waiting for the gangplank to be lowered, I spotted Louise on the dock. I was overjoyed. But my happiness was tempered when I caught sight of Eleanor Embree—Ralph's widow. She was standing bravely next to Louise, putting on the best face she could, determined to welcome home the air group her husband had died leading. Despite my happiness at finally being home, the sight of Eleanor made for my saddest single moment of the war. It was heartrending. But for luck, I might just as easily have been gone, and Louise would also have been wearing the brave face.

They finally got the gangplank down and we rushed—pushing and shoving—ashore. I grabbed Louise and gave her a very long kiss and then just held her in my arms. I still could hardly believe that I had survived a third combat cruise and was finally back home.

After Louise and I managed to pull apart I took time to speak with Eleanor. Although I'm sure she already knew the answer, she wanted to hear it from someone who had known Ralph; she wanted to know what had happened and if there was any possibility that he could have survived. It was very hard for me to look into her eyes and tell her that, from what we knew, there was little chance that Ralph was alive. I admired her courage and didn't mind the interruption of my reunion with Louise.

Louise's parents were also there and they took us to the home of one of their friends where we spent the rest of the day and that night. The next morning,

I went back to the air station and found that I had received orders to serve as a flight instructor at Corpus Christi, Texas. I wasn't too pleased with the orders—the duty seemed chickenshit after what I had seen and done. But anything that kept me from going back into combat was more than welcome. Several other squadron mates received the same orders. So once again—as when I left VF-9—I had to say farewell to friends I had shared combat with, while moving on to a new duty station with other friends from the same unit.

I had 30 days of leave coming to me, so Louise and I went up to Long Beach and spent a few days with her parents before we climbed into our trusty Dodge and headed east to visit my family. It was slow, hot traveling. What I remember most about that trip happened in a rather sleazy motel somewhere in Louisiana. We hadn't noticed before we went to bed that the screen door from the room to the carport had a big hole in it. When we woke up the next morning, Louise had hundreds of mosquito bites on her body and was practically hysterical. I, on the other hand, didn't have a single bite. We deduced that the dusting with DDT that I had received after my trip to Yontan Airfield on Okinawa had somehow kept the mosquitoes from biting me. My good fortune did not make Louise feel any better.

We arrived in Athens on August 1, and had a wonderful reunion with my family and relatives. One of my uncles insisted that I go to his Rotary Club meeting and regale the members and guests with a few tales of my exploits. And, of course, I went out to the airfield to see my old instructors. Driving the Dodge, I retraced the route I had pedaled on my bike so many years before. Bill Quinby was no longer there, but Ben Bradley, my advanced CPT flight instructor, was. I could not help but see the envy in his eyes when I told him about how it was in combat. He may have envied my combat experiences, but without living it, he could hardly have understood the losses and hurt that came with those experiences.

A few days later, another of my uncles offered us the use of his cabin on Lake Rabun in North Georgia, about 100 miles away. Louise and I were about halfway there on August 6, 1945, when we heard on the car radio that the first atom bomb had been dropped on Japan. When my air group had passed through Guam on the way back to the States, we had heard rumors about some sort of superbomb or wonder weapon. At the time I hadn't given the rumors a great deal of thought, but when I heard about the incredible destructiveness of the atom bomb, I knew that they were true. In spades.

Over the next few days, we enjoyed the cabin, and the fishing, and cruising around the lake in my uncle's little motorboat. It was during this idyllic bit of time alone with Louise that the second atom bomb was dropped, on Nagasaki.

A few days later, on August 14, 1945, Japan agreed to accept terms for surrender.

There was an incredible sense of relief in knowing that I wouldn't have to go back into combat, nor would anyone else. I could hardly believe it!

That night Louise and I went out on the lake and celebrated the surrender. I fired tracer bullets into the air from my .38 caliber pistol. I didn't need them anymore.

Epilogue

I was 24 years old, more worldly-wise and much more tired than a man my age ought to have been. And with the war's end, many thousands more young men just like me were streaming home every day. Tired or not, though, I was grateful that I was still alive.

So many of the others I served with had perished. More than 20 of my close friends and squadron mates had been shot down and killed. Many more were lost in noncombat accidents. I missed them then, and I miss them now. Almost daily I still wonder, more than half a century later, why I survived when so many did not. It was such a close thing.

Surviving combat is often just a matter of inches. It was just a matter of inches when the Vichy bullet crashed through my windscreen in North Africa in 1942. It was just a matter of inches at Rabaul when the Zero sprayed machinegun bullets into both of my wings but somehow missed my cockpit. It was just a game of inches again when my wing—rather than my cockpit—was engulfed in flames over Yap. Similarly, had things been skewed just a few inches over Kikai Shima, the 40-millimeter shell that holed my horizontal stabilizer would have blown the tail of my airplane off. And there is no doubt that the Japanese kamikaze pilot—the one who had attacked the *Randolph* on the morning I was preparing to retrieve Jay Finley—would have surely killed me had he moved his controls by just a few inches.

It is difficult to understand or explain. Sometimes I pass it off as plain good luck; at other times I am sure that someone was watching out for me. Either way, I am here, and for that I am thankful.

The biggest reason for my thankfulness has to do with the best thing that ever happened to me—my wife, Louise. Throughout the war, her love and her letters made what I was doing more bearable, and somehow gave it a keener, more bittersweet edge. I had to make certain that I returned home to her!

Louise and I made the decision that I would stay in the service. She had been raised in the Navy, and I was given a regular commission in 1944. The life appealed to us. Soon after the war I was promoted to the rank of lieutenant commander. For the next 24 years we moved all over the country while we raised a beautiful family of four sons and one daughter. I had a good career and was lucky enough to serve as a squadron commander. It's fitting, somehow, that the squadron I was privileged to lead was VF-12.

There were other rewarding assignments as well—too many to review. Through it all I was proud to serve with the remarkable enlisted men and officers who made—and still make—the Navy so great. My final assignment took me to Naval Air Station Miramar in San Diego, California. There, I served first as the station operations officer and then as the executive officer—and worked for my wartime squadron mate Chick Smith. I retired from the Navy in 1969 and still live in the San Diego area.

Doing research for this book brought back many long-forgotten memories. Some of them were good, but many were not. The way my mind worked as I dredged up these recollections surprised me. For whatever reason, events from early in the war came to me much more easily than things that happened later. Perhaps the gruesome grind off the coast of Okinawa—the relentless campaign that forced me to set aside my emotions while it was actually happening—caused me to block out those events and others related to them. I don't know.

Over the years I have been asked about my feelings toward my former enemies, the Japanese. While I certainly abhorred the cruelty practiced by the Empire of Japan, and though I absolutely could not fathom the kamikaze mentality, I held no burning animosity toward the Japanese pilots I fought. They were doing what they were told to do. They were flying under orders, just as I was. Even today I hold no ill will toward the individual Japanese pilots from that time.

The dropping of the atomic bombs comes up as a related issue. I cannot understand how others can question the legitimacy of the decision. As horrible as they were, those bombs saved more lives—particularly Japanese lives—than they took. Had the home islands been invaded—as they surely would have been had the bombs not been dropped—many, many more Japanese would have been killed. And so would have many more of my friends. In fact, it's reasonable to think that even I would have had to do another combat tour. For all these reasons I am thankful that the bombs were dropped.

With any reflection at all, I know that the war was the defining event of my life. Everything I did subsequent to those years was shaped in some manner by what happened to me, or around me, during the war. Out of all those experiences I built a life with my wife. And I wouldn't trade either for anything in the world.

Afterword

Mac "went West" in 2008 and I've missed him ever since. As kind, modest, skilled, and intelligent as he seems within these pages, he was even more so in real life. When we worked together on the book, he was almost embarrassed to discuss his successes, and was always considerate when talking of others. He was a gentleman, a devoted father, and a man who was as much in love with his wife as anyone I've ever met.

These are the attributes I most want people to know about Mac.

—Jay A. Stout, August 11, 2023